REDEEMING
THE TIME

REDEEMING
THE TIME

Gospel Perspectives on the Challenges of the Hour

ROBERT BARRON

FOREWORD BY JOHN L. ALLEN JR.

Published by Word on Fire, Park Ridge, IL 60068
© 2022 by Word on Fire Catholic Ministries
Printed in the United States of America
All rights reserved

Cover design, typesetting, and interior art direction
by Cassie Pease, Marlene Burrell, and Rozann Lee.

25 24 23 22   1 2 3 4

ISBN: 978-1-685780-05-0

Library of Congress Control Number: 2021922708

CONTENTS

CONTENTS

CONTENTS

PART VI – NAVIGATING POLITICAL POLARIZATION

PART VII – FACING COVID-19 AND THE PROBLEM OF EVIL

PART VIII – SHINING THE LIGHT OF THE NATIONS

FOREWORD

With regard to current events, the perennial temptation of Christianity is to become either too vertical or too horizontal. That is, we end up either so obsessed with otherworldly contemplation as to be completely detached from what's happening just outside the doors of the chapel, or so invested in a social or political program as to all but ignore the spiritual dimension of human existence and destiny. The more subtle form of the same temptation, probably, is to think the solution is a neat mathematical 50/50 split, with half one's time devoted to the here and now and the other half to the life beyond.

Naturally, the proper Catholic answer is something different entirely—it's "both/and." The aim is a life utterly tied up in the hurly and burly of the day, and, at the same time, totally permeated by the transcendent. Put simply, the trick is to be completely horizontal and completely vertical at the same time.

In recent Catholic life, the best example was St. John Paul II, the would-be Carmelite mystic whose entire life radiated spiritual depth, but who was also at least as well-informed and engaged in the nitty-gritty of geopolitics and the movements of history as most secular politicians and diplomats of his era. In today's America, the best public example we have of that capacity to fully incarnate the horizontal and the vertical is probably Auxiliary Bishop Robert Barron of Los Angeles, founder of Word on Fire, as this collection of essays abundantly illustrates.

Certainly no one could accuse Barron of paying short shrift to the spiritual. His best-known works aren't commentaries on current affairs but artful expositions of the perennial faith of the Catholic Church, crafted by someone who's clearly drenched in belief. While Catholicism has many fine evangelists, however, Barron's particular gift is to make the Church's timeless tradition nevertheless seem timely by addressing it to the peculiar zigs and zags of the postmodern era, from our quasi-Jansenist fundamentalism about science to our toxic addiction to snark.

At one point Barron evokes St. John Henry Newman to the effect that the Church moves through a culture like a foraging animal in a forest, taking advantage of what it can and fighting off what it must. This book captures Barron at both his foraging and his fighting best.

I've always known that Bishop Robert Barron is a keen consumer of journalism, and that he appreciates the pressures journalists face in compiling the first draft of history; the Fellowship I hold at the Word on Fire Institute devoted to St. Francis de Sales, patron saint of journalists, is one proof of the point. Unlike many religious figures one meets in this line of work, Barron doesn't expect journalists to be the fifth evangelist instead of the fourth estate; he understands that journalism is a different animal, with its own logic and principles of tradecraft, and he wants it to be probing, critical, and unbeholden to other agendas. When he's critical of the journalistic enterprise, it's because he wants us to do better journalism, not to be spokespersons for the system or advocates for some other cause.

I make my living covering the Vatican, and, over the years, I've had more conversations than I can count with bishops about whatever the latest madness unfolding in or around the Eternal City happens to be. I can testify that I've rarely been asked smarter questions than those I've taken from Barron, and it's because he's got the heart of a priest and the mind of a professor, but also the savvy of a good beat reporter. (To this day, a question he once asked about papal elections haunts me because I still don't have a good answer to it, but that's for another time.)

What I hadn't realized until reading this collection of essays, however, is that Barron is actually a fellow member of the tribe, a journo flying below radar. He's so well known for his video projects, his homilies, his lectures and speeches, that it's easy to miss the fact that he's also an old-school newspaper columnist, a sort of Walter Winchell in a mitre and cassock. Had most of these essays been printed on the op-ed page of the *New York Times* or *Wall Street*

Journal, they would have been right at home—and, frankly, the level of our civic discourse in America would be much higher if they were.

Strictly as an essayist—the word for which in my professional neighborhood is "columnist"—Barron exhibits three towering strengths, all abundantly illustrated in this collection.

First, Barron writes with real intelligence. His piece on the fiasco surrounding ex-Cardinal Theodore McCarrick, now also ex-priest, begins with a reference to Luca Signorelli's image of the Antichrist in the Orvieto Cathedral and veers quickly into exegesis of René Girard, with no apologies for the eggheaded discursions. He's also in the habit of dropping words such as "evanesce" and "deracinate" into sentences, with no sense of artifice. Barron assumes his reader is smart enough to handle high-level content and makes no effort, like so many contemporary columnists, to dumb things down or to smother an absence of insight with clichés and one-liners.

I mean, no one who ends columns with quirky slogans such as "Down with Kantian reductionism!" is really appealing to the lowest common denominator, is he?

Second, Barron takes a stand. There's never any mistaking which side of an argument he's on; just read his essay on Bill Nye the Science Guy's views on philosophy, for example, and you won't come away muddled about what Barron thinks. (I'm too old to have watched Nye's 1990s-era program, which was pitched at the youth of the day, but I share Barron's skepticism that hosting a TV kids show necessarily qualifies someone to make pronouncements on metaphysics.)

Yet while Barron can be critical, even caustic, he's never mean. In fact, he's emerged as the great opponent of twenty-first-century Catholic snark, especially on social media. A whole section of this collection is devoted to calling out what Barron calls a "culture of contempt" online, which is hardly just a Catholic problem, but which Catholics arguably have a higher calling to resist. Carefully ponder his diagnosis of social media comboxes in the essay on "The Internet and Satan's Game," and you'll never again be confused about the difference between argument (good) and calumny (bad).

Third, Barron is just a flat-out good writer. Consider, for instance, the way he wraps up an essay on the movie *The Shape of Water*, in which Barron makes the argument that the film exalts freedom and individualism at the expense of structure and participation in something larger than the self: "If all we have is the shape of water—which is to say, no shape at all," Barron writes, "we're actually in bad shape." (Fair warning: someday, I will find a context to steal that line.)

In the essay in this volume on misuse of the term "culture warrior," which he considers a good example of treating an abstraction as if it's a real thing, Barron suggests following Bernard Lonergan's epistemic imperatives:

- Be attentive (see what is really there to be seen).
- Be intelligent (form plausible hypotheses to explain a given phenomenon).
- Be reasonable (make judgments so as to determine which of a variety of bright ideas is in fact the right idea).
- Be responsible (accept the full implications of the judgment made).

You'll find no better example of a spry Catholic mind trying to put those principles to work than the essays collected here. As we say in Italian, *Buona lettura*!

John L. Allen Jr.

PART I

FIGHTING THE SEXUAL ABUSE CRISIS

Tintoretto and the
Reform of the Church

At the close of a long session of walking and musing in the National Gallery of Art, I was drawn by an empty and comfortable-looking couch situated at the end of one of the galleries. Plopping down to rest, I looked up at the picture right in front of me. At first glance, given the color scheme and the peculiar modeling of the figures, I thought it was an El Greco, but closer examination revealed that it in fact was Tintoretto's depiction of Christ at the Sea of Galilee. The drama at the center of the composition is the Apostles' boat, buffeted by choppy waves, and St. Peter taking a gingerly, tentative step onto the bounding main at the invitation of the Lord, who beckons to him. My seated posture conduced toward contemplation, and I spent a good deal of time with this painting, first admiring the obvious technical skill of the painter, especially in the rendering of the water, but eventually moving to a deeper perception of its spiritual theme, of particular resonance today.

Whenever the Gospels present the disciples of Jesus in a boat, they are, of course, symbolically representing the Church. So Tintoretto is showing the Church in its practically permanent condition across the ages: at sea, rocked by waves, in danger of going under. Indeed, with a handful of remarkable exceptions, every age has been, in some way, a perilous one for the Mystical Body of Christ. The boat is filled with the specially chosen Apostles of the Lord, those who spent years with the Master, learning his mind, watching his moves, witnessing his miracles with their own eyes, taking in his spirit. One would think that even if everyone else failed to follow the Lord, these men would hold steady. And yet we see them cowering, timorous, obviously at a loss as the storm rages around them. And the Gospels, in a manner that sets them apart from most other literature dealing with religious founders

3

and their disciples, do consistently portray Jesus' inner circle as deeply flawed. Peter denied the Lord at the moment of truth; James and John succumbed to petty ambition; Thomas refused to believe the report of the Resurrection; Judas betrayed his master; all of them, with the exception of John, abandoned him on the cross, protecting their own hides. And yet Tintoretto shows Peter tentatively placing his foot upon the sea, commencing to walk toward Jesus. The great spiritual lesson—shopworn perhaps to the point of being a cliché, but still worth repeating—is that as long as the Church keeps its eyes fixed on Christ, it can survive even the worst of storms. It can walk on the water.

The Catholic Church is once more enduring a moment of extreme trial in regard to sexual abuse. This time, the focus of attention is on the failure of some bishops to protect the vulnerable, and in at least one terrible case, the active abuse perpetrated by a cardinal archbishop. The whole world is rightly outraged by these sins, and the Church appropriately feels ashamed. Many wonder, understandably, how those specially devoted to Christ could fall into such depravity. But then we recall that every bishop today is a successor of the Apostles—which is to say, of that band that both sat in easy familiarity with Jesus and denied, betrayed, and ran from their Master. In stormy times, the first Apostles cowered, and their successors, we have to admit, often do the same.

But there are grounds for hope. They are found, however, not in institutional reform (as important as that is), not in psychological analysis (as indispensable as that might be), not in new programs and protocols (as helpful as they might prove), but rather in a return to Jesus Christ. Eyes fixed on him, hearts attuned to him, minds beguiled by him, action determined by him, the leaders of the Church can, even now, walk on the water.

Tintoretto sheds considerable light on this issue of apostolic weakness and strength in the very manner in which he has arranged the figures in his composition. The painting is foreshortened in such a way that the disciples appear very small, almost doll-like, whereas Jesus, looming in the extreme foreground, looks gigantic. As John the Baptist put the principle: "He must increase, but I must decrease" (John 3:30). When our anxieties and egos are

4

placed in the foreground, Christ necessarily recedes. Crucial to the reformation of the Church is the reversal of that perspective.

The McCarrick Mess

This article was released on August 9, 2018. That October, the Holy See announced an investigation into Theodore McCarrick's abuse, culminating in a report released in November 2020.

When I was going through school, the devil was presented to us as a myth, a literary device, a symbolic manner of signaling the presence of evil in the world. I will admit to internalizing this view and largely losing my sense of the devil as a real spiritual person. What shook my agnosticism in regard to the evil one was the clerical sex abuse scandal of the nineties and the early aughts. I say this because that awful crisis just seemed too thought-through, too well-coordinated, to be simply the result of chance or wicked human choice. The devil is characterized as "the enemy of the human race" and particularly the enemy of the Church. I challenge anyone to come up with a more devastatingly effective strategy for attacking the Mystical Body of Christ than the abuse of children and young people by priests. This sin had countless direct victims of course, but it also crippled the Church financially, undercut vocations, caused people to lose confidence in Christianity, dramatically compromised attempts at evangelization, etc., etc. It was a diabolical masterpiece.

Sometime in the early aughts, I was attending a conference and found myself wandering more or less alone in the area where groups and organizations had their booths. I came over to one of the tables and the woman there said, "You're Fr. Barron, aren't you?" I replied affirmatively, and she continued, "You're doing good work for the Church, but this means that the devil wants to stop you. And you know, he's a lot smarter than you are and a lot more powerful." I think I just mumbled something to her at that moment, but she was right, and I knew it. All of this has come back to me in the wake of the McCarrick catastrophe. St. Paul warned us that we battle not against flesh and blood but against "powers and principalities." Consequently, the principal work of the Church at this devastating moment ought to be prayer, the conscious and insistent invoking of Christ and the saints.

Now, I can hear people saying, "So Bishop Barron is blaming it all on the devil." Not at all. The devil works through temptation, suggestion, and insinuation—and he accomplishes nothing without our cooperation. If you want to see the principle illustrated, Google Luca Signorelli's image of the Antichrist in the Orvieto Cathedral. You'll see what I mean. McCarrick did wicked things, and so did those, it appears, who enabled him. And we have to come to terms with these sins.

Before I broach the subject of how to do this, permit me to say a few words about unhelpful strategies being bandied about. A first one is indiscriminate scapegoating. The great philosopher René Girard taught us that when communities enter into crisis, people typically commence desperately to cast about for someone or some group to blame. In the catharsis of this indiscriminate accusation, they find a kind of release, an ersatz peace. "All the bishops should resign!" "The priesthood is a cesspool of immorality!" "The seminaries are all corrupt!" As I say, these assertions might be emotionally satisfying at some level, but they are deeply unjust and conduce toward greater and not less dysfunction. The second negative strategy is the riding of ideological hobby horses. So lots of commentators—left, center, and right—have chimed in to say that the real cause of the McCarrick disaster is, take your pick, the ignoring of *Humanae Vitae*, priestly celibacy, rampant homosexuality in the Church, the mistreatment of homosexuals, the sexual revolution, etc. Mind you, I'm not saying for a moment that these aren't important considerations and that some of the suggestions might not have real merit. But I *am* saying that launching into a consideration of these matters that we have been debating for decades and that will certainly not admit of an easy adjudication amounts right now to a distraction.

So what should be done? The United States Conference of Catholic Bishops (USCCB) has no juridical or canonical authority to discipline bishops. And even if it tried to launch an investigation, it has, at the moment, very little credibility. Only the pope has juridical and disciplinary powers in regard to bishops. Hence, I would suggest (as a lowly back-bencher auxiliary) that the bishops of the United States—all of us—petition the Holy Father to form a team, made up mostly of faithful lay Catholics skilled in forensic investigation, and to empower them to have access to all of the relevant documentation and financial records. Their task should be to determine how McCarrick managed, despite his widespread reputation for iniquity, to rise through the ranks of the hierarchy and to continue, in his retirement years, to function as a roving ambassador for the Church and to have a disproportionate influence on the appointment of bishops. They should ask the ecclesial version of Sen. Howard Baker's famous questions: "What did the responsible parties know and when did they know it?" Only after these matters are settled will we know what the next steps ought to be.

In the meantime, and above all, we should ask the heavenly powers to fight with us and for us. I might suggest especially calling upon the one who crushes the head of the serpent.

Sowing the Wind and Reaping the Whirlwind:
A Reflection on the Irish Referendum

I will confess that as a person of Irish heritage on both sides of my family, I found the events in Ireland in May 2018 particularly dispiriting. Not only did the nation vote, by a two-to-one margin, for the legal prerogative to kill their children in the womb, but they also welcomed and celebrated the vote with a frankly sickening note of gleeful triumph. Will I ever forget the unnerving looks and sounds of the frenzied crowd gathered to cheer their victory in the courtyard of Dublin Castle? As the right to abortion now sweeps thoroughly across the Western world, I am put in mind of Gloria Steinem's mocking remark from many years ago to the effect that if men could get pregnant, abortion would be a sacrament. I say this because abortion has indeed become a sacrament for radical feminism, the one absolutely sacred, nonnegotiable value for so-called progressive women.

One of the features of the lead-up to the vote—and this has become absolutely commonplace—was the almost total lack of moral argument on the part of the advocates of abortion. There was a lot of political talk about "rights," though the rights of the unborn were never mentioned; and there were appeals to "health care," though the lethal threat to the health of the child in the womb was a nonissue. There was, above all, an attempt to manipulate people's feelings by bringing up rare and extreme cases. But what one hardly ever heard was a real engagement of the moral argument that a direct attack on a human life is intrinsically evil and as such can never be permitted or legally sanctioned.

Accompanying the entire process, of course, was the subtext of the Catholic Church's cultural impotence, even irrelevance. Every single story that I read in advance of the vote and subsequent to it mentioned the fact that overwhelmingly Catholic Ireland had shaken off the baleful influence of the Church and had moved, finally, into the modern world. How sad, of course, that being up-to-date is apparently a function of our capacity to murder the innocent. But at the same time I must admit—and I say it to my shame as a Catholic bishop—that, at least to a degree, I understand this reaction. The sexual abuse of children on the part of some Irish priests and brothers, not to mention the physical and psychological abuse of young people perpetrated by some Irish nuns, as well as the pathetic handling of the situation by far too many Irish bishops and provincials, produced a tsunami of suffering and deep injustice.

And we must remember a principle enunciated by my colleague Fr. Stephen Grunow—namely, that the abuse of children in any society, but especially in one as insular and tight-knit as Irish society, has a tremendously powerful ripple effect. When a young person is sexually abused, particularly by a figure as trusted as a priest, that child is massively and permanently hurt; but once the abuse becomes known, so are his siblings, his parents, his friends, his extended family, his parish. Now multiply this process a dozen times, a hundred times, a thousand times—again, especially in a country as small as Ireland—and you will find that, in very short order, the entire nation is filled with anger, indignation, and a legitimate thirst for setting things right. I do believe that what we witnessed last week was a powerfully emotional reaction to the great crimes of the last several decades. The deeply sad truth is that the abuse of young men and women has given rise to an even more dramatic abuse of unborn children. When you sow the wind, you reap the whirlwind.

Is there a way forward for Ireland? I think a significant sign of hope is the considerable number of people who took the extremely unpopular stance against this legislative innovation. Knowing full well that they would likely lose and that they would be subject to ridicule and perhaps even the loss of their professional positions, they courageously argued for life. On that foundation, much of value can be built. But what Ireland most needs at this moment—and indeed for the next hundred years—are saints and mystics. Moral arguments can and should be made, but if the Church wants to recover its standing as a shaper of the Irish culture, it has to produce men and women who give themselves radically to the Gospel. It needs figures in the mold of Teresa of Kolkata, Oscar Romero, Francis of Assisi, Dorothy Day—indeed of St. Patrick, St. Brendan, St. Columbanus, and St. Brigid. And it requires men and women of prayer, like the founders of the great Benedictine, Franciscan, Dominican, Cistercian, and Trappist houses that still dot the Irish countryside—and like the strange denizens of Skellig Michael, who for six centuries clung to the edges of the world off the coast of Ireland and lived in total dependence upon God.

Finally, only prayer, witness, radical trust in divine providence, honest preaching, and the living of the radical Gospel will undo the damage done last week.

Letter to a Suffering Church:
Conclusion

The sexual abuse scandal has been for me, for millions of other Catholics, and especially for the victim-survivors, lacerating. I know many Catholics are sorely tempted just to give up on the Church, to join another religious group, or perhaps to become one of the religiously unaffiliated. But this is not the time to leave; it is the time to stay and fight. If I may, I'd like to make a historical reference to a key moment in our political history. By the 1850s, it had become unmistakably clear to Abraham Lincoln that slavery was not only a moral outrage but also an institution that posed a mortal threat to American democracy. One can hear his arguments along these lines in the great speeches he gave while debating Stephen Douglas during the 1858 Illinois senatorial campaign. But nowhere was his case more pithily put than in his famous address before the Illinois General Assembly just after his nomination for the Senate: "A house divided against itself cannot stand. I believe that this government cannot endure permanently half-slave and half-free."

It was this conviction that led Lincoln, upon becoming president in 1861, to accept and prosecute a terrible war. Midway through that conflict, while dedicating a cemetery for those who died in its decisive battle, Lincoln explained why he continued to fight: "Four score and seven years ago our fathers brought forth on this continent a new nation, conceived in liberty, and dedicated to the proposition that all men are created equal. Now we are engaged in a great civil war, testing whether that nation, or any nation so conceived and so dedicated, can long endure." There were indeed many people in the North who, appalled at the losses on the battlefield and less than persuaded of the utility of the war, were rancorously calling for Lincoln to give up, to let the Confederacy have what it wanted. But the president knew that something more than military victory or national pride was at stake in the struggle; he knew that slavery constituted a rot upon American democracy, a disease that undermined the principles of our founders. Therefore, despite the pain, he had to fight.

I understand that it's not a perfect analogy, but I think it sheds at least some light on the present situation in the Church. The sexual abuse of young people by some priests and the countenancing of that abuse by some bishops is more than a moral problem; it is a rot, a disease, a threat to the great principles of the Church that we hold dear. Yes, an easy option is to cut and run, to give up on the operation. But if you believe, as I do, in the doctrines and practices and convictions of the Church, if you think it is indispensable that the Mystical Body of Jesus Christ abides as a light to the world, then take the Lincoln option: stay and fight!

Fight by raising your voice in protest; fight by writing a letter of complaint; fight by insisting that protocols be followed; fight by reporting offenders; fight by pursuing the guilty until they are punished; fight by refusing to be mollified by pathetic excuses. But above all, fight by your very holiness of life; fight by becoming the saint that God wants you to be; fight by encouraging a decent young man to become a priest; fight by doing a Holy Hour every day for the sanctification of the Church; fight by coming to Mass regularly; fight by evangelizing; fight by doing the corporal and spiritual works of mercy.

God is love, and he has won the victory through the cross and Resurrection of Jesus. Therefore, we inhabit what is finally a divine comedy, and we know that the followers of Jesus are on the winning side. Perhaps the very best way to be a disciple of Jesus right now is to stay and fight for his Church.

PART II

REACHING THE "NONES"

The Least Religious Generation
in US History:
A Reflection on Jean Twenge's *iGen*

Jean Twenge's book *iGen* is one of the most fascinating—and depressing—texts I've read in the past decade. A professor of psychology at San Diego State University, Dr. Twenge has been, for years, studying trends among young Americans, and her most recent book focuses on the generation born between 1995 and 2012. Since this is the first cohort of young people who have never known a world without iPads and iPhones, and since these devices have remarkably shaped their consciousness and behavior, Twenge naturally enough has dubbed them the "iGen."

One of her many eye-opening findings is that iGen'ers are growing up much more slowly than their predecessors. A baby boomer typically got his driver's license on his sixteenth birthday (I did), but an iGen'er is far more willing to postpone that rite of passage, waiting until her eighteenth or nineteenth year. Whereas previous generations were eager to get out of the house and find their own way, iGen'ers seem to like to stay at home with their parents and have a certain aversion to "adulting." And Twenge argues that smartphones have undeniably turned this new generation in on itself. A remarkable number of iGen'ers would rather text their friends than go out with them and would rather watch videos at home than go to a theater with others. One of the upshots of this screen-induced introversion is a lack of social skills, and another is depression.

Now, there are many more insights that Dr. Twenge shares, but I was particularly interested, for obvious reasons, in her chapter on religious attitudes and behaviors among iGen'ers. In line with many other researchers, Twenge shows that the objective statistics in this area are alarming. As recently as the 1980s, 90% of high school seniors identified with a religious group. Among iGen'ers, the figures are now around 65% and falling. And religious practice is even more attenuated: only 28% of twelfth graders attended services in 2015, whereas the number was 40% in 1976. For decades, sociologists of religion have been arguing that, though explicit affiliation with religious institutions was on the decline, especially among the young, most people remained "spiritual"—that is to say, convinced of certain fundamental religious beliefs. I remember many conversations with my friend Fr. Andrew Greeley along these lines.

But Twenge indicates that this is no longer true. Whereas even twenty years ago, the overwhelming number of Americans, including youngsters, believed in God, now fully one-third of eighteen-to-twenty-four-year-olds say that they don't believe. As late as 2004, 84% of young adults said that they regularly prayed; by 2016, fully one-fourth of that same age cohort said that they never pray. We find a similar decline in regard to acceptance of the Bible as the Word of God: one fourth of iGen'ers say that the Scriptures are a compilation of "ancient fables, legends, history, and moral precepts recorded by men." Her dispiriting conclusion: "The waning of private religious belief means that young generations' disassociation from religion is not just about their distrust of institutions; more are disconnecting from religion entirely, even at home and even in their hearts."

Now, what are some of the reasons for this disconnect? One, Twenge argues, is the iGen preoccupation with individual choice. From their earliest years, iGen'ers have been presented with a dizzying array of choices in everything from food and clothes to gadgets and lifestyles. And they have been encouraged, by practically every song, video, and movie, to believe in themselves and follow their own dreams. All of this self-preoccupation and stress upon individual liberty stands sharply athwart the religious ideal of surrendering to God and his purposes. "My life, my death, my choice" (a rather iGen-friendly motto that I recently saw emblazoned on a billboard in California) sits very uneasily indeed with St. Paul's assertion "Whether we live or whether we die, we are the Lord's" (Rom. 14:8). A second major reason for iGen dissatisfaction with religion is one that has surfaced in lots of surveys and polls—namely, that religious belief is incompatible with a scientific view of the world. One young man that Twenge interviewed is typical: "Religion, at least to people my age, seems like it's something of the past. It seems like something that isn't modern." Another said, "I knew from church that I couldn't believe in both science and God, so that was it. I didn't believe in God anymore." And a third reason—also attested to in lots of studies—is the "antigay attitudes" supposedly endemic to biblical Christianity. One of Twenge's interviewees put it with admirable succinctness: "I'm questioning the existence of God. I stopped going to church because I'm gay and was part of a gay-bashing religion." One survey stated the statistical truth bluntly enough: 64% of eighteen-to-twenty-four-ackground tasksyear-olds believed that Christianity is antigay, and for good measure, 58% of those iGen'ers thought that the Christian religion is hypocritical.

Dismal stuff, I know. But Dr. Twenge performs a great service to all those interested in the flourishing of religion, for she lays out the objectivities unblinkingly, and this is all to the good, given our extraordinary capacity for wishful thinking and self-deception. Further, though she doesn't tell religious educators and catechists how to respond, she unambiguously indicates what is leading this most unreligious generation in our history away from the churches. Her book should be required reading for those who wish to evangelize the next generation.

Spinoza, Secularism, and
the Challenge of Evangelization

Throughout Anthony Gottlieb's breezy and enjoyable history of modern philosophy, entitled *The Dream of Enlightenment*, his treatment of such figures as Descartes, Hobbes, Locke, and Voltaire reveals his own rather strong bias in favor of the rationalism and anti-supernaturalism advocated by these avatars of modern thought. Toward the end of his chapter on Spinoza, Gottlieb avers that what he calls "the religion of Spinozism" is more or less identical to the secularist worldview espoused by so many in the West today, including himself.

I found his summary extremely clarifying and indeed useful as a foil for what I take to be a properly religious view of things. Answering him point by point is a good exercise for anyone who would aspire to evangelize the culture today. First, he argues, "It [Spinoza's view] insists that morality has nothing to do with the commands of a supremely powerful being, and that it does not require a priesthood . . . to sustain it." Of course, some healthy demythologizing is in order: no serious religious person imagines that God is like an earthly potentate, sitting on a throne and barking out arbitrary commands. But serious religious people do indeed think that absolute moral norms—that is to say, laws prohibiting acts intrinsically wrong in themselves (slavery, the direct killing of the innocent, the sexual abuse of children, etc.)— must be grounded in something other than personal whim, social convention, or biological evolution. They must, in fact, find their justification in the deepest structures of reality, which is another way of saying in the very being of God.

What about Gottlieb's second observation regarding a priesthood? Well, I'm not going to make an argument here for the fullness of the Catholic liturgical life, but to speak of priesthood is roughly to speak of worship, and worship is none other than the formal and ritual ordering of one's life to God. Thus, if God is indeed the ground for morality, then something like worship is in point of fact required for the cultivation and exercise of morality. According to the famous dictum of Will Herberg, morality severed from its religious source is like cut flowers placed in a vase. It will flourish for a short time, but without the enacted praise of God, it will fade quickly enough.

Gottlieb goes on: "[Spinoza's philosophy] rejects the idea of a personal God who created, cares about and occasionally even tinkers with the world." Spinoza did indeed eschew the notion of the personhood of God, identifying the deity, more or less, with nature as such—and this has made him agreeable to atheists, pantheists, and worshipers of nature for the past several centuries. But does this finally make sense? A close analysis reveals that the universe, in every nook and cranny, is marked by contingency or dependency. Things don't exist through themselves, but through the influence of a whole nexus of causes extrinsic to themselves. But those causes are themselves contingent upon further causes. If we want to give a sufficient reason why individual phenomena and things exist, we cannot go on endlessly appealing to conditioned causes. We must come, finally, to some reality that exists simply through the power of its own nature. And we recognize that this unconditioned being is the source of the being of everything outside of itself; we acknowledge, in a word, that it is the Creator of the universe.

But is Spinoza at least correct in characterizing this uncaused cause as fundamentally impersonal? We must answer no, since that which is absolutely unconditioned remains incapable of being further actualized and hence is in possession of any and all perfections of being, very much including mind, will, and freedom. "It" must be, therefore, a "he," a person. Now, if we grant that the Creator is a person, can we still agree with Spinoza (and modern secularism) that he doesn't care for the world? No! To love is to will the good of the other. If existence is a good (and it surely is), and if the universe itself exists only through the will of the Creator (and it surely does), then the very being of the world from moment to moment is the fruit of the unconditioned reality's *love* for the world.

Finally, Gottlieb argues that the Spinozan philosophy rejects the supernatural and "places its faith in knowledge and understanding, rather than in faith itself." By "supernatural," he probably means the superstitious belief in ghosts, goblins, and such, but properly speaking, the supernatural is that which transcends the world of ordinary experience, of the visible and the measurable. Why should this be ruled peremptorily out of court? We've already shown that it is eminently reasonable to believe in God, who is undoubtedly supernatural. And isn't it just a crude prejudice to claim that reality is limited to what we human beings can take in with our senses and measure with our puny instruments? In point of fact, Gottlieb gives away the game with his frank admission that secular rationalism "puts its faith" in reason, thereby hoisting itself on its own petard. Why is faith a bad thing until it is used to justify the limiting of the rational to the empirically verifiable?!

If you have time, do read Gottlieb's history of modern philosophy. It will show you the ideas, prejudices, and questionable assumptions that have trickled down into the minds of many people, especially the young, today. And it will help thereby to prepare you to evangelize our religiously skeptical culture.

Getting Out of the Sacristy:
A Look at Our Pastoral Priorities

Throughout all the years of my involvement with the Church, the parish has been taken as *the* crucial ecclesial institution. Talk to almost anyone involved in Catholic ministry over the past fifty years and you will hear ample criticism of lots of aspects of Church life, but you will, almost without exception, hear praise of the parish. I think here of Fr. Andrew Greeley's lyrical evocations of the parish as a uniquely successful social and religious institution. Certainly within the context of diocesan priesthood, parish work is the unquestioned default position. Ministry outside of the parochial setting—hospital work, seminary work, teaching, administration, etc.—is acceptable, but it is generally seen as not quite what a diocesan priest ought to be doing. I think it's fair to say that the overwhelming amount of our money, time, energy, and personnel go into the maintenance of parish structures.

Now, please don't misunderstand me: *I love the parish and believe in its importance passionately.* Worship, instruction in discipleship, the building up of the community, formation for mission—all of this happens typically within the parish. I did full-time parish work for several years, and I've been involved in numerous parishes for the full thirty-two years of my priesthood. Now as a regional bishop in the largest archdiocese in the country, I supervise and regularly visit roughly forty parishes. However, I do wonder whether, given the unique demands of our time, it might be wise to ask a few questions about our hyper-stress on the parish.

Survey after survey has shown that the number of the "nones," or the religiously unaffiliated, is increasing dramatically in our country. Whereas in the early 1970s, those claiming no religion was around 3%, today it is close to 25%. And among the young, the figures are even more alarming:

40% of those under forty have no religious affiliation, and fully 50% of Catholics under forty claim to be "nones." For every one person who joins the Catholic Church today, roughly six are leaving. And even those who identify as Catholic are spending very little time in and around parishes. Most studies indicate that perhaps 20 to 25% of baptized Catholics attend Mass on a regular basis, and the numbers of those receiving the sacraments—especially Baptism, Confirmation, Marriage—are in noticeable decline. Furthermore, objective analysis reveals—and I can testify from a good deal of personal experience—that a tiny percentage of the already small percentage who attend Mass typically participate in parish programs of education, social service, and spiritual renewal. The point—and again, this is to say absolutely nothing against those who do wonderful work within the parish—is that perhaps we should reconsider our priorities and focus, above all, on active evangelization, the great mission *ad extra*.

Pope Francis memorably told us to "get out of the sacristies and into the streets," and to go "to the existential margins." Especially in our Western context, the streets and the existential margins are where we find the "nones." Two or three generations ago, we could trust that many people (Catholics certainly) would come to our institutions—schools, seminaries, and parishes—to be evangelized, but we absolutely cannot assume that today. But yet we still seem to devote most of our money, time, and attention to the maintenance of these institutions and their programs. Might it not be wiser to redirect our energies, money, and personnel outward, so that we might move into the space where the unevangelized, the fallen-away, the unaffiliated dwell? My humble suggestion is that a serious investment in social media and the formation of an army of young priests specifically educated and equipped to evangelize the culture through these means would be a desideratum. But that's a subject for another column.

The last time Cardinal George addressed the priests of Chicago, at a convocation just about nine months before his death, he made a prophetic remark. He told the Chicago presbyterate that, at the beginning of the Church, there were no dioceses, no schools, no seminaries, and no parishes.

But there were evangelists. He said that, in light of our present challenges, this is worth thinking about. He was right.

Blasting Holes through
the Buffered Self

The Soul's Upward Yearning by Fr. Robert Spitzer, the intergalactically smart Jesuit who once served as president of Gonzaga University and who now directs the Magis Center on matters of faith, reason, and science, is, in my judgment, the best challenge to what the philosopher Charles Taylor calls the "buffered self"—that is to say, a self isolated from any sense of the transcendent. Taylor observes that, prior to 1500, almost everyone believed in God and held that life would be meaningless apart from some reference to goods lying beyond our ordinary experience. But today, at least in the West, one can find armies of people who both deny God and affirm that the goods of this world are sufficient to make us happy. This buffered existence makes evangelization nearly impossible, for it closes a listener to the proposal that true fulfillment and God are tightly linked together. Spitzer's strategy is to show from literature, philosophy, the popular arts, theoretical physics, and epistemology that the human soul yearns for and is in fact already linked to a transcendent or transphysical dimension. By the sheer accumulation of evidence from this wide variety of sources, he punches hole after hole in the buffer that surrounds the modern self.

There is a brilliant idea on practically every page of *The Soul's Upward Yearning*, but I will focus simply on three. First, Spitzer draws our attention to the remarkably universal sense of the transcendent described by philosophers, mystics, and seekers across time and cultures. Limiting ourselves to some key Western figures, Rudolf Otto, for example, speaks of the experience of the *mysterium tremendum et fascinans* (the mystery at the same time fearsome and compelling). This numinous reality overwhelms us and simultaneously draws us into itself, and in its presence we intuit that we are more than physical, that there is a dimension of ourselves that links us to the realm where this mysterious reality dwells. We can find echoes of Otto's speculation in Paul Tillich's "ultimate concern," Karl Rahner's "absolute mystery," and C.S. Lewis' "longing for joy." Now, we might imagine the skeptic wondering whether this is just so much fantasy and subjective projection. Spitzer's answer is that the properly numinous puts us in touch with the good and the true and the holy in their unconditioned form, and this implies that the experience cannot be sequestered within subjectivity alone, for such an experience would be *ipso facto* a conditioned one.

A second major connection to the transcendent is in the very dynamic of human knowing, an idea articulated by myriad philosophers across the centuries—Plato, Aristotle, Aquinas, Newman, etc.—but given particularly clear expression by the twentieth-century Jesuit philosopher Bernard Lonergan. Lonergan maintained that each particular act of knowing takes place within the heuristic context of what can be further known. In any field of intellectual endeavor, every answered question gives rise to a dozen more questions, precisely because the mind is never satisfied with anything less than total knowledge. It wants, in Lonergan's language, "to know everything about everything." This means, Spitzer explains, that the mind is always already in possession of an at least inchoate awareness of what is completely and radically intelligible, that which, in itself, provides answers to every possible question. But this is none other than the unconditioned reality, that which is utterly real, for a conditioned thing, by definition, would beg the question of its own existence and hence would not be utterly intelligible. All of this is to argue, in a word, that the mind is ordered to God, or as Thomas Aquinas put it, that "in every particular act of knowing, God's existence is implicitly co-known."

If these last two arguments seem too abstract, consider a third route of access that Spitzer presents—namely, the phenomenon of near-death experience. Such experiences have been studied carefully for the past forty years, and most of us are well aware of their characteristics: moving out of the body and seeing its surroundings clearly, passing through walls and ceilings, following a tunnel toward a bright light radiating love and compassion, often meeting deceased loved ones along the way. Those who have had such experiences usually swear by them and remain utterly convinced that there is a dimension of the self that survives physical death. Nevertheless, as Spitzer acknowledges, critics have emerged, arguing that these can be explained as hallucinations produced by the brain as it is deprived of oxygen or the fruit of endorphins released by the dying brain. But how can such reductive accounts begin to explain the fact that those who have exited their bodies can describe their environments with such remarkable accuracy? Indeed, in one extraordinary case, a woman left her body on the operating table, traveled through a variety of corridors in the hospital, left the building on the far side of the operating room, and saw a single tennis shoe on the ledge. Afterward, the shoe was found, just as she had described it. And how can the physicalist theories possibly explain how people blind from birth correctly see objects and colors in the environs of the sites where they died? Is it not far more likely, Spitzer speculates, that these experiences demonstrate the existence of a transphysical dimension to the self?

As you have undoubtedly guessed by now, I would enthusiastically endorse Fr. Spitzer's book. And I might suggest that, after you've read it, you pass it along to a bright young person who has soaked too long in the acids of postmodern skepticism and materialism and who has lived too long in the musty confines of the buffered self.

Bill Nye Is Not the Philosophy Guy

Reliable sources have informed me that for the millennial generation Bill Nye is a figure of great importance, due to his widely watched program from the 1990s called *Bill Nye the Science Guy*. Evidently, he taught a large swath of American youth the fundamentals of experimental science and became for them a sort of paragon of reason. Well, I'll take their word for it.

But judging from a recent video in which Bill Nye discussed the relation between science and philosophy, I can only tell you that he sure is not the "philosophy guy."

In a rambling and largely incoherent response to an interlocutor who wondered whether philosophy is still relevant, Nye denigrated the discipline, stating that philosophy never deviates from common sense, that it doubts the reality of sense experience, and that it engages in speculation about whether we might be part of an intergalactic ping-pong match! In regard to the first observation, I would say that, pretty much from Socrates on, philosophers have practically specialized in deviating from common sense. In regard to the second (which flatly contradicts his first assertion), I would say that some philosophers—Descartes most famously—speculated along these lines in order to perform a sort of epistemological experiment and certainly not to prove the nonexistence of the physical world. In regard to the third, I can only say that this has more to do with someone on an LSD trip than any serious philosopher that I'm aware of.

I don't want to spend any more time engaging Nye's rather silly claims, but I do want to address an issue that undergirds everything he says and that is infecting the minds of many young people today—namely, scientism. Not to put too fine a point on it, scientism is the reduction of all knowledge to the scientific form of knowledge. In other words, it is a strict identification of the rational with the deliverances of the scientific method developed in the late sixteenth century. That this method—empirical observation, followed by hypothesis, followed by experimentation, followed by confirmation through repeated experimentation—has indeed rendered abundant fruit is obvious to anyone. And that its accompanying technology has benefitted the world in countless ways is beyond dispute. But the very success of the sciences invites the distortion of scientism, an epistemological imperialism that consigns extra-scientific forms of rationality to the intellectual ash heap. And what an impoverishment this produces!

At the very dawn of philosophy, Plato spoke to us of prisoners chained up inside a cave. All they can see are flickering shadows on the cave wall. One prisoner managed to free himself from the chains, escape from the cave, and find an upper world of light and substance. He realized that the shadows that he had spent his life watching were but simulacra of what is truly real. Finally, he gazed up to the sun, whose brilliant light made all things visible. This splendid fable is the metaphorical representation of the process by which one moves from knowledge of the evanescent world of nature to knowledge of the more permanent things and finally to the source of all knowledge and being. Plato's disciple Aristotle presented the same idea in a more prosaic manner, speaking of the transition from physics (the study of matter in motion) to mathematics (the study of numeric relations) and finally to metaphysics (the study of being as such). Neither philosopher despised what we would characterize today as science—in fact, Aristotle can credibly claim the title as father of Western science—but they both recognized that there are things the sciences can't know, things that are, in point of fact, the most important, lasting, and fascinating.

The physical sciences can reveal the chemical composition of ink and paper, but they cannot, even in principle, tell us anything about the meaning of *Moby Dick* or *The Waste Land*. Biology might inform us regarding the process by which nerves stimulate muscles in order to produce human action, but it could never tell us anything about whether a human act is morally right or wrong. Optics might disclose how light and color are processed by the eye, but it cannot possibly tell us what makes the Sistine Chapel ceiling beautiful. Speculative astrophysics might tell us truths about the unfolding of the universe from the singularity of the Big Bang, but it cannot say a word about why there is something rather than nothing or how contingent being relates to noncontingent being. How desperately sad if questions regarding truth, morality, beauty, and existence *qua* existence are dismissed as irrational or prescientific.

The scientism that I've been describing and criticizing is but a symptom of a more far-reaching problem—namely, the fading away of the humanities in our schools. If the study of literature, the arts, and philosophy is regarded as impractical and "soft" in comparison to the study of the sciences, we will produce a generation of, I'm sorry to say, prisoners chained inside of Plato's cave. They will know a great deal about the evanescent world of nature, but they won't know anything about how to live a decent life, how to differentiate between the sublime and the mundane, how to recognize God. So listen to Bill Nye as he leads you through an experiment, but please don't listen to him in regard to the higher questions and the more permanent things.

Stephen Hawking: Great Scientist, Lousy Theologian

S tephen Hawking was a great theoretical physicist and cosmologist, perhaps the most important since Einstein. It is only right that his remains have been interred alongside those of Isaac Newton in Westminster Abbey. He was, furthermore, a person of tremendous courage and perseverance, accomplishing groundbreaking work despite a decades-long struggle with the debilitating effects of Lou Gehrig's disease. And by all accounts, he was man of good humor with a rare gift for friendship. It is practically impossible not to admire him. But boy was he annoying when he talked about religion!

In the last year of his life, Hawking was putting the finishing touches on a book that is something of a follow-up to his mega-bestselling *A Brief History of Time*. Called *Brief Answers to the Big Questions*, it is a series of short essays on subjects including time travel, the possibility of intelligent life elsewhere in the universe, the physics that obtains within a black hole, and the colonization of space. But chapter 1 is entitled simply "Is There a God?" To the surprise of no one who has been paying attention to Hawking's musings on the subject the last several years, his answer is no. Now, to anyone involved in the apologetics or evangelization game, this is, of course, depressing, since many people, especially the young, will say, "Well, there you have it: the smartest man in the world says that God does not exist." The problem is that one can be exceptionally intelligent in one arena of thought and actually quite naïve in another. This, I'm afraid, is the case with Stephen Hawking, who, though uniquely well-versed in his chosen field, makes a number of blunders when he wanders into the domains of philosophy and religion.

Things get off to a very bad start in the opening line of the chapter: "Science is increasingly answering questions that used to be the province of religion." Though certain primitive forms of religion might be construed as attempts to answer what we would consider properly scientific questions, religion, in the developed sense of the term, is not asking and answering scientific questions poorly; rather, it is asking and answering qualitatively different kinds of questions. Hawking's glib one-liner beautifully expresses the scientistic attitude, by which I mean the arrogant tendency to reduce all knowledge to the scientific form of knowledge. Following their method of empirical observation, hypothesis formation, and experimentation, the sciences can indeed tell us a great deal about a certain dimension of reality. But they cannot, for example, tell us a thing about what makes a work of art beautiful, what makes a free act good or evil, what constitutes a just political arrangement, what are the features of a being *qua* being—and indeed, why there is a universe of finite existence at all. These are all philosophical and/or religious matters, and when a pure scientist, employing the method proper to the sciences, enters into them, he does so awkwardly, ham-handedly.

Let me demonstrate this by drawing attention to Hawking's treatment of the last issue I mentioned—namely, why there should be a universe at all. Hawking opines that theoretical physics can confidently answer this question in such a way that the existence of God is rendered superfluous. Just as, at the quantum level, elementary particles pop into and out of existence regularly without a cause, so the singularity that produced the Big Bang simply came to be out of nothing, without a cause and without an explanation. The result, Hawking concludes, is that "the universe is the ultimate free lunch." The first mistake—and armies of Hawking's followers make it—is to equivocate on the meaning of the word "nothing." In the strict philosophical (or indeed religious) sense, "nothing" designates absolute nonbeing; but what Hawking and his disciples mean by the term is in fact a fecund field of energy from which realities come and to which they return. The moment one speaks of "coming from" or "returning to," one is not speaking of nothing! I actually laughed out loud at this part of Hawking's analysis, which fairly gives away the game: "I think the universe was spontaneously created out of nothing, according to the laws of science." Well, whatever you want to say about the laws of science, they're not nothing! Indeed, when the quantum theorists talk about particles popping into being spontaneously, they regularly invoke quantum constants and dynamics according to which such emergences occur. Again, say what you want about these law-like arrangements, they are not absolute nonbeing. And therefore, we are compelled to ask the question: Why should contingent states of affairs—matter, energy, the Big Bang, the laws of science themselves—exist at all? The classical response of religious philosophy is that no contingency can be explained satisfactorily by appealing endlessly to other contingencies. Therefore, some finally noncontingent reality, which grounds and actualizes the finite universe, must exist. And this uncaused cause, this reality whose very nature is to be, is what serious religious people call "God." None of Hawking's speculations—least of all his musings about the putative "nothing" from which the universe arises—tells against this conviction.

May I say by way of conclusion that I actually rather liked Stephen Hawking's last book. When he stayed within the confines of his areas of expertise, he was readable, funny, informative, and creative. But could I encourage readers please to take him with a substantial grain of salt when he speaks of the things of God?

Doctor Strange, Scientism, and the Gnostic Way Station

S cott Derrickson's film *Doctor Strange* received rave reviews for its special effects, its compelling storytelling, and the quality of its actors, but I would like to focus on the spirituality implicit in it. *Doctor Strange* is far from a satisfying presentation of the spiritual order, but it represents a significant step in the right direction, which proves especially helpful for our time.

Played by the always splendid Benedict Cumberbatch, Dr. Strange is dashing, handsome, ultra-cool, a brilliant neurosurgeon called upon to handle only the most delicate and complex surgeries. He is also unbearably arrogant, pathologically self-absorbed, utterly dismissive of his colleagues, something of a first-class jerk. While racing in his Lamborghini to an evening soiree, he runs his car off the road and suffers grievous injuries to his hands. Despite the heroic efforts of the best surgeons, his fingers remain twisted, incapable of performing the operations that made him rich and famous.

In his desperation, he travels to a mysterious treatment center in Kath-mandu, where people with horrific and irreversible physical damage have, he hears, been cured. There he confronts a bald-pated female figure, played by Tilda Swinton, who claims that she has healed severed spinal cords through the manipulation of spiritual forces. When he hears this, the rationalist Dr. Strange explodes in anger and, poking her in the chest, asserts his conviction that matter is all there is and that we human beings exist for a brief moment in the context of an indifferent universe. With that, she shoves him backward and, to Dr. Strange's infinite astonishment, his astral body suddenly leaves his ordinary body. This is his introduction to a world that he never knew existed, and the beginning of his mystical apprenticeship. (By the way, if you want a compelling Christian take on this phenomenon, look at Fr. Robert Spitzer's musings on "transphysical consciousness," or in more ordinary language, the "soul.")

What I particularly liked about this confrontation in Kathmandu is how it represents a challenge to the comically arrogant scientism of our time, by which I mean the fallacy of reducing all forms of knowing to the scientific manner of knowing. This attitude, though widespread today through the influence of the "new" atheists, is utterly self-refuting. How, precisely, did the advocate of scientism see, measure, or empirically verify through experimentation the truth of the claim that only empirically measurable things are true? Though as I say widely held in many circles today, this crude attitude was not characteristic of the founders of the modern sciences, many of whom—Descartes, Copernicus, Galileo, and Newton come readily to mind—were devoutly religious, nor was it embraced by such key scientific figures as Gregor Mendel, an Augustinian friar, or Georges Lemaître, the formulator of the Big Bang theory of cosmic origins and a Catholic priest. The coolly arrogant but hopelessly narrow Dr. Strange is an apt representation of the clueless advocates of scientism on the contemporary scene, those who have simply closed themselves off to what a thousand generations of human beings have taken for granted.

In order to participate in the dynamics of the higher world, Dr. Strange has to go through a lengthy and demanding training, not unlike, his master explains, the formation he went through to become a neurosurgeon. But now he has to leave his ego aside and surrender to something he can't entirely understand. This disciplining of the grasping self, of course, is at the heart of monastic and spiritual traditions the world over. Therefore, in the measure that it reminds young people that there is more to reality than meets the eye, and in the measure that it encourages them to embark upon a properly spiritual path, *Doctor Strange* performs, I would argue, an important service.

However, all is not well with this film from a spiritual point of view, for it stops, as many contemporary movies do, at a sort of way station to the real thing. As does Star Wars, which also features a young man going through a needed apprenticeship, *Doctor Strange* initiates us into a fundamentally Gnostic space, a realm of spiritual powers, both good and evil, engaged in a relentless and never-ending struggle. (Dark and light side of the Force, anyone?) And its basic game is the learning of spells and incantations—secret gnosis—that will enable one to manipulate the higher powers to a good purpose. To be sure, there are elements of the biblical story in *Doctor Strange* as there are in Star Wars—for instance, the theme of salvific suffering and embrace of mission on behalf of others. But Gnostic visions always miss the essential teaching contained in biblical revelation—namely, that God is a personal power, who can never, even in principle, be manipulated by us, and who reigns supreme and victorious over any and all powers of evil at work in the cosmos. The point of the spiritual life, on the biblical reading, is not to control the powers through knowledge but to surrender in faith to the purposes of God and to accept from God a mission to incarnate his love in the world.

I'm sure it's asking too much to expect escapist popcorn movies to get biblical spirituality right. And if *Doctor Strange* can beguile young people out of a deadening and self-contradictory scientism, opening them to a world beyond ordinary experience, I say "two cheers" for it.

The Jordan Peterson Phenomenon

L ike many others, I have watched the Jordan Peterson phenomenon unfold with a certain fascination. If you don't know what I'm talking about, you don't spend a lot of time on social media, for Peterson, a mild-mannered psychology professor from the University of Toronto, has emerged as one of the hottest personalities on the internet. He is followed by millions of people, especially young men. His lectures and presentations—cool, understated, brainy, and blunt—are avidly watched and commented upon. And his book *12 Rules for Life: An Antidote to Chaos* is a number one bestseller all over the world. Moreover, Peterson's spirited and articulate opposition to the imposition of speech codes in his native Canada has made him a controversial political player, a hero of free speech to his supporters and a right-wing ideologue to his detractors. His interview with Cathy Newman of Channel 4 News, during which Peterson's interlocutor revealed herself as a hopelessly biased social justice warrior, has been viewed tens of millions of times.

In many ways, Peterson is doing for this generation what Joseph Campbell did for the previous one—namely, reintroducing the archetypal psychology of C.G. Jung in an appealing and provocative manner. Jung's theorizing centered around what he termed the archetypes of the collective unconscious—which is to say, those primordial instincts, insights, and memories that influence much of our behavior and that substantially inform the religions, philosophies, and rituals of the human race. The Jungian template enables Peterson to interpret many of the classical spiritual texts of Western culture in a fresh way—those very texts so often excoriated by mainstream intellectuals as hopelessly patriarchal, biased, and oppressive. It also permits him to speak with a kind of psychological and spiritual authority to which young people are not accustomed but to which they respond eagerly.

His book, an elaboration of twelve basic psychological rules for life, makes for bracing and satisfying reading. Peterson's considerable erudition is on clear display throughout, but so is his very real experience in the trenches as a practicing psychotherapist. His advice is smart indeed, but it never seems abstract, detached, or unrealistic. In the course of this brief article, I can only hint at some of his fascinating findings and recommendations. A theme that runs through the entire book is that of the play between order and chaos, symbolized most neatly by the intertwining fish of the Tao image. Human consciousness itself, Peterson argues, sets one foot in the former and the other in the latter, balancing the known and the unknown, the settled and the unexplored. Too much of one, and we fall into complacency, routine, and, at the limit, tyranny; too much of the other, and we lose our bearings completely, surrendering to the void.

The great myths of the hero—from Gilgamesh to Luke Skywalker and Bilbo Baggins—typically recount the story of someone who leaves complacent domesticity behind in order to venture into the dangerous unknown, where he manages to find something of enormous value to his family or village or society. One key to psychological/spiritual fulfillment is to embody this archetype of the hero, to live one's life as an adventurous exploration of the unknown. So Peterson tells his readers—especially young men, who have been cowed into complacency for various reasons—to throw back their shoulders, stand tall, and face the challenges of life head on. This archetype of the hero also allows us to read the story of Adam and Eve with fresh eyes. In paradise (the word itself denotes "walled garden"), our first parents were secure and innocent, but in the manner of inexperienced children. Leaving paradise was, in one sense, a positive move, for it permitted them to grow up, to engage the chaos of the unknown creatively and intelligently. This reading of Genesis, which has roots in Tillich, Hegel, and others, permits us to see that the goal of the spiritual life is not a simple return to the garden of dreaming innocence, but rather an inhabiting of the garden on the far side of the cross, that place where the tomb of Jesus was situated and in which the risen Christ appeared precisely as "gardener."

Peterson's investigation of the psyche of Aleksandr Solzhenitsyn was, for me, one of the most illuminating sections of the book. Solzhenitsyn, of course, was a victim of both Hitler and Stalin, a terrorized and dehumanized inmate in the Gulag Archipelago, and one of the most tortured of souls in the terrible twentieth century. It would have been surpassingly easy for him simply to curse his fate, to lash out in anger at God, to become a sullen figure scurrying about the margins of life. Instead, he endeavored to change his own life, to turn the light of his moral consciousness on himself, to get his psychological house in order. This initial move enabled him to see the world around him with extraordinary clarity and, eventually, to tell the story of Soviet depravity with such devastating moral authority. The lesson that Peterson draws from this example is this: if you want to change the corrupt world, "start to stop doing what you know to be wrong. Start stopping today."

I have shared just a handful of wise insights from a book that is positively chockablock with them. So do I thoroughly support Jordan Peterson's approach? Well, no, though a full explication of my objection would take us far beyond the confines of this brief article. In a word, I have the same concern about Peterson that I have about both Campbell and Jung—namely, the Gnosticizing tendency to read biblical religion purely psychologically and philosophically and not at all historically. No Christian should be surprised that the Scriptures can be profitably read through psychological and philosophical lenses, but at the same time, every Christian has to accept the fact that the God of the Bible is not simply a principle or an abstraction, but rather a living God who acts in history. As I say, to lay this out thoroughly would require at least another article or two or twelve.

On balance, I like this book and warmly recommend it. I think it's especially valuable for the beleaguered young men in our society, who need a mentor to tell them to stand up straight and act like heroes.

Listening to Jordan Peterson
and Sam Harris

Of the many Jordan Peterson videos, the ones that intrigued me the most were his dialogues with Sam Harris, one of the "four horsemen of the new atheism" and perhaps the most strident critic of religion on the scene today. The reason that Peterson was paired with Harris is that the former has begun to explore, in remarkably perceptive ways, the psychological and archetypal significance of the biblical stories and hence implicitly to question the wholesale dismissal of religion that one finds in the new atheists.

In the discussions I watched, Harris, like his colleagues, the late Christopher Hitchens and Richard Dawkins, focused his attention on the ways that religion, due to its dogmatism and allergy to self-critique, has given rise to myriad forms of oppression and violence. We can find this, of course, in the Bible itself, which seems to condone slavery, countenance genocide, encourage the mistreatment of women, and sanction the brutal elimination of conquered people. And we see it, Harris argues, throughout religious history, finding expression in inquisitions, witch hunts, pogroms, etc. Behind all of this mayhem, the atheist contends, is the typically religious tendency to accept things on the basis of faith, to set aside critical reason, and to embrace authoritarianism. In answer to this familiar objection, Jordan Peterson spoke of two extremes that dog the intellectual and moral project throughout the ages—namely, fundamentalism and chaotic relativism. The first—uncritical, oppressive, arrogant, and violent—produced and continues to produce the very negativities that Harris legitimately complains of; but the second—anchorless, impotent, without moral seriousness—has proven to be just as dangerous. The responsible moral actor and intellectual explorer lives in the space in between those two extremes.

41

If I am reading Peterson correctly, he feels that Harris and his atheist colleagues fall into the trap of identifying the dogmatic and fundamentalist shadow that inevitably accompanies religion with religion *tout court*. And they accordingly tend to overlook the substantial and very positive contributions religious thinkers and agents have made in helping us avoid the chaos of sheer relativism, especially in regard to matters of ultimate concern. Here I would substantially agree with Peterson, for I have simply found it impossible to take seriously a view that rules out of court the massive contribution that religion has made to human culture. At the same time, I would also signal a sympathy with Harris in the measure that I, humbly and gratefully, acknowledge that it was the Enlightenment critique of Christianity that compelled the churches to reconsider some of their patterns of behavior and strategies of biblical interpretation. We did indeed need some of the luminosity of the Enlightenment to eliminate the shadow that he correctly identifies.

So what precisely does Jordan Peterson propose in regard to religion? I'll confess that things can get a bit murky, due in part to his meandering and ruminative style. With his stress on archetypal psychology, he is obviously a Jungian, but what became clear to me as I watched these videos is how deeply Kantian his approach is. The great eighteenth-century philosopher opined that we cannot know the existence of God through the exercise of theoretical reason. The classical metaphysical approaches to God through cosmology and metaphysical speculation are ruled out (see the *Critique of Pure Reason* for the details). However, Kant maintained, we *can* come to a kind of working knowledge of God through what he called practical or moral reasoning. The idea of God as the *summum bonum*, he argued, is one of the conditions for the possibility of undertaking the moral enterprise at all. In other words, we would never endeavor to do any good thing unless we implicitly accepted the supposition that God is. A variation of this approach can be found in Kant's *Religion within the Limits of Reason Alone*. In that text, Kant argues that the story of Jesus presents the "archetype of the person perfectly pleasing to God," and hence provides, at least for Westerners, the narrative substrate for the moral undertaking. We do not have to worry particularly about the historical veracity of what the Gospels communicate, for it is the story as such that matters.

I think that Peterson is reviving this Kantian approach for our time. He usually backs away from metaphysical speculation about the existence of God; he doesn't seem particularly interested in classical arguments for a first cause or necessary being. But he does indeed think that the archetype of God, expressed typically in narrative form, is essential for moral thought and moral behavior. Biblical language regarding devotion to God or following the will of God reflects and gives expression to this inchoate supposition.

So where does this leave us? I think that Jordan Peterson represents a great step beyond the one-sided (though necessary) critique offered by Sam Harris and his atheist colleagues. He has helped an awful lot of people who have been malformed by a doctrinaire secularism to open their minds and hearts to the truth embedded in the Bible and the great religious traditions. But he remains stuck, it seems to me, on one side of the Kantian divide. The living and personal God of the Bible remains, for him, an archetype, an idea, a heuristic device.

The USCCB Meeting, Jordan Peterson, and the "Nones"

n June 2019, I gave a presentation at the USCCB Spring Meeting in Baltimore. My topic was what I identified as the second greatest crisis facing the Church today—namely, the massive attrition of our own people, especially the young. I trust that the first—around which most of our discussions that week revolved—is obvious to everyone. Judging from the extremely positive reaction of my brother bishops and the lively conversation that followed my presentation, the talk was well received. I was also delighted it apparently prompted a spirited conversation on social media.

After laying out the rather dismal statistics regarding the "nones" or the religiously unaffiliated—50 percent of millennial Catholics now claim no religious identity, for every one person who joins our Church, six are leaving, etc.—I commenced to offer some reasons why so many are exiting. I told my brother bishops that these were not the fruit of idle speculation, but rather of the many statistical and sociological studies that have been conducted regarding the phenomenon. The number one reason—reiterated in survey after survey—is that young people are quitting the Church because they don't believe in the teachings of classical Christianity. Moreover, the studies consistently maintain that this lack of belief is often because religion is seen as conflicting with science. Other factors, I continued, include the general secularism and moral relativism of the culture, the difficulty many young people have with the Church's sexual teachings, and the supposed correlation between religion and violence.

Having presented these findings, I then shared what I take to be signs of hope. The first is that, among the unaffiliated, there are relatively few fierce atheists or determined opponents of religion. Most are indifferent to faith and have drifted rather than stormed away from the Church. A second indicator of hope is the massive presence of young people on social media platforms that trade in religious topics. I mentioned my own participation in a Reddit AMA (Ask Me Anything), which yielded almost twelve thousand comments and questions, making it the third most discussed exchange of its kind the previous year. Even though many, if not most, of those who joined in that conversation proposed challenging questions, or made skeptical observations, the undoubted interest in matters religious is something to build on. Finally, I referenced what I called "the Jordan Peterson phenomenon." I was drawing my brothers' attention to the rather extraordinary fact that a mild-mannered, soft-spoken psychology professor, speaking of serious matters in a sober way, could attract tens of thousands to arenas and millions to his social media sites. I told my fellow bishops that most recently Peterson had been lecturing on the Bible, causing armies of people, especially young men, to take a fresh look at the Scriptures. I explicitly said that my reference to Peterson in no way signaled a one-sided or uncritical endorsement of his teaching. Nevertheless, his emergence and his success are, I argued, indicators that we could get a serious message across to a wide audience.

The reaction to my talk outside the walls of the bishops' conference ballroom was, as I say, interesting. Most reacted very positively to my observations and suggestions, but some, on both the extreme left and the extreme right, took exception to what I said. On the starboard side of the spectrum, there were comments to the effect that I had underplayed the importance of the clerical sex abuse scandals. Well, no one has been more vehement in his denunciation of these outrages than I (see my *Letter to a Suffering Church* for the details), but judging from the available data, it's simply not the case that the scandals are a major driver of disaffiliation. They indeed appear as a factor, but not a significant one, certainly in comparison with the causes I named above. I get the passion around this issue, but it shouldn't prompt us to draw conclusions not supported by objective evidence.

But I was especially surprised, and more than a little amused, by the overheated response from some on the far-left end of the spectrum. It appears that the mere mention of the name Jordan Peterson is enough to send some into irrational conniptions. Though I had unambiguously stated that my reference to the Canadian was in no way meant as an endorsement of the entirety of his thought, some commentators and combox denizens characterized me as a Peterson disciple, an apologist for his program, a lackey. One particularly hysterical observer had me "basing my apologetics" on Jordan Peterson! Oy vey. As I have made clear in my own articles and videos, Peterson reads the Bible through a Jungian, psychodynamic lens, and hence, by definition, does not read it adequately. It is not even evident that the Canadian believes in God in the accepted sense of the term. "Basing my apologetics" on him?! Give me a break.

What is particularly sad to me is that the commentariat, especially in regard to religion, has become so polarized and ideologically driven that the most elementary distinctions aren't made and the most broad-brush analyses are commonplace. What makes it sadder still is that these distortions and projections stand in the way of addressing the vitally important issue under consideration. As left and right defend their respective ideological bailiwicks, the Church continues to hemorrhage young people. If we want to get serious about a problem that ought to concern everyone in the Church, it would be wise to attend to objectivities.

What I Learned Talking with Thousands of Skeptics on Reddit

In September 2019, I made my second dive into the Reddit AMA world. One of the most popular websites in the world, Reddit is a forum for all sorts of online conversations and presentations. The AMA (for Ask Me Anything) is a twenty-first-century version of the medieval *quodlibetal* questions, during which a game theology professor would entertain any inquiry that came from the floor. Now, things are a bit cruder and more rough and ready on Reddit than they were in the universities of the Middle Ages, but you get the idea. When I engaged in the exercise last year, I received almost twelve thousand questions and comments, making mine the third most commented-on AMA after those of Bill Gates and Jordan Peterson. This time, I received over fifteen thousand comments and counting, making mine the *second* most commented-on AMA of the past year, just after Bill Gates and ahead of Bernie Sanders! I mention this not to show how popular I am with the Reddit crowd (I'm sure most of them have never heard of me), but rather to demonstrate just how massively interested young people are in the questions of religion.

If you can make it through the plethora of obnoxious, juvenile, and insulting comments, you will actually learn a great deal about what is on the minds of the Reddit audience—mostly young men between the ages of eighteen and thirty—when it comes to religion. I would identify four major themes: proving the existence of God, the problem of suffering, the determination of why one would choose one religion over another, and homosexuality. Each of these issues was addressed hundreds, perhaps thousands, of times. Permit me to speak, very briefly, of each in turn.

So first of all, the question of proving God's existence came up again and again. Are there rational grounds for believing in God? How do I know that there is a God? Can God's reality be demonstrated to someone who does not believe in the Bible? What struck me very positively in this regard is that the young people on Reddit seemed to have a powerful interest in God—and that's no small thing. They weren't treating the proposal of God's existence as prescientific nonsense or self-serving fantasy. They were honestly wondering about God, restlessly searching for him. What struck me a bit more negatively is that there seemed to be little or no sense that Christian theologians and philosophers have been presenting and defending arguments for God's existence for centuries. That the Reddit audience hadn't an inkling of what these proofs and demonstrations might be is, at least in part, a failure of the churches in their ministry of education.

The second major theme was the problem of evil. Now, it has been said that all of theology commences with and ultimately centers around the issue of justifying the ways of God in the presence of great suffering; so in a way, the intense interest of young people in this question is another encouraging sign that they are eager to think theologically. It would obviously require a lengthy book even to scratch the surface of this matter, but I would make just this one observation. I told a number of my conversation partners that there is only one mystery more puzzling than the problem of evil, and that is the mystery of goodness. Evil does not, strictly speaking, exist. It is the lack of a good that ought to be there, and as such, it is always parasitic upon the good. So as deeply frustrating and confounding the problem of evil is, it is always outpaced by the "problem" of goodness—namely, why goodness and beauty should exist at all. This, I suggested, might be at least a fresh way to address the issue.

The third principal motif was this: How could one possibly know that one's religion is better or truer than any other? To a large extent, this query is born from the relativism that holds sway everywhere in the culture of the West and, relatedly, from the conviction that toleration is the one indisputable value. Behind the question is the assumption that any attempt to claim truth in regard to a given religion is simply tantamount to arrogance and bigotry. Those who posed it seem to feel that religions are more or less like hobbies.

You have yours and I have mine, but neither one of us would be justified in imposing them on each other or on anyone else. And what all of this reveals is the breakdown in anything like genuinely public religious argument. That a person can or should actually *make a case* rationally for a religious perspective strikes the Reddit audience as absurd. In response to one of these questioners, I offered a brief demonstration of how one might argue, on Thomist grounds, for the legitimacy of a Trinitarian monotheism. I would be flabbergasted if that little exercise actually convinced my interlocutor, but my more modest hope is that it might show him/her that objective argument is possible in regard to religious matters.

Finally, my Reddit friends were massively concerned with the issue of homosexuality. Repeatedly, probably a thousand times, I heard that the Church hates gays and is hopelessly behind the times in regard to welcoming and affirming homosexuals. I won't even attempt in the context of this article to address the moral issues here, but permit me to say that the reaction of the Reddit audience is ample proof that the language the Church has used to articulate its teaching in regard to this question has been ineffective to say the very least. Those well-versed in Aristotelian teleological ethics understand what is meant by the claim that homosexual acts are "intrinsically disordered," but I'm afraid that the vast majority of people took that language to mean that homosexual persons are twisted and contemptible. Was this a deeply incorrect reading of the Church's teaching? Absolutely. But is it an indication that we can and must do a great deal better in getting that teaching across with greater compassion and clarity? I think the question answers itself.

I will confess that my two forays into the Reddit space have been more than a little discouraging. If you dare, look at the dismaying number of just plain aggressive and mean-spirited comments. But at the end of the day, I take those fifteen thousand comments as a deeply encouraging sign that the restless human heart is still searching for the only one who will satisfy it.

Apologists, Catechists, Theologians: Wake Up!

After perusing a recent Pew Study on why young people are leaving the active practice of Christianity, I confess that I just sighed in exasperation. I don't doubt for a moment the sincerity of those who responded to the survey, but the reasons they offer for abandoning Christianity are just so uncompelling. That is to say, any theologian, apologist, or evangelist worth his salt should be able easily to answer them. And this led me (hence the sigh) to the conclusion that "we have met the enemy and it is us." For the past fifty years or so, Christian thinkers have largely abandoned the art of apologetics and have failed (here I offer a *j'accuse* to many in the Catholic universities) to resource the riches of the Catholic intellectual tradition in order to hold off critics of the faith. I don't blame the avatars of secularism for actively attempting to debunk Christianity; that's their job, after all. But I do blame teachers, catechists, evangelists, and academics within the Christian churches for not doing enough to keep our young people engaged. These studies consistently demonstrate that unless we believers seriously pick up our game intellectually, we're going to keep losing our kids.

Let me look just briefly at some of the chief reasons offered for walking away from Christianity. Many evidently felt that modern science somehow undermines the claims of the faith. One respondent said, "Rational thought makes religion go out the window," and another complained of the "lack of any sort of scientific evidence of a creator." Well, I'm sure it would come as an enormous surprise to St. Paul, St. Augustine, St. John Chrysostom, St. Jerome, St. Thomas Aquinas, St. Robert Bellarmine, St. John Henry Newman, G.K. Chesterton, C.S. Lewis, and Joseph Ratzinger—all among the most brilliant people Western culture has produced—that religion and reason are somehow incompatible. And to focus more precisely on the issue of "scientific evidence," the sciences, ordered by their nature and method to an analysis of empirically verifiable objects and states of affairs within the universe, cannot even in principle address questions regarding God, who is not a being in the world, but rather the reason why the finite realm exists at all. There simply cannot be "scientific" evidence or argument that tells one way or the other in regard to God. Mind you, this is by no means to imply that there are no rational warrants for belief in God. Philosophers over the centuries, in fact, have articulated dozens of such demonstrations, which have, especially when considered together, enormous probative force. I have found, in my own evangelical work, that the argument from contingency gets quite a bit of traction with those who are wrestling with the issue of God's existence. What these arguments have lacked, sad to say, are convinced and articulate defenders within the academy and in the ranks of teachers, catechists, and apologists.

One of the young people responded to the survey using the formula made famous by Karl Marx: "Religion just seems to be the opiate of the people." Marx's adage, of course, is an adaptation of Ludwig Feuerbach's observation that religion amounts to a projection of our idealized self-image. Sigmund Freud, in the early twentieth century, further adapted Feuerbach, arguing that religion is like a waking dream, a wish-fulfilling fantasy. This line of thinking has been massively adopted by the so-called "new atheists" of our time. I find it regularly on my internet forums. What all of this comes down to, ultimately, is a dismissive and patronizing psychologization of religious belief. But it is altogether vulnerable to a *tu quoque* (you do the same thing) counterattack. I think it is eminently credible to say that atheism amounts to a wish-fulfilling fantasy, precisely in the measure that it allows for complete freedom and self-determination: if there is no God, no ultimate moral criterion, I can do and be whatever I want. In a word, the psychologizing cuts just as effectively in the opposite direction. Hence, the two charges more or less cancel one another out—and this should compel us to return to real argument at the objective level.

A third commonly cited reason for abandoning the Christian churches is that, as one respondent put it, "Christians seem to behave so badly." God knows that the clergy sex abuse scandals of recent decades have lent considerable support to this argument, already bolstered by the usual suspects of the Inquisition, the Crusades, the persecution of Galileo, witch-hunts, etc., etc. We could, of course, enter into an examination of each of these cases, but for our purposes I am willing to concede the whole argument: yes indeed, over the centuries, lots and lots of Christians have behaved wickedly. But why, one wonders, should this tell against the integrity and rectitude of Christian belief? Many, many Americans have done horrific things, often in the name of America. One thinks of slave owners, the enforcers of Jim Crow laws, the carpet bombers of Dresden and Tokyo, the perpetrators of the My Lai Massacre, the guards at Abu Ghraib prison, etc. Do these outrages *ipso facto* prove that American ideals are less than praiseworthy, or that the American system as such is corrupt? The question answers itself.

Relatedly, a number of young people said that they left the Christian churches because "religion is the greatest source of conflict in the world." One hears this charge so often today—especially in the wake of September 11—that we tend to take it as self-evident, when in point of fact, it is an invention of Enlightenment-era historiography. Voltaire, Diderot, Spinoza, and many others in the seventeenth and eighteenth centuries wanted to undermine religion, and they could find no better way to achieve this end than to score Christianity as *the* source of violence. Through numberless channels this view has seeped into the general consciousness, but it simply does not stand up to serious scrutiny. In their exhaustive survey of the wars of human history (*The Encyclopedia of Wars*), Charles Phillips and Alan Axelrod demonstrate that less than 7 percent of wars could be credibly blamed on religion, and even the most casual reflection bears this out.

In point of fact, the bloodiest wars in history, those of the twentieth century, which produced over one hundred million dead, had practically nothing to do with religion. Indeed, a very persuasive case could be made that ideological secularism and modern nationalism are the sources of the greatest bloodshed. And yet the prejudice, first fostered by the *philosophes* of the Enlightenment, oddly endures.

An earlier Pew Study showed that for every one person who joins the Catholic Church today, six are leaving, and that many of those who leave are the young. This recent survey indicates that intellectual objections figure prominently when these drifters are asked why they abandoned their faith. My *cri de coeur* is that teachers, catechists, theologians, apologists, and evangelists might wake up to this crisis and do something about it.

A New Apologetics:
An Intervention at the Youth Synod

This intervention was offered at the Vatican during the 2018 Synod on Young People, the Faith, and Vocational Discernment.

Jesus' encounter with two erstwhile disciples on the road to Emmaus (Luke 24:13–35) provides a beautiful template for the Church's work of accompaniment across the ages. The Lord walks with the couple, even as they move away from Jerusalem—which is to say, spiritually speaking, in the wrong direction. He does not commence with a word of judgment, but rather with attention and quiet encouragement. Jesus continues to listen, even as they recount, accurately enough, all the data having to do with him. But then, knowing that they lack the interpretive pattern that will make sense of the data, he upbraids them ("Oh, how foolish you are, and how slow of heart to believe all that the prophets have declared!"), and then he lays out the form ("beginning with Moses and all the prophets, he interpreted to them the things about himself in all the scriptures"). He listens with love, and he speaks with force and clarity.

Innumerable surveys and studies over the past ten years have confirmed that young people frequently cite intellectual reasons when asked what has prompted them to leave the Church or lose confidence in it. Chief among these are the convictions that religion is opposed to science or that it cannot stand up to rational scrutiny; that its beliefs are outmoded, a holdover from a primitive time; that the Bible is unreliable; that religious belief gives rise to violence; and that God is a threat to human freedom. I can verify, on the basis of twenty years of ministry in the field of online evangelization, that these concerns are crucial stumbling blocks to the acceptance of the faith among young people.

What is vitally needed today, as an aspect of the accompaniment of the young, is a renewed apologetics and catechesis. I realize that in some circles within the Church, the term apologetics is suspect, since it seems to indicate something rationalistic, aggressive, condescending. I hope it is clear that arrogant proselytizing has no place in our pastoral outreach, but I hope it is equally clear that an intelligent, respectful, and culturally sensitive explication of the faith ("giving a reason for the hope that is within us"—see 1 Pet. 3:15) is certainly a desideratum. There is a consensus among pastoral people that, at least in the West, we have experienced a crisis in catechesis these last fifty years. That the faith has not been effectively communicated was verified by a recent Religious Landscape Study from the Pew Research Center in America. It indicated that, among the major religions, Catholicism was second to last in passing on its traditions. Why has it been the case, over the past several decades, that young people in our own Catholic secondary schools have read Shakespeare in literature class, Homer in Greek class, Einstein in physics class, but, far too often, superficial texts in religion? The army of our young who claim that religion is irrational is a bitter fruit of this failure in education.

Therefore, what would a new apologetics look like? First, it would arise from the questions that young people spontaneously ask. It would not be imposed from above, but would rather emerge organically from below, a response to the yearning of the mind and the heart. Here it would take a cue from the method of St. Thomas Aquinas. The austere texts of the great theological master in point of fact emerged from the lively give-and-take of the *quaestiones disputatae* that stood at the heart of the educational process in the medieval university. Thomas was deeply interested in what young people were really asking. So should we.

Secondly, a new apologetics should look deep and long into the question of the relationship between religion and science. For many people today, scientific and rational are simply equivalent or coextensive terms. And therefore, since religion is obviously not science, it must be irrational. Without for a moment denigrating the sciences, we have to show that there are nonscientific and yet eminently rational paths that conduce toward knowledge of the real. Literature, drama, philosophy, the fine arts—all close cousins of religion—not only entertain and delight; they also bear truths that are unavailable in any other way. A renewed apologetics ought to cultivate these approaches.

Thirdly, our apologetics and catechesis should walk the *via pulchritudinis* (way of beauty), as Pope Francis characterized it in *Evangelii Gaudium*. Especially in our postmodern cultural context, commencing with the true and the good—what to believe and how to behave—is often counter-indicated, since the ideology of self-invention is so firmly established. However, the third transcendental, the beautiful, often proves a more winsome, less threatening path. And part of the genius of Catholicism is that we have so consistently embraced the beautiful—in song, poetry, architecture, painting, sculpture, and liturgy. All of this provides a powerful matrix for evangelization. And as Hans Urs von Balthasar argued, the most compelling beauty of all is that of the saints. I have found a good deal of evangelical traction in presenting the lives of these great friends of God, somewhat in the manner of a baseball coach who draws young adepts into the game by showing them the play of some of its greatest practitioners.

When Jesus explained himself to the disciples on the road to Emmaus, their hearts began to burn within them. The Church must walk with young people, listen to them with attention and love, and then be ready intelligently to give a reason for the hope that is within us. This, I trust, will set the hearts of the young on fire.

Why Accompaniment Involves Apologetics

In July 2018, I granted an interview to the *National Catholic Reporter* concerning the Synod on Young People, the Faith, and Vocational Discernment, to which I was elected a delegate. We discussed a number of topics, including the rise of the "nones," the purpose of the synod, and creative ways of listening to the concerns of young people. In the course of the conversation, I also stated that I would bring the issue of apologetics before the synod, since so many young people have questions about, and objections to, the faith. But when the interview appeared, the author expressed her puzzlement that I would mention apologetics, though it is clear that the working document calls for "accompaniment" of young people. It seems many think doing apologetics and accompaniment are mutually exclusive. To my mind, they're mutually implicative. Of course, especially in our context today, a browbeating, "I've got all the answers" approach is counter-indicated. But apologetics as such is needed more than ever—and more to the point, is perfectly congruent with Pope Francis' insistence on walking with those who struggle with the faith.

I don't know any better illustration of what this looks like than the account of Jesus' conversation with two erstwhile disciples on the road to Emmaus (Luke 24:13–35). The story commences with the couple walking the wrong way. Everything in the Gospel of Luke moves toward Jerusalem, the city of the cross, the Resurrection, the sending of the Spirit, the birth of the Church. Thus, venturing away from the center, they are evocative of all of us sinners who, to varying degrees, wander on wrong paths. Suddenly, walking with them, though they are prevented from recognizing him, is the Lord Jesus. He does not announce himself; he does not launch into a discussion of theology; he does not tell them what to think or how to behave.

He walks with them in easy fellowship, even though they are going the wrong way, and he gently asks what's on their minds: "What are you discussing with each other while you walk along?"

All that the left quite rightly finds attractive in accompaniment is on display here: tolerance, the willingness to enter the psychological space of those who are lost, nonaggressiveness, listening, etc. And this patient approach indeed bears a good deal of evangelical fruit, for Jesus discovers that they know quite a bit about him: "Jesus of Nazareth . . . was a prophet mighty in deed and word before God and all the people. . . . Our chief priests and leaders handed him over to be condemned to death and crucified him. . . . Yes, and besides all this, it is now the third day since these things took place. Moreover, some women of our group astounded us . . . and told us that they had indeed seen a vision of angels who said that he was alive." But it also reveals how much they didn't know, and this invites a decisive turn; the patient, listening Christ becoming pretty directive: "Oh, how foolish you are, and how slow of heart to believe all that the prophets have declared!" And with that, Jesus launches into a very rich apologetic, placing the events of the cross and Resurrection within the interpretive context of the Old Testament, taking the couple through a master class in Scripture and theology.

It shouldn't be too difficult to see how this story provides a template for the evangelical accompaniment of young people today. Yes indeed, friendship and respectful listening are indispensable. Walking with even those who are alienated from the Church is always the right thing to do. Browbeating, moralizing, and haranguing are to be avoided. However, accompaniment does not simply mean wandering around with someone! As the Emmaus account clearly demonstrates, the gentle, invitational approach aroused questions that then called for answers. Jesus loved them, walked with them, elicited what they knew—and then he taught, with clarity, at length, and in depth. And so young people today (who, trust me, have myriad questions about religion) are hungry and thirsty—not just for friendly companions but for a word from the Church. The term "apologetics" is derived from the Greek *apologia*, which simply means "bringing a word to bear." It implies, therefore, giving a reason, providing a context, putting things in perspective, offering direction. How wonderful that, recalling Jesus' great apologetic intervention, the Emmaus disciples said, "Were not our hearts burning within us while he was talking to us on the road, while he was opening the scriptures to us?" Young people will feel the same way today if the Church both walks and talks with them.

As long as we're exploring etymology, it is instructive, by way of conclusion, to examine the roots of the word "accompaniment." It comes from the Latin *cum pane* (with bread). To accompany is not just to be with someone; rather, it is to share bread with that person, to give and to receive life. In the evangelical context, therefore, true accompaniment goes beyond fellowship. It has to do with offering the bread of life.

Black Elk and the Need
for Catechists

In his formal address to us at the commencement of the annual November meeting of the United States bishops in 2017, Archbishop Christophe Pierre, the Apostolic Nuncio to the United States, reiterated statistics that I have often remarked regarding the growing number of "nones" or religiously unaffiliated in our country. He especially noted the rise of this cohort among people under thirty years of age. For every one person who joins the Catholic Church today, he reminded us, six are leaving. We must make a renewed commitment, he concluded, to the indispensable work of handing on the faith. The archbishop's intuition in this regard was confirmed, over and again, by bishops who spoke, in various sessions and forums, of a crisis of catechesis in our church.

I had this wake-up call from the pope's representative very much in mind as my friend Bishop Robert Gruss, the Bishop of Rapid City, South Dakota, rose to speak on the second day of the meeting. Bishop Gruss' happy task was to present to us the case for the beatification and canonization of Nicholas Black Elk, a Lakota Indian medicine man who, at midlife, converted to Catholicism. After hearing the bishop's impassioned presentation, we enthusiastically voted to approve the advancement of Black Elk's cause. What especially struck me in Bishop Gruss' brief biographical sketch is that Black Elk, after his conversion, eagerly took up the task of catechesis within his community. Due to his impressive memory and acute mind, he was able to convey the complexities of the Bible and Church teaching to his fellow Lakotans who had embraced the faith. And very much in line with the Catholic conviction that grace builds on and perfects nature, Black Elk endeavored to incorporate his mystical sensibility and healing power into the fuller context of his Catholicism. It was his holiness and prayerful connection to God, even more than his learning, that brought his people closer to Christ.

My prayer is that, if the cause of Black Elk moves forward, we might one day invoke him as a real icon for catechists in the Catholic Church. There is an army of volunteers across our country who give generously of their time to pass on the faith to our young people, but I wonder how many of these laborers in the vineyard of the Lord truly realize the sacredness of their task. Without good catechists, more and more of our young people will fall into secularism and indifferentism. And as these unaffiliated in ever greater numbers come of age, our society will be adversely affected, for Christian ideas and values will be less and less in play.

So what can catechists today take from the example of Nicholas Black Elk? First, they can commit themselves to the assiduous study of the faith. As I have argued before, huge numbers of the young identify intellectual problems and questions as the reasons they are leaving the faith: religion in relation to science, the existence of God, the objectivity of moral values, etc. Without smart catechists, the kids abandon the faith. It's as blunt and as simple as that. My nephew, who is starting his first year at the Massachusetts Institute of Technology (MIT) this fall, went through religious education as he was coming of age. To be frank, he found the vast majority of his training superficial and remembers almost none of it. But one year stays in his mind. In his sixth grade religious education class, he had a catechist who had a master's degree in theology and who took the young people, with some rigor, through a study of the Bible. Please don't tell me that the kids can't handle that sort of challenge; on the contrary, it's what they remember—and savor.

Secondly, they can see their work as a true vocation, a sacred calling, a mystical obligation. As Pope Paul VI put it so memorably, men and women of today listen to witnesses more than to teachers, and to teachers in the measure that they are also witnesses. Or as the cliché has it: the faith is caught more than taught. Some years ago, I read a study that indicated what drew young people to the faith were not gimmicks or histrionics or the pathetic attempt to be "relevant" to them. What drew them were teachers who knew their subject matter and were obviously committed to it.

Catechists, the Church needs you! We're losing our kids to secularism. If anyone of sharp mind and faithful heart is reading these words, take seriously the possibility that God is calling you to this sacred work. And I pray that one day catechists can look to Nicholas Black Elk as exemplar and heavenly friend.

Go in Haste! Be Amazed! Treasure!

A recent survey from the Public Religion Research Institute showed that now fully one-fourth of Americans belong to no religion at all—that's approximately eighty million people. And among those in the eighteen to twenty-nine age group, the percentage of "nones" goes up to 40! This increase has been alarmingly precipitous. Fifty years ago, only a fraction of the country would have identified as unreligious, and even a decade ago, the number was only at 14 percent. What makes this situation even more distressing is that fully 64 percent of young adult "nones" were indeed raised religious but have taken the conscious and active decision to abandon their churches. Houston, we definitely have a problem.

I have written frequently regarding practical steps that religious leaders ought to be taking to confront this rising tide of secularist ideology, and I will continue to do so. But for the moment, I would like to reflect on a passage from the Gospel of Luke that sheds considerable light on this issue. It has to do with the visit of the shepherds to Mary and the Christ child in the stable at Bethlehem (Luke 2:15–19), and it hinges on three words: haste, amazed, and treasured.

We hear that, upon receiving the angel's message, the shepherds "went with haste" to visit the holy family. This echoes a passage from a bit earlier in Luke's Gospel: having heard the news of her own pregnancy and that of Elizabeth, Mary, we are told, "went with haste" to the hill country of Judah to help her cousin (Luke 1:39). The spiritual truth that both of these pericopes disclose is that energy, verve, enthusiasm, and a sense of mission come precisely from a good that is perceived to be both objective and transcendent to the ego. If I might borrow the language of Dietrich von Hildebrand, it is only the objectively valuable—as opposed to the merely subjectively satisfying—that fills the mind and soul with passion and purpose. When the sense of objective and transcendent value is attenuated—as it necessarily is within the context of a secularist worldview—passion and mission fade away. John Henry Newman said that what gives a river verve and movement is precisely the firmness of its banks. When those banks are broken down, in the interest of a supposed freedom, the once energetic body of water spreads out into a great lazy lake. What we have in our secularist culture, which denies the transcendent good, is a subjectivism that gives rise to the "whatever" attitude. Toleration and self-assertion reign supreme; but no one goes anywhere with haste. Rather, we all rest on our individual air mattresses in the midst of the placid but tedious lake.

The second word I want to emphasize is "amazed." Luke tells us that those who heard the shepherds' testimony were "amazed" (or "astonished") at the news. The King James Version renders this as "they wondered at" the message. Wonder, amazement, and astonishment happen when the properly transcendent power breaks into our ordinary experience. The findings of the sciences delight and inform us, but they don't astonish us, and the reason for this is that we are finally in control of the deliverances of the scientific method. We observe, we form hypotheses, we make experiments, and we draw conclusions. Again, this is all to the good, but it doesn't produce amazement. Dorothy Day witnessed to the astonishing when she said that, upon the birth of her first child, she felt a gratitude so enormous that it would correspond to nothing or no one in this world. Mother Teresa was properly amazed when, on a lengthy train journey to Darjeeling, she heard a voice calling her to minister to the poorest of the poor. The Apostles of Jesus fell into wonder when they saw, alive again, their Master who had been crucified and buried. These are the most precious kinds of experiences that we can have, and if St. Augustine is right, they alone can satisfy the deepest longing of the heart. A secularist ideology—the worldview embraced by the "nones"—produces the clean, well-lighted space of what we can know and control. But it precludes true astonishment, and this leaves the soul impoverished.

The final word from Luke upon which I'd like to reflect is "treasured." The evangelist tells us that Mary "treasured all these words and pondered them in her heart." Newman said that Mary, precisely in this contemplative, ruminative frame of mind, is the model of all theology. I'd press it further. She is the real symbol of the Church in its entire function as the custodian of revelation. What is the Sistine Chapel? What is Notre Dame Cathedral? What is the *Divine Comedy* of Dante? What is the *Summa contra Gentiles* of Thomas Aquinas? What are the sermons of John Chrysostom? What are the teachings of the great ecumenical councils? What is the liturgy in all of its complexity and beauty? These are all means by which the Church stubbornly, century in and century out, treasures the astonishing events of God's self-manifestation. Up and down the ages, the Church ponders what God has done so that the memory of these mighty deeds might never be lost. As such, she performs an indispensable service on behalf of the world—though the world might not have any sense of it. She keeps holding up the light against the darkness.

So to the "nones" and to those who are tempted to move into secularism, I say, don't float on the lazy lake; rather, go in haste! Don't settle for something less than astonishment; be amazed! Don't fall into spiritual amnesia; treasure!

PART III

RESISTING THE CULTURE OF CONTEMPT

Social Media and
the Culture of Contempt

Years ago, when I first started posting articles and videos on the internet, I frequently engaged the so-called "new atheists." Predictably, they weren't overjoyed at my contributions, and they often commented bitterly on my sites. Sometimes, atheist web-meisters would direct their followers to fill the comboxes of my videos with disparaging and *ad hominem* remarks. After dealing, in more recent years, with some archconservative Catholics in these same forums, I can honestly say: I prefer the atheists!

I must admit that the vitriol, negativity, personal attacks, and outright calumny that come regularly from self-professed Catholics is just dismaying and disedifying in the extreme. The most recent example is the reaction to an article that I wrote regarding the right relationship between clergy and laity in their shared engagement of the culture. Relying on the Vatican II document *Lumen Gentium*, which I extensively cited, I calmly made my argument. I attacked no one; I indulged in no character assassination; I never made an *ad hominem* remark. I simply laid out the clear teaching of an ecumenical council and tried to apply it to our present situation. Now, was my article susceptible to criticism? Of course. As Cardinal George used to say, in the spirit of St. Thomas Aquinas, "No matter what you argue, there is always a *sed contra*." He meant that even the most finely articulated demonstration has left something important unsaid, or some angle unexplored, or some nuance undeveloped. And so are people justified in bringing up objections and counterarguments? Naturally.

But in the wake of my article, armies of commenters, encouraged by certain internet provocateurs, inundated Twitter and all of my social media sites with wave upon wave of the most hateful, vituperative, and venomous words that one could imagine. I was called "spineless," "gutless," and "cowardly," and that's just to mention the most benign and nonobscene remarks. For four days, I had to engage three of my coworkers at Word on Fire full time simply to remove the most poisonous comments. When a Fellow of the Word on Fire Institute, a home-schooling mother of four and devout Catholic, had the temerity to send a tweet defending my article, she was similarly overwhelmed with foul-mouthed verbal sludge.

I realize that it is much easier to engage in this sort of mean-spirited mob action than it used to be. Years ago, if you were angry about an article that you read and really wanted to let the author have it, you would have been obliged to write a note, find an envelope and a stamp, and send your diatribe to the editor of the paper or journal. Then you would have been at the mercy of that editor, who, most likely, would have thrown your cruel and poorly argued letter away. Now all you have to do is type your words into a computer and they appear, in a matter of seconds, unedited, for all the world to see. And furthermore, you can do this more or less anonymously. Hence, the prevalence and virulence of Twitter mobs.

But may I, as a spiritual father, issue a sort of pastoral *cri de coeur* to my fellow Catholics who practice this sort of thing? *Cut it out!* The kind of attack that I endured and that remains sadly rampant on social media is a moral outrage. The technical and traditional word for it is calumny—which is to say, the mean-spirited and unjust accusation of another person. Precisely because it is a violation of both charity and justice, calumny is properly categorized as a mortal sin. Could I pose a question to the army of Catholics who posted outrageous comments on my social media sites? Though I know you want to appear tough-minded in front of your colleagues, can you honestly say, when you reread your remarks, that you're proud of them? Honestly.

I have been at this social media work for a long time, and I'm well acquainted with Harry Truman's *mot*: "If you can't stand the heat, get out of the kitchen." When you make an argument in the public space, you have to expect opposition. I completely get that. But once again, there is a sharp distinction between legitimate argument and calumny. A real argument—

involving the marshaling of evidence, the citation of authorities, the fair and careful reporting of one's opponent's position, etc.—is morally praiseworthy, for it fosters both truth and love. It seeks to shed light on what is really the case and to invite others to see more clearly. Calumny, on the other hand, is indifferent to truth and is inimical to love.

If I may be permitted a final observation: I cannot imagine a more effective evangelical countersign to the wider world than the kind of mob action that I witnessed last week. Can you imagine a non-Catholic, a non-Christian, a religious seeker, or a nonbeliever coming on one of my social media sites out of genuine curiosity and seeing how *Catholics* were responding to a bishop who had made an argument? Who could possibly blame them for thinking, "I don't want any part of that group"?

As Tertullian reminded us, what first attracted many pagans to Christianity was the obvious love that Christians showed to one another. What effect do you think Catholic Twitter mobs are having?

The Internet and Satan's Game

In early 2019, a video surfaced showing a supposedly racist confrontation, in front of the Lincoln Memorial, between a grinning young high school student and a Native American elder chanting and beating a drum. The immediate and ferocious judgment of the internet community was that the boy was effectively taunting and belittling the elder, but subsequent videos from wider angles as well as the young man's own testimony cast considerable doubt on this original assessment. My purpose in this article is not to adjudicate the situation, which remains, at best, ambiguous, even in regard to the basic facts. It is to comment, rather, on the morally outrageous and deeply troubling nature of the response to this occurrence, one that I would characterize as, quite literally, Satanic.

When the video in question first came to my attention, it already had millions of views on Facebook and had been commented upon over fifty thousand times. Eager to find out what this was all about, I began to scroll through the comments. They were practically one hundred percent against the young man, and they were marked, as is customary on social media, by stinging cruelty. As I continued to survey the reactions, I began to come across dozens urging retribution against the boy, and then dozens more that provided the addresses and email contacts of his parents, his school, and his diocese. I remember thinking, "Oh my goodness, do they realize what they're doing? They're effectively destroying, even threatening, this kid's life."

At this point, my mind turned, as it often does today, to René Girard. The great Franco-American philosopher and social commentator is best known for his speculations on what he called the scapegoating mechanism. Sadly, Girard maintained, most human communities, from the coffee klatch to the nation state, are predicated upon this dysfunctional and deeply destructive instinct. Roughly speaking, it unfolds as follows. When tensions arise in a group (as they inevitably do), people commence to cast about for a scapegoat, for someone or some group to blame. Deeply attractive, even addictive, the scapegoating move rapidly attracts a crowd, which in short order becomes a mob. In their common hatred of the victim, the blamers feel an ersatz sense of togetherness. Filled with the excitement born of self-righteousness, the mob then endeavors to isolate and finally eliminate the scapegoat, convinced that this will restore order to their roiled society. At the risk of succumbing to the *reductio ad Hitlerum* fallacy, nowhere is the Girardian more evident than in the Germany of the 1930s. Hitler ingeniously exploited the scapegoating mechanism to bring his country together—obviously in a profoundly wicked way.

Girard's theory was grounded in his studies of Shakespeare, Dostoevsky, and other literary figures, but his profoundest influence was the Bible, which not only identified the problem but showed the way forward. Take a good, long look at the story of the woman caught in adultery in the eighth chapter of John's Gospel to see what Girard saw regarding both the sin and the solution. It is surely telling that one of the principal names for the devil in the New Testament is *ho Satanas*, which carries the sense of the accuser. And how significant, thought Girard, that it is precisely *ho Satanas* who offers all of the kingdoms of the world to Jesus, implying that all forms of human community are tainted, at least to a large degree, by the characteristically Satanic game of accusation, blaming, scapegoating.

All of which brings me back to the incident in Washington and the nasty reaction to it on the internet. I have used the internet to great positive effect in my evangelical work for many years, so I certainly don't agree with those who denounce it in an unnuanced way. However, there is something about social media comboxes that makes them a particularly pernicious breeding ground for Girardian victimizing. Perhaps it's the anonymity, or the ease with which comments can be made and published, or the prospect of finding a large audience with little effort—but these forums are increasingly fever swamps in which hatred and accusation breed. When looking for evidence of the Satanic in our culture, don't waste your time on special effects made popular by all of the exorcism movies. Look no further than your computer and the twisted "communities" that it makes possible and the victims that it regularly casts out.

A few weeks ago, the *Wall Street Journal* published a piece on me and my work. The author referred to me as "the Bishop of Social Media," a title which I find more than a little strange. But for the moment, I'm going to claim it, only so I can make a pastoral pronouncement to all those who use social media. When you're about to make a comment, ask yourself a very simple question: Am I doing this out of love, out of a sincere wish for the good of the person or persons I'm addressing? If not, shut up. If it becomes clear that your comment is simply spleen-venting, scapegoating, or virtue-signaling, shut up. The internet can be a marvelous tool, and it can be a weapon used for Satanic purposes. Applying the test of love can very effectively undermine the scapegoating mechanism and drive the devil out.

Pride, Humility, and
Social Media

recently came across an article by a woman named Sarah Menkedick entitled "Unfiltered: How Motherhood Disrupted My Relationship with Social Media." The piece was not only wittily and engagingly written; it also spoke to some pretty profound truths about our cultural situation today and the generation that has come of age under the influence of the internet.

She argues that to have swum in the sea of Instagram, Facebook, Pinterest, and YouTube from the time that one was a child was to live one's life perpetually in front of an audience. Most millennials never simply had experiences; they were conditioned to record, preserve, and present those experiences to a following who were invited to like what they saw, to comment on it, to respond to it. To be sure, she acknowledges, the social media, at their best, are powerful means of communication and connection, but at their worst, they produce this odd distantiation from life and a preoccupation with the self. Here is how Menkedick puts it: "I've come of age as a writer at a time when it is no longer enough just to write. A writer must also promote her work and in the process promote herself as a person of interest. . . . I learned the snarky, casually intellectual voice of feminist and pop culture bloggers, the easy outrage, the clubby camaraderie."

But then something extraordinary happened to the author: she became a mother. On the front porch of her home, nursing her baby, she discovered that she had a visceral aversion to snark and absolutely no desire to share her experience with an audience or curry favor from it. She didn't want to cultivate any ironic distance from motherhood; rather, she wanted to believe in it with all her heart, to let it wash over her. "Before I had a child, I took it for granted that no intellectual writer-type could ever be taken seriously were she to cave into conventional sentiment. As a mother, I was swept away by these huge, ancient, universal emotions I'd previously dismissed as uncomplicated." Her baby, in a word, broke through the carapace of her self-regard and let in some real light. Again, granting all that is truly good about social media (which I use massively in my own ministry), they can easily produce the conviction that we are the stars of our own little dramas, always playing for an eager audience. Authentic spirituality always gives rise to the opposite conviction: *your life is not about you.*

To grasp this distinction more completely, let me propose two scenarios to you. In the first, you are engaged in conversation with someone that you desperately want (or need) to impress—say, a prospective employer or a popular figure whose friendship you crave. In this context, you are indeed speaking, listening, laughing, looking pensive, etc., but more importantly, you are watching yourself perform these moves, and you are exquisitely attentive to the reaction of your interlocutor. Is she laughing at your jokes? Does she look bored? Did your witticism land effectively in her consciousness? The point is that you are not really experiencing reality directly, but rather through a sort of veil. It is as though you are looking at a beautiful landscape, but through a foggy window. Now a second scenario: you are in lively conversation with a friend, and there is no ulterior motive, no egotistic preoccupation. You become quickly lost in the discussion, following the argument where it leads, laughing when you are truly amused, watching your partner, but not in order to see how she's reacting to you, but just because she's interesting. In this case, you are immersed in reality; you are looking at the landscape through a clear pane of glass, taking in its colors and textures in all of their vividness.

Now, to use the language of the classical moral and spiritual tradition, the first situation I described is marked, through and through, by pride, and the second by humility. Don't think of pride, first and foremost, as self-exaltation, which is, in fact, but a face or consequence of pride. In its most proper nature, pride is seeing the world through the distorting lens of the ego and its needs. On the other hand, humility, from the Latin *humus* (earth), is getting in touch with reality directly, being close to the ground, seeing things as they are.

This is why Thomas Aquinas famously says "*humilitas est veritas*" (humility is truth). What makes the first scenario so painful and cringeworthy is that it is out of step with the truth of things. What makes the second scenario so exhilarating, so fun, is that it is full of reality.

What Sarah Menkedick intuited was the manner in which the social media environment can be a breeding ground for the unique type of spiritual distortion and dislocation that we traditionally call pride. What made all the difference for her was the arrival of her baby, in all of his densely textured *reality*—a reality that she could appropriate only through humility.

Thomas Aquinas and the
Art of Making a Public Argument

There is, in many quarters, increasing concern about the hyper-charged political correctness that has gripped our campuses and other forums of public conversation. Even great works of literature and philosophy—from *Huckleberry Finn* and *Heart of Darkness* to, believe it or not, Kant's *Critique of Pure Reason*—are now regularly accompanied by "trigger warnings" that alert prospective readers to the racism, sexism, homophobia, or classism contained therein. And popping up more and more at our colleges and universities are "safe spaces" where exquisitely sensitive students can retreat in the wake of jarring confrontations with points of view with which they don't sympathize. My favorite example of this was at Brown University, where school administrators provided retreat centers with Play-Doh, crayons, and videos of frolicking puppies to calm the nerves of their students *even before a controversial debate commenced*! Apparently even the prospect of public argument sent these students to an updated version of daycare. Of course, a paradoxical concomitant of this exaggerated sensitivity to giving offense is a proclivity to aggressiveness and verbal violence; for once authentic debate has been ruled out of court, the only recourse contesting parties have is to some form of censorship or bullying.

There is obviously much that can and should be mocked in all of this, but I won't go down that road. Instead, I would like to revisit a time when people knew how to have a public argument about the most hotly contested matters. Though it might come as a surprise to many, I'm talking about the High Middle Ages, when the university system was born. And to illustrate the medieval method of disciplined conversation, there is no better candidate than St. Thomas Aquinas. The principal means of teaching in the medieval university was not the classroom lecture, which became prominent only in the nineteenth-century German system of education; rather, it was the *quaestio disputata* (disputed question), which was a lively, sometimes raucous, and very public intellectual exchange. Though the written texts of Aquinas can strike us today as a tad turgid, we have to recall that they are grounded in these disciplined but decidedly energetic conversations.

If we consult Aquinas' masterpiece, the *Summa theologiae*, we find that he poses literally thousands of questions and that not even the most sacred issues are off the table, the best evidence of which is article three of question two of the first part of the *Summa*: *"Utrum Deus sit"* (Whether there is a God). If a Dominican priest is permitted to ask even that question, everything is fair game; nothing is too dangerous to talk about. After stating the issue, Thomas then entertains a series of objections to the position that he will eventually take. In many cases, these represent a distillation of real counterclaims and queries that Aquinas would have heard during *quaestiones disputatae*. But for our purposes, the point to emphasize is that Thomas presents these objections in their most convincing form, often stating them better and more pithily than their advocates could. In proof of this, we note that during the Enlightenment, rationalist *philosophes* would sometimes take Thomistic objections and use them to bolster their own anti-religious positions. To give just one example, consider Aquinas' devastatingly convincing formulation of the argument from evil against the existence of God: "If one of two contraries were infinite, the other would be destroyed . . . but God is called the infinite good. Therefore, if God exists, there would be no evil." Thomas indeed provides a telling response, but, as stated, that is a darn good argument. Might I suggest that it would help our public discourse immensely if all parties would be willing to formulate their opponents' positions as respectfully and convincingly as possible?

Having articulated the objections, Thomas then offers his own magisterial resolution of the matter: *"Respondeo dicendum quod . . ."* (I respond that it must be said . . .). One of the more regrettable marks of the postmodern mind is a tendency to endlessly postpone the answer to a question. Take a look at Jacques Derrida's work for a master class in this technique. And sadly, many today, who want so desperately to avoid offending anyone, find refuge in just this sort of permanent irresolution. But Thomas knew what Chesterton knew—namely, that an open mind is like an open mouth: it is designed to close finally on something solid and nourishing. Finally, having offered his *Respondeo*, Aquinas returns to the objections and, in light of his resolution, answers them. It is notable that a typical Thomas technique is to find something right in the objector's position and to use that to correct what he deems to be errant in it.

Throughout this process—in the objections, *Respondeos*, and answers to objections—Thomas draws on a wide range of sources: the Bible and the Church Fathers of course, but also the classical philosophers Aristotle, Plato, and Cicero; the Jewish scholar Moses Maimonides; and the Islamic masters Averroes and Avicenna. And he consistently invokes these figures with supreme respect, characterizing Aristotle, for example, as simply "the Philosopher" and referring to Maimonides as "Rabbi Moyses." It is fair to say that, in substantial ways, Thomas Aquinas disagrees with all of these figures, and yet he is more than willing to listen to them, to engage them, to take their arguments seriously.

What this Thomistic method produces is, in its own way, a "safe space" for conversation, but it is a safe space for adults and not timorous children. It wouldn't be a bad model for our present discussion of serious things.

Kathy Griffin and
the Vanishing of Argument

In 2017, the comedian Kathy Griffin posed for an appalling staged photo of herself holding a mock-up of the bloody, severed head of Donald Trump. Despite her rather pathetic apology, a firestorm of protest broke out pretty much everywhere. To say that this stunt was in poor taste or, in the parlance of our times, "offensive," would be the understatement of the decade. At a time when the most barbarous people on the planet were, in point of fact, decapitating their enemies and holding up the heads as trophies, it simply beggared belief that Griffin would have imagined this escapade as an acceptable form of social protest.

But I would like to situate what Griffin did in a wider context, for it is but a particularly brutal example of what is taking place throughout our society, especially on university campuses. Speakers of a more conservative stripe, ranging from serious academics such as Charles Murray and Heather Mac Donald to provocateurs such as Ann Coulter and Milo Yiannopoulos, have been shouted down, obstructed, insulted, and in extreme cases physically assaulted on the grounds of institutes of higher learning throughout the United States. Very recently, at Evergreen State College in Olympia, Washington, a tenured professor was compelled to hold his biology class in a public park. His crime? He had publicly criticized a planned "Day of Absence" during which white students, staff, and faculty were coerced into leaving the campus, since people of color claimed they felt "unsafe" at the college. For calling this blatantly racist move by its proper name, the professor was, of course, himself labeled a racist, and mobs of angry students shut down his classes, forcing him to lecture in the park.

81

What is most striking to me in all of this is the obvious lack of anything resembling rational argument. Students are not posing counterpositions, marshaling evidence, drawing logical conclusions, proposing more convincing scenarios, etc. In a word, they are not *arguing* with their opponents. They are bullying them, drowning them out, intimidating them, physically attacking them. This is not only irrational; it is deeply disrespectful, for it fundamentally denies the humanity of their adversaries. Nowhere is this dehumanization more patently evident than in the case of Kathy Griffin's protest. And the impatience with argument is rooted in a more basic assumption of many on the left—which is precisely why this violence is breaking out in environments where a radical ideology holds sway. I'm talking about the questioning of objective truth and the concomitant hyper-valorization of the self-assertive will. It is a commonplace on the left that claims to objective truth are thinly veiled plays of power, attempts by one group to impose its views on another. Accordingly, "truth" is construed as a function of the will of the individual. I determine the meaning of my life, and you determine the meaning of yours; I decide my gender and you decide yours—and therefore the best we can do together is tolerate one another's choices.

But when there is no truth, there can be no argument, for argument depends upon a shared appeal to certain epistemic and ethical values. If I might propose an analogy, it's something like the common rules that make a game possible. Precisely because the players all agree to certain strictures and delimitations, real play can ensue. If every participant is making up the rules as he goes along and according to his whim, the game promptly evanesces. Indeed, if we continue with this analogy, the game, in fact, doesn't simply disappear; it devolves into bickering and finally into violence, since the players have no other recourse for the adjudication of their disputes. Now we can see why it is a very short step indeed from epistemic and moral relativism in the classroom to violence on the quad. Since I can't argue with my opponent, I can only silence him, dehumanize him, shut him down.

The valorization of will over intellect is described by the technical term "voluntarism," and the roots of this ideology are tangled indeed. Jean-Paul

Sartre and Michel Foucault were advocates of it in the twentieth century, and they both found their inspiration in the nineteenth-century German theoretician Friedrich Nietzsche. Nietzsche's *Übermensch* (Superman or Over-man) stood blithely beyond the conventional categories of good and evil and determined the meaning of his life through his limitless will to power. The problem, of course, is what happens when two Supermen clash, when two limitless wills collide. The only path forward, Nietzsche correctly intuited, would be warfare—and let the strongest survive. What should be clear to everyone is that this has remained anything but high theorizing, that in fact, Nietzsche's vision now dances in the heads of most young people in our society today.

Are we surprised, therefore, that stridency, anger, violence, censorship, and the will to power dominate the public conversation? I realize that it might sound a bit frumpy to put it this way, but the path forward is better epistemology.

Violence against Christians and the Waning of Reason

There were more Christian martyrs in the twentieth century than in all of the previous nineteen centuries combined. Hitler, Stalin, Mao, Pol Pot, and many of their lesser-known totalitarian colleagues put millions of Christians to death for their faith in that terrible hundred-year period. One of the saddest features of the still-young twenty-first century is that this awful trend is undoubtedly continuing. By far the most persecuted religious group in the world today are Christians, and they are dying by the thousands, especially in the Middle East and in Africa. Though Hindus and Buddhists have indeed been targeting Christians, their most egregious aggressors, by leaps and bounds, have been radicalized Muslims, the 2019 mass killings in Sri Lanka being but one recent example of this kind of violence. I have stated this fact simply and bluntly, because I am convinced that no solution can be found unless and until, at the very least, we speak truthfully.

As many commentators have pointed out, the cultural and media elites in the West have been comically dissembling and obfuscating in this regard. The statements of former President Barack Obama and former Secretary of State Hillary Clinton regarding the Sri Lanka bombings, which referred to the victims not as Christians or Catholics but as "Easter worshippers," are a particularly pathetic case in point. But little better are the hundreds of editorials, opinion pieces, articles, and books that characterized these attacks as primarily motivated by economics and politics, or the fruit of cultural resentment. I have no doubt whatsoever that all of these factors played a role, but we are blind not to see that the chief driver of this violence has been, first and foremost, religion. Now, I certainly understand it is to no one's advantage to stir up religious tensions, especially in pluralist societies, but the denial of religion as the chief cause of these outrages is disingenuous at best, dangerously stupid at worst.

A good deal of this is due to a theory, still stubbornly persistent among the elite commentariat in the West, that religion is (or at least ought to be) fading away. The "secularization hypothesis," proposed from the time of Comte, Nietzsche, and Marx, is, despite significant evidence to the contrary, widely subscribed to among Western opinion-makers. On this reading, the religious is never what is "really" going on; rather, it is a superstructural cover for economics or politics or race relations or the struggle for cultural hegemony. But until we see religious disagreement as indeed what is really going on in the present violence, we aren't going to solve the problem. Hans Küng is a theologian I rarely agree with, but he was dead right when he commented that there will be no peace among the nations until there is peace among the religions. And there will be no such peace until the religions find some common ground on which to stand, some context in which a real dialogue and conversation can take place.

But what could possibly constitute such ground? Aren't Christianity and Islam—to stay with the two faiths that are clashing most dramatically today—simply incommensurable and mutually exclusive systems of belief? Aren't they based on revelations repugnant to one another? Might I suggest an answer to these questions by hearkening back to an earlier time? In the thirteenth century, Thomas Aquinas constructed an intellectual system, cathedral-like in its beauty and complexity, on the basis of both faith and reason. As he articulated the meaning of Christian revelation, he used the tools provided by the science and philosophy that were available to him. In constructing this rational edifice, he relied on pagan, Jewish, and Christian philosophers, but among the most important of his influences were philosophers and theologians of the Islamic tradition. Aquinas' metaphysics is, quite simply, unthinkable apart from the work of Averroes, Avicenna, and Avicebron, Muslim theorists all. During the High Middle Ages, Christians and Muslims did indeed dialogue on the basis of a shared intellectual heritage, but it is precisely the waning of the influence of these great philosophic masters within Islam and the rise of a will-based, positivistic approach that has contributed mightily to the conflicts we witness today. And if we might set aside the passions roused by his admittedly awkward use of an example of a dysfunctional Christian-Muslim conversation, it would be helpful to return to the famous Regensburg Address of Pope Benedict XVI. What the pope was calling for in that speech was an enthusiastic retrieval of a tradition embedded deep within Christianity—namely, the use of reason, grounded in the conviction that Jesus is the incarnation precisely of the Logos (reason) of God. As long as religion is marked primarily by will (and he was indeed critiquing contemporary radical Islam on this score), it will tend to resort to violence. And in bringing forward the Logos tradition, he was summoning Islam to return to a perhaps forgotten or underutilized dimension of its own heritage.

Are certain Muslims attacking Christians today on religious grounds and for religious reasons? Yes. Is at least a significant part of the problem a strain of voluntarism and irrationality within Islam? Yes. What's the way forward? If I might cite a prophet sacred to both Christianity and Islam: "Come now, let us reason together" (Isa. 1:18 RSV-CE).

Love an Enemy This Lent

The three classical spiritual practices that the Church urges us to embrace during Lent are prayer, fasting, and almsgiving. I would strongly encourage every one of my readers to follow this recommendation, perhaps intensifying each one of the three during the holy season. But there is another Lenten discipline that I would like to put forward: forgiving an enemy.

There is enough anger in the Catholic community to light up the eastern seaboard for a year. I say this not to pick on Catholics in particular; I would say it of any group of human beings. We are—all of us—sitting on a lot of unresolved rage. Thomas Aquinas defines the deadly sin of anger in his typically pithy manner as an irrational or excessive desire for revenge. Every one of us has been hurt by someone else, aggressed, unjustly harmed, insulted—perhaps to an extreme degree. And so, naturally enough, we harbor a desire to respond in kind. Now, there is such a thing as justified anger, which is nothing but a passion to right wrongs. Think of the "anger" displayed by Jesus as he cleansed the temple or by Martin Luther King as he led the civil rights movement. That righteous indignation is to be praised. But many of us, let's be honest, cultivate an excessive, unreasonable passion to get back at those who have harmed us. We spend an extraordinary amount of time fantasizing about what we might say and do to our enemies if we ever had the opportunity or the requisite power. This is what Thomas Aquinas means by the "deadly sin" of anger.

And this is exactly what Jesus is urging us to extricate from our souls precisely through the admittedly wrenching act of forgiving our enemies. In the Sermon on the Mount, the Lord teaches, "You have heard that it was said to those of ancient times, 'You shall not murder.' . . . But I say to you that if you are angry with a brother or sister, you will be liable to judgment. . . . So when you are offering your gift at the altar, if you remember that your brother or sister has something against you, leave your gift there before the altar and go; first be reconciled to your brother or sister" (Matt. 5:21–24). And in what constitutes, in my judgment, the rhetorical and spiritual high point of the Sermon, Jesus says, "You have heard that it was said, 'You shall love your neighbor and hate your enemy.' But I say to you, Love your enemies" (Matt. 5:43–44). This teaching makes no sense unless we are assuming that we have real enemies—that is to say, people who have unfairly and aggressively harmed us. But the Lord is summoning us beyond the desire for revenge, even beyond the strict justice of the *lex talionis*, the "eye for an eye" principle. He is insisting that we *love* those who have made us angry, that we desire their good.

About twenty-five years ago, Joseph Cardinal Bernardin of Chicago was accused by a young man named Steven Cook of sexual misconduct. In a speech given at Mundelein Seminary shortly thereafter, the cardinal said that he was devastated by this charge, indeed so demoralized and traumatized that he had taken to praying, spread-eagle on the ground in his chapel, that the Lord might deliver him from the shame and hurt that he felt. After two agonizing months, Cook withdrew the charge, admitting that it was based on a false memory. Who would have blamed Cardinal Bernardin if he had said, "Good riddance!" and never had a thing further to do with Steven Cook? But the cardinal didn't do that. Instead, he traveled to see the young man, brought him the gift of a Bible, anointed him (Cook was dying of AIDS), and offered his forgiveness. That's what loving, and not just tolerating, one's enemy looks like. Some decades ago, an Amish family—mother, father, and son—was making their way, as is their custom, by horse-drawn buggy. A car filled with rowdy teenagers came up behind them and commenced to tailgate them impatiently. Finally, they swerved around the buggy, and one of the boys hurled a brick in the direction of the horse. The projectile missed the animal but struck the young man, killing him instantly. Who could possibly have blamed the grieving parents if they had turned on their son's killer? Instead, they appeared at the teenager's trial and begged the judge for leniency—and then, during the time of his imprisonment, they visited him regularly. That is another icon of enemy love.

Might I urge all of my readers to call to mind an enemy? Hold an image of him or her in your mind—someone who has done you real harm. This Lent, contrive a way to love that person, to heal that relationship. It might be a phone call, an email, a visit, a gesture—but as a salutary Lenten practice, do it.

PART IV

CONFRONTING MORAL CHAOS

The Crown and the
Fundamental Values of a Society

The Netflix original series *The Crown*, which has to do with the last months of the reign of King George VI and the first years of the reign of his daughter, Queen Elizabeth II, is just the kind of program that Americans in particular seem naturally to love. It features beautiful photography of palaces, processions, and formal receptions; and it provides a behind-the-scenes look at the *ne plus ultra* of the British aristocracy. Consider it *Downton Abbey* on steroids.

Some of the more affecting scenes in the entire series center around the transition from father to daughter, a time of trauma for the nation and deep personal pain for the family of the relatively young king. After Elizabeth, just returned from an African sojourn, had viewed the body of her beloved father, she meets her grandmother, Queen Mary, in one of the corridors of Buckingham Palace. The old lady, swathed in black Victorian garb, spies her granddaughter, and then with tremendous dignity and through considerable discomfort, contorts herself into a formal curtsy. Taking in this unaccustomed display, Elizabeth registers her astonishment and feels, perhaps for the first time, that she is now the monarch.

Queen Mary had composed an extraordinary letter to her granddaughter, just after the death of the king. In it, she specified that, as queen, Elizabeth would not be beholden to Parliament, for it had not chosen her, nor to the people, for they had not voted for her, but rather to God, in whose name she would be coronated. This is how the letter concludes: "I have seen three great monarchies brought down through their failure to separate personal indulgences from duty. . . . While you mourn your father, you must also mourn someone else: Elizabeth Mountbatten, for she has now been replaced by another person, Elizabeth Regina. The two Elizabeths will frequently be in conflict with one another. The fact is, the crown must win—must always win."

As if to prove Queen Mary's point with as much visual panache as possible, the filmmakers emphasize the sacred, ordination-like dimension of Elizabeth's coronation. Not only does she receive a crown, but she is also anointed, by the Archbishop of Canterbury, "as priests, prophets, and kings were anointed." That's according to a tradition that, the archbishop explicitly tells her, goes back to King Solomon's consecration by "Zadok the priest and Nathan the prophet." And all of it is done under the aegis and in the name of "the Father, the Son, and the Holy Spirit."

As the series unfolds, we see Queen Mary's prediction of conflict coming to pass. On a number of occasions, Queen Elizabeth is torn between her obligation to the church and her affection for her sister, Margaret, who has fallen in love with a divorced man whom she wishes to marry. All of her personal instincts and feelings lead her to grant permission to her beloved sister, but her duty to God compels her to refuse. Even in the face of popular opinion, which runs strongly in Margaret's direction, and despite the bitter tears of her sister, the queen follows the precepts of the Lord. Elizabeth Regina triumphs over Elizabeth Mountbatten.

Now, I bring all of this up, not to address so much the issue of divorce and remarriage within the Christian dispensation, but rather something deeper and more abiding—namely, the presence within any healthy society of values that are grounded in God. We are quite naturally at home with practical decisions that result from majority vote or with allegiances consequent upon strong personal feelings. But finally, both practical strategies and personal feelings must rest upon objective goods that are not themselves up for debate, values that flow from God. In Great Britain, the monarch—anointed and not appointed—is the personification of this dimension of the society's moral life. In the American context, the Declaration of Independence and the Constitution, which enshrine and defend fundamental human rights, play a similar role.

If you doubt me on this score, I might recommend a close reading of the prologue to the Declaration, which states, "We hold these truths to be self-evident, that all men are created equal, that they are endowed by their Creator with certain unalienable Rights." Thomas Jefferson is not speaking here of values consequent upon the people's will, but rather of the proper ethical matrix for any and all legislative deliberation. When this feature of public life is forgotten, everything becomes a matter of majority vote or private whim—and the society necessarily drifts.

There is another scene in *The Crown* that brings this point home. When they were children, King George brought Elizabeth and Margaret together and invited them to pledge that they would always remain faithful to one another and that nothing would ever supersede their mutual loyalty. When the moment of truth came many years later, and Elizabeth was forced to choose God's way over her sister's desire, Margaret bitterly reminded her of this oath. Though he was a good man and though the two sisters dearly loved one another, King George should never have compelled his daughters to make that pledge. For nothing can be permitted to violate the God-given moral values upon which a society is rightly constructed. God bless the makers of *The Crown* for helping us to see this in a most dramatic way.

Paul Tillich and *The Shape of Water*

knew that *The Shape of Water* would win the Academy Award for Best Picture. It checked three of the major Hollywood boxes: celebration of oppressed people, valorization of complete sexual freedom, and a Christian villain. It used to be that a black hat or shifty eyes or a foreign accent would give someone away as the bad guy, but now, it is the quoting of the Bible.

Of course, this shouldn't surprise us in regard to *The Shape of Water*, for the auteur behind the film is the Mexican director Guillermo del Toro, who has gone on record many times as a despiser of religion, especially Catholicism. In a conversation with Charlie Rose, he admitted to being "a raging atheist," and in a 2007 interview, he said, "I hate structure; I'm completely anti-structural in terms of believing in institutions. I hate them. I hate any institutionalized social, religious, or economic holding." One might wonder what he makes of the studios that produce his films or the banks that invest his money, but I'll leave those considerations for another day.

The title of his award-winning movie gives away the game, for the one thing that water does not have is shape. Its very essence is fluidity, formlessness, and freedom from structure. And this is precisely what is celebrated in the film. Against all odds and despite enormous obstacles, the heroine, a young, fearful, and marginalized woman, falls in love with an amphibian creature whom the government (structure: boo!) keeps locked up in a laboratory facility. The lady and the aqua-man build up over time a mutual trust, give their consent to one another, and finally, with the help of well-intentioned friends, manage to do the deed. I gathered that the hope of the director was that the viewer would thrill to this brave flouting of convention and rejoice in the trans-species love on display. For sex, apparently, has no proper form, objective structure, or natural end; it has the shape of water, flowing according to the desires of those who engage in it.

All of this actually put me in mind of Paul Tillich, one of the most significant Christian theologians of the last century. In his massive *Systematic Theology*, Tillich presented what he called the three ontological polarities—that is to say, tensions or contraries that characterize living things at every level. A good part of the drama and difficulty of human life follows upon our consciousness of living in the midst of these polarities. The first is dynamics and form. Plants, animals, and human beings could not live unless they were marked by novelty, movement, change, and the constant adaptation to the environment in which they find themselves. At the same time, all such organisms possess a fundamental structure that preserves their identity and stability across time. Without a reliable cellular, molecular, muscular, and nervous system, no animal or plant could subsist; instead it would be, in short order, absorbed by its surroundings. What we call "life" is in fact a subtle and carefully calibrated balancing act between dynamics and form; too much of one or the other would spell disaster.

The second of the ontological polarities is freedom and destiny. The former is liberty to choose, to move, to be different, to find one's own path. Without freedom, no living thing could possibly thrive. Tillich remarks that the uniqueness of each tree, plant, animal, and person is, to a large extent, a function of this capacity. However, freedom is in tension with destiny, by which Tillich means the substrate upon which freedom stands, the givens with which freedom works. Liberty never operates in a vacuum, nor is it capable of positing itself; rather, it works with the raw material of one's family experience, education, language, body, and culture. Throughout life, these two poles remain in creative tension with one another, but any one-sided resolution would result in collapse: either the chaos of pure arbitrariness or the petrification of static traditionalism.

The third polarity is individualization and participation. Each person wants to be herself, to find her path, to stand out from the crowd. In fact, if individualization doesn't take place, one remains in a good deal of psychological peril, permanently infantilized or simply a cog in some societal structure. But at the same time, everyone longs to belong to something beyond herself, to participate with others in a shared political, religious, or cultural endeavor. Tillich saw the Germany of the 1930s as a society that had oscillated dangerously in the direction of pure participation: as the Nazi slogan had it, "one people, one nation, one Führer." But he saw the Western countries as having moved (admittedly not as drastically) in the opposite direction, toward pure individualism. Once again, the delicate balance between the two is the key.

A film called *The Shape of Water*, produced by someone who, by his own admission, hates structure, is sadly emblematic, I fear, of a society that is indeed in danger of oscillating to one side of the Tillich polarities. Is it not the case that the leading avatars of our culture consistently valorize dynamics, freedom, and individualization, while they just as consistently denigrate form, destiny, and participation? And is not sexuality the thin edge of the blade? Increasingly, any limits that have been classically set to sexual expression are swept away as fussy holdovers from a primitive time, and any sense that sexuality possesses a form and finality independent of individual free choice is mocked as an arbitrary imposition.

But if Tillich is right, this one-sidedness is a sign of sickness. The biblical authors appreciated water as a positive symbol for life, but they also understood it as a symbol of chaos and formlessness. Think of the *tohu wabohu* (watery abyss) from which God drew creation. We do indeed need dynamics, freedom, and individualism, but if all we have is the shape of water—which is to say, no shape at all—we're actually in bad shape.

Breaking Out of the Prison
of Self-Invention

For the past many years, I have been maintaining an internet ministry that allows me, through comment boxes, to listen in on the questions, complaints, and pontifications of thousands of people in regard to religion. I have noticed that these commentaries sort themselves out in fairly predictable ways, centering around issues of God's existence, the problem of suffering, the uniqueness of Christianity among the religions of the world, and the whole range of the Church's sexual teachings.

But another theme that presents itself with remarkable regularity is the denial of the objectivity of truth and moral value. I have encountered this position frequently over the years, but a spate of such objections surfaced in the wake of a recent video of mine on the subject. Here is one typical response: "Thirty seconds in, and he's ["he" means me] obviously dumb: objective moral values? Those aren't real." Though this gentleman focused on moral values, many of the commentators on this score have equal disdain for the objectivity of truth claims.

Though, as I said, this is a commonly held view, a moment's reflection reveals how silly this position is. Since he has bothered to complain about my point of view, he obviously holds that there is something the matter with articulating an incorrect opinion, that this is something I *shouldn't* do. Furthermore, since he is appealing to the public, he must think that this standard of rectitude is not merely a subjective whim of his own but a standard that is generally known. In a word, he is holding to the very principle that he denies—namely, that some objective and universal moral value exists. Moreover, in making bold to call me "dumb," he also indirectly affirms the objectivity of truth, since he could make no such determination of my mental acuity unless he believed in some clear epistemic criterion. In a word, he is hoisted on his own petard. Even the most radical and thoroughgoing skeptic is necessarily standing on some ground when he launches his criticism. He might quarrel with someone's understanding of a moral or intellectual value, but the one thing he cannot coherently say is that there is no such thing as moral or intellectual value.

C.S. Lewis, arguably the greatest Christian apologist of the last century, saw this problem and endeavored to address it in his short but marvelous book *The Abolition of Man*. He took as his starting point a famous story told of Samuel Taylor Coleridge. As Lewis recounts it, the poet was standing with two acquaintances in the presence of a stunning waterfall. One of his interlocutors announced that the sight was "sublime," and the other that it was indeed "pretty." Coleridge enthusiastically confirmed the first characterization and apparently turned away in disgust at the second. The authors of a popular book of English composition (with which Lewis was familiar) opined that Coleridge's discrimination was baseless, since each person was simply describing the emotions that he felt in the presence of the waterfall and not anything intrinsic to the waterfall. C.S. Lewis thought this was so much nonsense. Rather, as Coleridge correctly intuited, the reaction of the first person was appropriate to the real quality of the cascade, and the reaction of the second person was pathetically inappropriate to it. The objective rules the subjective and not vice versa.

Lewis' discussion vividly calls to mind Dietrich von Hildebrand's distinction between the objectively valuable and a subjective value response. For Hildebrand, the point of good mentoring is to help a student recognize value in the aesthetic, ethical, and epistemic orders, and then to call forth from her the response, both affective and intellectual, commensurate with the value. Once again, value language doesn't refer to feelings, but rather to the things and events that awaken the feelings. And both Lewis and Hildebrand hearken in this sense back to Aristotle, who said that the aim of education is to make the pupil like and dislike what he *ought*. In short, feelings and affections should be *trained* and not simply valorized.

I mention all of this because what C.S. Lewis saw in that book of English composition some eighty years ago is now everywhere in our culture; it is in fact the default position of practically everyone under the age of forty. It is commonly held that what we call "values" are just projections of our feelings and subjective whims, and consequently, anyone who dares to speak of properly objective truth or objective moral value is engaging in an oppressive play of power. The upshot of all this is that we have locked ourselves into millions of little prisons from which we have little choice but to hurl invective at one another. Perhaps the principal advantage of acknowledging objective value is that it provides the opportunity for all of us to fall in love together with something good, true, and beautiful. It permits us to break free of the prison of our egotism and to enter, together, a journey of exploration.

So don't let people seduce you with the rhetoric of self-invention and being free to make up one's own values. In the final analysis, there is no project duller and more suffocating than that.

The Doritos Commercial and the
Revival of Voluntarism

In a lighthearted Super Bowl commercial produced to advertise Doritos, a pregnant mother, undergoing an ultrasound, is annoyed by her husband, who is absentmindedly munching Doritos while their baby's image is displayed on the screen. But as the father moves the corn chip, the baby in the womb moves with it; and when the mother throws the bag across the room, the child reacts so keenly and purposively that he decides this is the moment to be born.

Cute, funny, harmless—right? Oh, not according to the National Abortion Rights Action League (NARAL), who complained (and one is compelled here to stifle laughter) that the commercial dangerously "humanized" the fetus. We are tempted to ask, "What do you think was gestating in the womb? A monkey? A rabbit?"

It has, of course, long been established scientifically that even a conceptus (a fertilized ovum) is already in full possession of human DNA distinct from that of his parents. Moreover, the developing embryo has a heartbeat and her own circulatory system twenty-two days after conception; at twenty weeks, the baby in the womb is capable of hearing his mother's voice, and responding to light, music, and other external stimuli. So though the Doritos commercial is, of course, playful, it exaggerates something quite real.

Yet according to NARAL, the child in the womb should not be "humanized," lest the absolute right to murder that child at any stage of its prenatal development should be denied. And mind you, that right, in our country, extends even to the moment when the baby is emerging from the womb (partial-birth abortion), indeed to the time after his birth, since many states place no restrictions on the killing of a newborn who has miraculously survived the abortion procedure (see born-alive legislation). For many people, the bottom line is this: all objective evidence to the contrary, the unborn are not human because defenders of abortion don't want them to be.

And here, philosophically speaking, is the rub. There is an ancient and enduring philosophical position that goes by the name of voluntarism—which is to say, the systematic favoring of the will over the intellect. In the Middle Ages, this view was on display in certain theologians who insisted that God's will is his primary attribute and therefore that the divine choice trumps all, including the evident truths of reason. William of Ockham, for example, famously distinguished between God's *potentia absoluta* (absolute power) and his *potentia ordinata* (ordained power). The former is what God, in the pure sense of the term, could do, his totally rangy capacity, while the latter designates what God actually did. So, for example, God in fact commanded us not to commit adultery, and he in fact made a world in which circles cannot be squares and vice versa. But in his absolute power, presumably, he could have determined that adultery is a virtue and that square circles are possible. This late medieval theorizing was picked up on by the founder of modern philosophy, René Descartes, who speculated that two plus two in point of fact is equal to four but that God could determine, should he please, that it be equal to five.

A philosopher who had no sympathy for this nonsense was St. Thomas Aquinas, who held that God's freedom is grounded in the truth of his being. God can indeed do anything, but he can't do the impossible, precisely because the impossible is a modality of nonbeing. To say that God cannot make two plus two equal to five or turn adultery into a virtue is not to limit God; it is to say that whatever he wills is consistent with the integrity of his own being. In a word, Aquinas insisted that the will and the intellect are partners and that freedom, accordingly, ought always to be consistent with the truth of things.

In 2006, Pope Benedict XVI, who as an academic was very familiar with the controversy I have just rehearsed, gave an oration at the University of Regensburg that came down on the side of Thomas Aquinas. The central theme of his presentation was the essential role that reason ought to play in relation to religion. At the heart of his argument was the concern that voluntarism was asserting itself in the religious realm (God's absolute power) and that this was conducing to violence, since without a common consensus regarding the truth, all that rival groups can do is resort to force, the assertion of the will.

I hope it is becoming clear why I feel that this somewhat arcane academic discussion is of crucial relevance in our time. As silly as it is to say that two plus two could be equal to five, it is just as silly to say that a child in the womb is anything but human. What makes both assertions possible is the claim that will (whether God's or our own) supposedly trumps intellect, that the sheer desire that something be true can make it true. And what makes all of this more than merely silly is, as Pope Benedict saw, that the divorce between will and mind unleashes violence, indeed *potentia absoluta*.

The revival of voluntarism is on rather massive display in our society, and the principle of the primacy of the will is behind much of our discussion of moral issues. As has always been the case, this has led to a distortion of speech and to the unchaining of some pretty dark forces.

Hannah Arendt, Totalitarianism, and the Distinction between Fact and Fiction

D. C. Schindler's marvelous book *The Politics of the Real: The Church Between Liberalism and Integralism* will be of interest to anyone passionate about the vexed and much-discussed issue of the relation between religion and politics. But I would like to draw particular attention to the epigraph that Schindler chose for his book, an observation that is meant to haunt the minds of his readers as they consider his particular arguments. It is drawn from the writings of Hannah Arendt, the twentieth-century German-Jewish scholar most famous for her lucubrations on the phenomenon of totalitarianism, and it is of remarkable relevance to our present cultural conversation. She said: "The ideal subject of totalitarian rule is not the convinced Nazi or the convinced Communist, but people for whom the distinction between fact and fiction (i.e., the reality of experience) and the distinction between the true and the false (i.e., the standards of thought) no longer exist."

We might define totalitarianism as the controlling of every aspect of life by the arbitrary will of a powerful individual or group. If this is accurate, we see why Arendt worried about the blurring of distinctions between the real and the unreal, between truth and falsity. The objectively good and the objectively true have their own intrinsic *authority*—that is to say, they command, by their very excellence, the obedience of the receptive mind and the responsive will. So, for example, in the presence of mathematical truths, scientific data, and philosophical arguments, the mind surrenders, and rejoices in its surrender. It does not arbitrarily impose itself on things as with totalitarianism; rather, the intrinsic truth of things imposes itself on the mind and thereby awakens it to its purpose. In the language of Thomas Aquinas, the intelligibility of the world *actualizes* the mind.

In a similar way, the intrinsic goodness of things engages, excites, and actualizes the will. Aquinas said that the will is simply the appetitive dimension of the intellect, by which he meant that the good, understood as such, is automatically desired. The point is that, once again, the subjective faculty does not impose itself on reality, making good whatever it wants to be good; rather, on the contrary, what is densely and objectively good commands the will by its own authority. And, as I have argued often before, this acquiescence of the will is not a negation of freedom but the discovery of authentic freedom: the same St. Paul who said that he was a slave of Christ Jesus also said that it was for freedom that Christ had set him free. That apparent contradiction is in fact the paradox produced by the fact that the will is most itself when it accepts the authority of the objective good.

Now, does anyone doubt that we are living in a society that puts such stress on the feelings and desires of individuals that it effectively undermines any claim to objectivity in regard to truth and goodness? Does anyone doubt that the default position of many in our culture is that we are allowed to determine what is true and good *for us*? Some years ago, as part of a social experiment, a five-foot, nine-inch white man went on a university campus and randomly asked students passing by whether they would consider him a woman if he said he felt he was a woman. A number of students said they were okay with that. Then he inquired whether they would accept that he was a Chinese woman, if that's what he claimed to be. One student answered: "If you identified as Chinese, I might be a little surprised, but I would say good for you—be who you are." Finally, he wondered whether they would agree that he was a six-foot-five Chinese woman. This last suggestion seemed to throw his interlocutors a bit. But one young man answered: "If you . . . explained why you felt you were six-foot-five, I feel like I would be very open to saying you were six-foot-five, or Chinese, or a woman." Do you recall the Academy Award–winning film *The Shape of Water*, in which a woman falls in love with an aquatic creature? The title of that movie gives away the game: a dispiriting number of people in our culture feel that the only shape is the shape of water—which is to say, no shape at all, except the one that we choose to provide.

With all of this in mind, let us return to Hannah Arendt. What opens the door to totalitarianism is, she thought, the radical indifference to objective truth, for once objective value has been relativized or set aside entirely, then all that remain are wills competing for dominance. And since the war of all against all is intolerable in the long run, the strongest will shall eventually emerge—and inevitably impose itself on the other wills. In a word, totalitarianism will hold sway. Notice, please, that one of the features of all totalitarian systems is strict censorship, for an authoritarian regime has to repress any attempt at real argument—which is to say, an appeal to an objective truth that might run counter to what the regime is proposing. The great Václav Havel was the first president of the Czech Republic after the breakup of the Soviet bloc and a famously dissenting poet who had been imprisoned for his positions against communism. He commented that, through his writings, he had opened up a "space for truth." Once that clearing was made, he said, others commenced to stand in it, which made the space bigger, and then more could join. This process continued until so many were in the space for truth that the regime, predicated upon the denial of truth, collapsed of its own weight.

I do believe that we are in a parlous condition today. The grossly exaggerated valuation of private feelings and the concomitant denial of objective truth and moral value have introduced the relentless war of wills—and evidence of this is on display in practically every aspect of our culture. Unless some of us open up a space for truth and boldly stand in it, despite fierce opposition, we are poised to succumb to the totalitarianism that Hannah Arendt so feared.

Paul VI, Prophet

July 2018 marked the fiftieth anniversary of Pope Paul VI's deeply controversial encyclical letter *Humanae Vitae*. I won't bore you with the details of the innumerable battles, disagreements, and ecclesial crises that followed upon this text. Suffice it to say that this short, pithily argued letter became a watershed in the postconciliar Catholic Church and one of the most significant points of contention between liberals and conservatives. Its fundamental contention is that the moral integrity of the sexual act is a function of the coming together of its "procreative and unitive" dimensions. That is to say, sexual intercourse is ethically upright only in the measure that it is expressive of love between married partners and remains open to the conception of a child. When, through a conscious choice, the partners introduce an artificial block to procreation—when, in a word, they separate the unitive and procreative finalities of the sexual act—they do something that is contrary to God's will.

Again, within the context of this brief article, I won't detail the arguments for and against this position. But I would like to draw particular attention to a remarkable passage in *Humanae Vitae*—namely, section 17, in which Paul VI plays the prophet and lays out, clearly and succinctly, what he foresees as consequences of turning away from the Church's classic teaching on sex. Though he is convinced that artificial contraception is morally bad in itself, he's also persuaded that it would, in the long run, adversely affect general societal attitudes regarding sex. Here is a first observation: "Let them first consider how easily this course of action could open wide the way for marital infidelity and a general lowering of moral standards. Not much experience is needed to be fully aware of human weakness and to understand that human beings—and especially the young, who are so exposed to temptation—need incentives to keep the moral law, and it is an evil thing to make it easy for them to break that law." Does anyone doubt that, in the last fifty years, we have seen a profound attenuation of marital fidelity? Could anyone possibly contest that the last half century has witnessed a significant breakdown of the institution of marriage? Is anyone so blind as not to see that during the last five decades a "lowering of moral standards" has taken place? To be sure, there are multiple causes of these declines, and certainly not all the blame can be ascribed to artificial contraception. However, Paul VI was intuiting something of great moment—namely, that once we commenced to redefine the nature of the sexual act, we placed ourselves on a very steep and slippery slope toward a complete voluntarism, whereby we utterly determine the meaning of sexuality, of marriage, and even of gender. And the rapid rise in pornography use, the sexual exploitation of children, and human trafficking are functions of this same arbitrariness. What was only vaguely envisioned and feared fifty years ago is now accepted more or less as a matter of course.

In that same section, Paul VI continues to prophesy: "Another effect that gives cause for alarm is that a man who grows accustomed to the use of contraceptive methods may forget the reverence due to a woman, and, disregarding her physical and emotional equilibrium, reduce her to being a mere instrument for the satisfaction of his own desires, no longer considering her as his partner whom he should surround with care and affection." In the post-Weinstein era, we hear practically every day of another celebrity who has treated women with disrespect, turning them indeed into objects for his own use and manipulation. The entire society is rightly outraged at this behavior, but precious few cultural commentators have noted the link between this kind of objectification and the conscious disassociation of the twin ends of the sexual act. When we are permitted casually to separate love from procreation—or as one analyst had it, to sever the link between sex and diapers—we place ourselves on a short road to reducing sexual intercourse to a form of self-indulgent recreation.

Section 17 of *Humanae Vitae* concludes with a startling act of prescience regarding the political implications of countenancing artificial contraception: "Finally, careful consideration should be given to the danger of this power passing into the hands of those public authorities who care little for the precepts of the moral law. Who will blame a government which in its attempt to resolve the problems affecting an entire country resorts to the same measures as are regarded as lawful by married people in the solution of a particular family difficulty? Who will prevent public authorities from favoring those contraceptive methods which they consider more effective? Should they regard this as necessary, they may even impose their use on everyone." What might have seemed exaggerated, perhaps even slightly paranoid, in 1968 is now a commonplace. The HHS Mandate, which would require even Catholic institutions to provide insurance coverage for contraception and abortifacients, has been so aggressively pursued that even the Little Sisters of the Poor found themselves battling for their rights in court. Pope Francis, an ardent admirer of Paul VI, has picked up on this theme, bemoaning the "ideological colonization" that takes place when the Western powers attempt, through threat of economic sanctions, to impose their sexual program on the underdeveloped world.

In the wake of its fiftieth anniversary, it is a good time to take another look at *Humanae Vitae*. I might suggest we commence with section 17.

Porn and the Curse
of Total Sexual Freedom

A recent issue of *Time* magazine featured a fascinating and deeply troubling article on the prevalence of pornography in our culture. The focus of the piece is on the generation of young men now coming of age, the first generation who grew up with unlimited access to hardcore pornography on the internet. The statistics on this score are absolutely startling. Most young men commence their pornography use at the age of eleven; there are approximately 107 million monthly visitors to adult websites in this country; twelve million hours a day are spent watching porn globally on the adult video site Pornhub; 40 percent of boys in Great Britain say that they regularly consume pornography; and on and on.

All of this wanton viewing of live-action pornography has produced, many are arguing, an army of young men who are incapable of normal and satisfying sexual activity with real human beings. Many twenty-somethings are testifying that when they have the opportunity for sexual relations with their wives or girlfriends, they cannot perform. And in the overwhelming majority of cases, this is not a physiological issue, which is proved by the fact that they can still become aroused easily by images on a computer screen. The sad truth is that, for these young men, sexual stimulation is associated not with flesh and blood human beings but with flickering pictures of physically perfect people in virtual reality. Moreover, since they start so young, they have been compelled, as they get older, to turn to ever more bizarre and violent pornography in order to get the thrill that they desire. And this in turn makes them incapable of finding conventional, nonexotic sex even vaguely interesting.

This state of affairs has led a number of men from the affected generation to lead the charge to disenthrall their contemporaries from the curse of pornography. Following the example of various anti-addiction programs, they are setting up support groups, speaking out about the dangers of porn, advocating for restrictions on adult websites, getting addicts into contact with sponsors who will challenge them, etc. And all of this, it seems to me, is to the good. But what really struck me in the *Time* article is that neither the author nor anyone that he interviewed or referenced ever spoke of pornography use as something morally objectionable. It has apparently come to the culture's attention only because it has resulted in erectile dysfunction! The Catholic Church—and indeed all of decent society until about forty years ago—sees pornography as, first and foremost, an ethical violation, a deep distortion of human sexuality, an unconscionable objectification of persons who should never be treated as anything less than subjects. That this ethical distortion results in myriad problems, both physical and psychological, goes without saying, but the Catholic conviction is that those secondary consequences will not be adequately addressed unless the underlying issue be dealt with.

It is precisely on this point that we come up against a cultural block. Though Freud's psychological theorizing has been largely discredited, a fundamental assumption of Freudianism remains an absolute bedrock of our culture. I'm referring to the conviction that most of our psychological suffering follows as a consequence from the suppression of our sexual desires. Once we have been liberated from old taboos regarding sex, this line of argument runs, we will overcome the neuroses and psychoses that so bedevil us. What was once the peculiar philosophy of a Viennese psychiatrist came to flower in the 1960s, at least in the West, and then made its way into practically every nook and cranny of the culture. How often have we heard some version of this argument: as long as you're not hurting anyone else, you should be allowed to do whatever pleases you in the sexual arena. What the *Time* article articulates in regard to the specific issue of pornography has been, in point of fact, glaringly obvious for quite some time: Freud was wrong. Complete sexual freedom has not made us psychologically healthier; just the contrary.

It has deeply sickened our society. The valorization of unrestricted freedom in regard to sex—precisely because it is morally corrupt—proves psychologically debilitating as well.

Whereas Freud, in the manner of most modern thinkers, principally valorized freedom, the Church valorizes love—which is to say, willing the good of the other. Just as moderns tend to reduce everything to freedom, the Church reduces everything to love; by which I mean, it puts all things in relation to love. Sex is, on the biblical reading, good indeed, but its goodness is a function of its subordination to the demand of love. When it loses that mooring—as it necessarily does when freedom is reverenced as the supreme value—it turns into something other than what it is meant to be. The laws governing sexual behavior, which the Freudian can read only as "taboos" and invitations to repression, are in fact the manner in which the relation between sex and love is maintained. And upon the maintenance of that relation depends our psychological and even physical health as well. That to me is the deepest lesson of the *Time* article.

Michelle Wolf and
the Throwaway Culture

At the 2018 White House Correspondents' Dinner, Michelle Wolf, who I'm told is a comedian, regaled the black-tie and sequin-gowned crowd with her "jokes." Almost all were in extremely bad taste and/or wildly offensive, but one has become accustomed to that sort of coarseness in the comedy clubs and even on mainstream television. However, she crossed over into the territory of the morally appalling when she indulged in this bit of witticism regarding Vice President Mike Pence: "He thinks abortion is murder, which, first of all, don't knock it until you've tried it. And when you do try it, really knock it. You know, you gotta get that baby out of there." One is just at a loss for words. I mean, even some in the severely left-leaning crowd in Washington groaned a bit at that remark.

It might be helpful to remind ourselves what Ms. Wolf is referencing when she speaks of "knocking that baby out of there." She means the evisceration, dismemberment, and vivisection of a child. And lest one think that we are just talking about "bundles of cells," it is strict liberal orthodoxy that a baby can be aborted at any stage of its prenatal development, even while it rests in the birth canal moments before birth. Indeed, a child who somehow miraculously survives the butchery of an abortion should, according to that same orthodoxy, be left to die or actively killed. Sure sounds like fun to me; hey, don't knock it until you've tried it.

I realize that these attitudes have been enshrined in American law for some time, but what particularly struck me about the Correspondents' Dinner was how they were being bandied about so shamelessly for the entertainment of the cultural elite. Let's face it, the people in that room—politicians, judges, writers, broadcasters, government officials—are the top of the food chain, among the most influential and powerful people in our society. And while the killing of children was being joked about—especially, mind you, the children of the poor, who are disproportionately represented among the victims of abortion—most in this wealthy, overwhelmingly white, elite audience guffawed and applauded.

And this put me in mind of Friedrich Nietzsche. I've spoken and written often of the influence of this nineteenth-century thinker, whose musings have trickled their way down through the universities and institutions of the high culture into the general consciousness of many if not most people today. Nietzsche held that the traditional moral values have been exposed as ungrounded and that humanity is summoned to move, accordingly, into a previously unexplored space "beyond good and evil." In such a morally unmoored universe, the *Übermensch* (Superman or Over-man) emerges to assert his power and impose his rule on those around him. Nietzsche had a special contempt for the Christian values of sympathy, compassion, and love of enemies, characterizing them as the ideals of a "slave morality," repugnant to the noble aspirations of the *Übermensch*. Through his many avatars in the twentieth century—Sartre, Heidegger, Foucault, Ayn Rand, etc.—Nietzsche, as I said, has exerted an extraordinary influence on contemporary thought. Whenever a young person today speaks of traditional ethics as a disguised play of power or of her right to determine the meaning of her own life through an exercise of sovereign freedom, we can hear the overtones of Friedrich Nietzsche.

All of which brings me back to the White House Correspondents' Dinner. When we live in the space beyond good and evil, when morality is construed as entirely the invention of personal freedom, when nothing counts as intrinsically wicked, when any claim to moral authority is automatically shouted down—in other words, when we live in the world that Nietzsche made possible—then the will of the most powerful necessarily holds sway. And when something or someone gets in the way of what the powerful want, well then, they just "gotta knock it out of there." Michelle Wolf's comment was not just a bad joke; it was a brazen display of power, designed to appeal precisely to those who have reached the top of the greasy pole.

One of the extraordinary but often overlooked qualities of a system of objective morality is that it is a check on the powerful and a protection of the most vulnerable. If good and evil are objective states of affairs, then they hem in and control the tendency of cultural elites to dominate others. When objective moral values evanesce, armies of the expendable emerge, and what Pope Francis aptly calls a *cultura del descarte* (a throwaway culture) obtains. One of the indicators that this has happened is lots of people in tuxedos and formal gowns, sipping from wine glasses, and laughing while someone jokes about the murder of children.

Seeing Abortion

We stand at a pivotal point in the great moral debate over abortion in our country—not because new arguments have emerged, but rather because laws so breathtaking in their barbarism have been passed, and a film so visceral in its presentation of the reality of abortion has found a wide audience. As John Henry Newman reminded us, assent to a proposition is rarely a matter of acquiescing to rational demonstration alone; instead, it often has to do with the accumulation of argument, image, impression, experience, and witness.

The legal protocols now in effect in New York, Delaware, and a number of other states allowing for the butchering of a child in the womb at any point in his or her nine-month gestation—and indeed, on the clinic or hospital table, should the child by some miracle survive the abortion—have sickened much of the country. And they have allowed people to see, in unmistakably clear terms, the full implications of the twisted "pro-choice" ideology. If a mother chooses to bring her baby to term and to be born, that child is, somehow by that choice, the subject of dignity and worthy of the full protection of the law; and if a mother chooses otherwise, even a newborn baby struggling to breathe on an operating table can be murdered and discarded like so much garbage. Biology and metaphysics be damned: our subjective decisions determine reality—and the result is state-sanctioned infanticide. So obviously insane, so clearly dangerous, so unmistakably wicked are these laws that they are causing many people to reconsider their position on abortion.

Unplanned, the story of Abby Johnson's wrenching transition from director of a Planned Parenthood clinic to vocal opponent of abortion, has proven to be a surprisingly popular film, despite its rather grim theme and despite considerable institutional opposition. As many have pointed out, Mrs.

Johnson is playing a role analogous to that played by Harriet Beecher Stowe in the nineteenth century. While there were plenty of arguments on both sides of the slavery debate at the time, many advocates of slavery underwent a conversion to abolitionism, not because of rational demonstrations, but precisely through the influence of Stowe's vivid presentation of the concrete reality of slavery in *Uncle Tom's Cabin*. So today, arguments and slogans on both sides of the abortion controversy are well known, and most people seem more or less locked in their respective camps. But *Unplanned* doesn't so much argue as show. "Abortion" becomes, accordingly, not an abstract issue, but an in-your-face, real, and bloody fact.

The film opens with the event that proved decisive for Abby Johnson herself. As director and administrator of a Planned Parenthood clinic, she was certainly aware of what was happening on the premises, but she had rarely been involved in an actual abortion. One afternoon, she was summoned to the operating room and asked to hold the device that allowed the doctor to see the ultrasound image of the child in the womb. As the physician went about his work, Abby could clearly see the child resting comfortably and then reacting violently as a suctioning device was inserted into the womb. To her horror, she then saw a tiny arm sucked off, only to reappear, moments later, as a bloody soup in a catheter next to her. As she watched, unable to take her eyes off of the horrific display, she saw the severely wounded baby continuing to evade the device, until a leg disappeared, then another arm, and finally the baby's head. And again, the remains of the living child surged like slush into the catheter. With that, she ran from the room, vomited in the bathroom, and resolved to dissociate herself forever from Planned Parenthood. The film makes clear that she had heard arguments against abortion all of her life, for her parents and husband were ardently and vocally pro-life, but she made the decision after she *saw* what it meant to end the life of an unborn child. Her hope, obviously, is that her film will have a similar effect on many others.

One of the most memorable scenes in *Unplanned* deals with an odd little party that took place at the clinic after hours. Abby, it turns out, was pregnant, and her colleagues, all female, gathered to give her a baby shower. Out came the balloons, the thoughtful presents, the encouraging hugs—all meant to show their joy at the birth of a new baby. But then we realize that these medical professionals, these good friends of Abby, have spent their entire day killing the babies of other women. Indeed, the blood of those procedures is on their shoes and scrubs. How is this scene possible? The condition for its possibility is the lunatic ideology of "choice" referenced above: if the baby is desired, let's have a party; if the baby is unwanted, kill him and cast his remains in a dumpster. Pro-choice advocates must know that this is the implication of their philosophy, but *Unplanned* makes them see it.

In 1850, lots of good and thoughtful people defended the institution of slavery. Now, only insane people would. Today, lots of decent and thoughtful people defend the pro-choice position. One can only hope that these recent laws, and this viscerally disturbing film, will hasten the day when only insane people would.

New York, Abortion, and a
Short Route to Chaos

I t was the celebration that was particularly galling. On the forty-sixth anniversary of the *Roe v. Wade* decision, the Governor of New York, Andrew Cuomo, signed into law a protocol that gives practically unrestricted access to abortion, permitting the killing of an unborn child up until the moment of delivery. In the wake of the ratification, the legislators and their supporters whooped, hollered, and cheered, a display depressingly similar to the jubilation that broke out in Ireland when a referendum legalizing abortion passed in 2018. Of course, all of the rhetoric about women's rights and reproductive health and empowerment was trotted out, but who can fail to see what was at stake? If an infant, lying peacefully in a bassinet in his parents' home, were brutally killed and dismembered, the entire country would rightfully be outraged and call for an investigation of the murder. But now the law of New York confirms that that same child, moments before his birth, resting peacefully in his mother's womb, can be, with utter impunity, pulled apart with forceps. And the police won't be summoned; rather, it appears, the killing should be a matter of celebration.

An ideology, taken in the negative sense, is a conceptual framework that blinds one to reality. The purpose of any ideational system, obviously, is to shed light, to bring us closer to the truth of things, but an ideology does the reverse, effectively obfuscating reality, distancing us from truth. All of the buzz terms I mentioned above are ideological markers, smokescreens. Or, if I can borrow the terminology of Jordan Peterson, they are the chattering of demons, the distracting hubbub of the father of lies. I recall that during the presidential campaign of 2016, Hillary Clinton was asked several times if the child in the womb, within minutes of birth, has no constitutional rights, and this extremely intelligent, experienced, and canny politician said, over and over again, "That's what our law dictates." Therefore, by a sheer accident of location, the unborn baby can be butchered, and the same baby, moments later and in the arms of his mother, must be protected by full force of law. That many of our political leaders can't or won't see how utterly ludicrous this is can only be the result of ideological indoctrination.

As I watched film of Andrew Cuomo signing this repulsive bill into law, my mind drifted back to 1984 and an auditorium at the University of Notre Dame where Cuomo's father, Mario—also Governor of New York at the time—delivered a famous address. In his lengthy and intellectually substantive speech, Governor Cuomo presented himself, convincingly, as a faithful Catholic, thoroughly convinced in conscience that abortion is morally outrageous. But he also made a fateful distinction that has been exploited by liberal Catholic politicians ever since. He explained that though he was personally opposed to abortion, he was not willing to pursue legal action to abolish it or even to limit it, since he was the representative of all the people, and not just of those who shared his Catholic convictions. Now, this distinction is an illegitimate one, which is evident the moment we draw an analogy to other public matters of great moral import: "I'm personally opposed to slavery, but I'll take no action to outlaw it or limit its spread"; "I personally find Jim Crow laws repugnant, but I will pursue no legal strategy to undo them"; etc. But at the very least, Mario Cuomo could declare himself deeply conflicted, anguished, and willing to support abortion law only as a regrettable political necessity in a pluralistic democracy.

But in a single generation, we have moved from reluctant toleration to unbridled celebration, from struggling Mario to exultant Andrew. And there is a simple reason for this. A privatized religion, one that never incarnates itself in gesture, behavior, and moral commitment, rapidly evanesces. Once-powerful convictions, never concretely expressed, devolve practically overnight into pious velleities—and finally disappear altogether. In Robert Bolt's magnificent play regarding St. Thomas More, *A Man for All Seasons*, we find a telling exchange between Cardinal Wolsey, a hard-bitten, largely amoral politico, and the saintly More. Wolsey laments, "You're a constant regret to me, Thomas. If you could just see facts flat on, without that horrible moral squint, with just a little common sense, you could have been a statesman." To which More responds, "Well . . . I believe when statesmen forsake their own private conscience for the sake of their public duties . . . they lead their country by a short route to chaos." Abandoning the convictions of one's conscience in the exercise of one's public duties is precisely equivalent to "I'm personally opposed but unwilling to take concrete action to instantiate my opposition."

And this abandonment—evident in Mario Cuomo's 1984 address—has indeed led by a short road to chaos, evident in Andrew Cuomo's joyful celebration of a law permitting the murder of children.

Love Is Both Tolerant
and Intolerant

Every community, inevitably, has a value or set of values that it considers fundamental, some basic good that positions every other claim to goodness. For most of the modern liberal democracies, for example, freedom and equality play this determining role in the moral discourse. In communist societies, economic justice, construed as the elimination of the class structure, would provide such a foundation. In the context of German National Socialism, the defense of the fatherland and the will of the Führer anchored the moral system, however corrupt. There is a rather simple means of identifying this ultimate value: in regard to any particular moral or political act, keep asking the question "Why is this being done?" until you come to the point where you find yourself saying, "Well, because that's just a good thing." The "just a good thing" is the value that your society or culture considers nonnegotiable and that in turn determines all subordinate values.

As a liberal society, ours has been, as I stated above, largely shaped by the values of liberty and equality, but in recent years, the ground has shifted a bit. Even a casual survey of the contemporary cultural scene reveals that the nonnegotiables, the values undetermined and all-determining, seem to be inclusivity, tolerance, and diversity. If you asked most people today, especially the young, why should you be inclusive, tolerant, and accepting of diversity, the answer, I imagine, would be a puzzled "Well, those are just good things to be."

And here I would like to draw a contrast with the community of the Church. Within a properly Christian context, the ultimate value, which positions and determines any other value, is neither tolerance, nor diversity, nor inclusivity, but rather love. I'll admit that things can get confusing at this

123

point, for the fundamental goods of the secular society today do have much in common with love, which is indeed often inclusive, tolerant, and encouraging of diversity. But not always—and thereupon hangs a tale.

To love is to will the good of the other as other. It is to break out of the black hole of one's own self-regard and truly desire what is best for another. Therefore, to be sure, love is inclusive in the measure that it recognizes the essential dignity of each individual; love is tolerant inasmuch as it respects the goodness of even those who hold errant points of view; and love encourages diversity to the degree that it eschews the imperialistic imposition of one's own ego upon another. However, sometimes love is exclusive, intolerant, and unaccepting of diversity—precisely because it wills the good of the other.

To illustrate this counterintuitive proposition, let me begin with a rather ordinary example. Suppose you are the coach of a college baseball team, and you are presiding over tryouts. You survey a number of players of varying skill levels, and you are compelled to make your selection of, say, twenty players out of a hundred candidates. Your choices will exclude far more than they include; they will sow unhappiness more abundantly than joy. But if you are a good man, they will be done out of love. You will be willing the good of those advanced players who can and should practice their skills through heightened competition and who will delight the fans who will attend their games; and you will be willing the good of those less advanced players who should not be permitted to compromise the integrity of the team and who should probably enter into some other arena of endeavor. In a word, both inclusion and exclusion will be acts of love, which proves that love is a more fundamental and positioning value.

Now a somewhat more elevated example. The Church of Jesus Christ is radically inclusive, for its ultimate purpose is to draw all people to the Lord. The Bernini Colonnade in St. Peter's Square, reaching out like arms to embrace the massive crowds, is evocative of this aspiration. Jesus said, "Go therefore and make disciples of *all* nations," and "proclaim the good news to the *whole creation*" (Matt. 28:19; Mark 16:15). Thus, inclusivity is without doubt one of the dimensions of the Church's love. However, the

Church is also exclusive and intolerant, for it discerns that certain forms of behavior are repugnant to its own integrity. Thus, for a variety of reasons, it excludes people from receiving Communion, and in extreme cases, it formally excommunicates others. It solemnly declares that those who are in the state of mortal sin are not worthy to approach the Eucharistic table unless they first receive sacramental absolution. And it unapologetically asserts that the Christian life has a formal structure, which by its very nature excludes certain styles of life that are incompatible with it. These discriminations, judgments, and exclusions are, if I might put it this way, modes of "tough love." Though they seem harsh, they are ways of willing the good of the other.

A song that has been widely played in Catholic circles in recent decades includes the line "All are welcome in this place." Cardinal Francis George once archly remarked, "Yes, all are welcome in the Church, but on Christ's terms, not their own." Real love both includes and excludes; real love is both tolerant and intolerant.

Why We Can't Do Evil
Even If Good May Come

There is a curious and intriguing passage in the third chapter of St. Paul's Letter to the Romans, which in the context of the missive seems almost tossed-off, but which has proven to be a cornerstone of Catholic moral theology for the past two thousand years. Responding to some of his critics, Paul says, "And why not say (as some people slander us by saying that we say), 'Let us do evil so that good may come?' Their condemnation is deserved!" (Rom. 3:8). One might formulate Paul's somewhat convoluted statement as follows: we should never do evil that good might come of it.

There are indeed truly wicked people who seem to take delight in doing evil for its own sake. Aristotle called them vicious or, in extreme cases, "beast-like." But most of us who do bad things typically can find a justification for our behavior through appealing to a good end that we were hoping through our action to achieve. "I'm not really proud of what I did," I might say to myself, "but at least it brought about some positive consequences." But the Church, following the prompt of St. Paul, has consistently frowned on this manner of thinking, precisely because it opens the door to moral chaos. Concomitantly, it has recognized certain acts—slavery, adultery, the sexual abuse of children, the direct killing of the innocent, etc.—as "intrinsically evil"; which is to say, they are incapable of being justified through appeal to motivation, extenuating circumstances, or consequences. So far, so obvious.

But this principle has come to my mind recently, not so much in regard to the moral acts of individuals, but to the moral assumptions that seem to be guiding much of our society. I might suggest that a sea change occurred in 1995 with the trial of O.J. Simpson. I think it's fair to say that the overwhelming majority of reasonable people would concur that Simpson committed the terrible crimes of which he was accused, and yet he was exonerated by a jury of his peers and vehemently supported by large segments in our society. How can we explain this anomaly? The exculpation of O.J. Simpson was justified, in the minds of many, because it was seen as contributing to the solution of the great social ill of the racial profiling and persecution of African Americans by the Los Angeles police department in particular and police officers across the country in general. Allowing a guilty man to go free and allowing a gross injustice to remain unaddressed were, at the very least, tolerated, because it appeared they conduced to some greater good.

The O.J. Simpsonization of our legal thinking was on gross display much more recently in the sad case of Cardinal George Pell. Once again, given the wild implausibility of the charges and the complete lack of any corroborating evidence, reasonable people were bound to conclude that Cardinal Pell, who was recently acquitted, should never have been brought to trial, much less convicted. And yet Pell was found guilty and sentenced to imprisonment, and a later appeal confirmed the original conviction. How could we possibly explain this disconnect? Many in Australian society, legitimately outraged at the abuse of children by priests and the subsequent cover-up by some in ecclesial authority, felt that the imprisonment of Cardinal Pell would somehow address this overarching issue. So, once again, in violation of Paul's principle, evil was done that good might come of it.

The same problem is evident in regard to sexual aggression against women. In the wake of the Harvey Weinstein situation and the subsequent #MeToo movement, no serious person doubts that numerous women have been unconscionably mistreated by powerful men and that this abuse is a cancer on the body politic. Therefore, in order to achieve the good of solving this problem, men are sometimes accused, harassed, or effectively condemned without investigation or trial. To show that I have no partisan axe to grind here, I will draw attention to the treatment of both Justice Brett Kavanaugh during his confirmation hearing and President Joe Biden in the days leading up to the 2020 election. The thinking seems, again, to be that the righting of a general wrong justifies morally irresponsible behavior in particular cases.

The prevalence of this moral consequentialism in our society is supremely dangerous, for the moment we say that evil can be done for the sake of the good, we have effectively denied that there are any intrinsically evil acts, and the moment we do that, the intellectual support for our moral system gives way automatically. And then the furies come. A very instructive example of the principle is the Terror that followed the French Revolution. Since there had been (undoubtedly) tremendous injustices done to the poor by the aristocratic class in eighteenth-century France, anyone perceived to be an enemy of the revolution was, without distinction or discrimination, swept to the guillotine. If innocents died alongside the guilty, so be it—for it served the building of the new society. I believe that it is no exaggeration to say that Western society has yet fully to recover from the moral chaos visited upon us by the lethal consequentialism of that time.

Therefore, even as we legitimately fight the great social evils of our time, we must remember Paul's simple but trenchant principle: never do evil that good might come of it.

PART V

DEFINING SOCIAL JUSTICE

Charlottesville
and America's Original Sin

I vividly remember my first visit to Charlottesville, Virginia. It was about twenty years ago, and I was on vacation with a good friend, who shared with me a passion for American history and for Thomas Jefferson in particular. We had toured a number of Civil War battlefields in Maryland and Virginia and then had made our way to Jefferson's University of Virginia in Charlottesville. Finally, we ventured outside the city to the little hilltop home that the great founder had designed and built for himself, Monticello. It was a glorious summer day, and the elegant manse shone in all of its Palladian splendor. We took in its classical lines, its distinctive red and white coloration, the understated beauty of its dome, its overall symmetry, balance, and harmony. On the inside, we saw all of Jefferson's quirky genius on display: scientific instruments, inventions, books galore. Just outside the house was the simple, unpretentious grave of Jefferson, the tombstone naming him as the author of the Declaration of Independence. There was no question that the very best of the American spirit was on display in that place.

But then we noticed something else. Below the sight lines of Monticello, literally underground, were the quarters of Jefferson's slaves. These were hovels, really little more than caves, with bare earth floors and flimsy roofs, and not even a hint of the elegance, comfort, and beauty of the great house. Jefferson had brought some of his slaves to France with him when he was the American ambassador to that country, and he had taught them the fine art of French cuisine. When he entertained at Monticello, these servants, dressed in the finery of courtiers at Versailles, would serve the savory meals that they had prepared. Afterward, they would return for the night to their underground hovels. A woman, who had been invited to stay for a time at Monticello, recorded in her diary that she woke up one morning to the sounds of horrific screaming. When she looked with alarm and concern out her window, she saw the author of the Declaration of Independence savagely beating one of his slaves.

Jefferson the morally upright sage; Jefferson the merciless slave owner. Splendid Monticello; its sordid slave quarters underground. One could literally see at this great American house the divide, the original sin, that has bedeviled our nation from its inception to the present day. The framers of the Constitution fought over slavery and race; the issue preoccupied the politics of America for the first half of the nineteenth century and finally drove the country to a disastrous and murderous civil conflict; it perdured in somewhat mitigated form in the segregation, both sanctioned and unofficial, that reigned in America in the decades following the Civil War; it came to a head during the great civil rights struggle of the mid-twentieth century, culminating in landmark legislation and in the assassination of Martin Luther King Jr.; it continued to assert itself in the Detroit riots of 1967, the Watts uprising, the unrest after the beating of Rodney King, the street violence in Ferguson, Missouri, and in many other events.

For me, it was weirdly fitting that a recent manifestation of it would be in Charlottesville, Virginia, where, twenty years ago, I had so vividly seen the moral contradiction at the heart of American history. Thomas Jefferson's principle that "all men are created equal, that they are endowed by their Creator with certain unalienable Rights," came face-to-face, on the streets of Charlottesville, with representatives of the most nefarious ideology of hatred and racial superiority. God knows that, since Jefferson's time, many, many battles have been won in this struggle, but the events in Charlottesville in August 2017 proved that the war is not yet over, that the original sin of America has not been thoroughly expunged.

I have been using the term "original sin" very much on purpose, for it is my conviction that both the problem and its solution are best articulated in theological categories. Finally, our awful tendency, up and down the ages and in every culture, to divide ourselves into opposing camps, to demonize the other, to scapegoat, to take away fundamental human rights, is a function of the denial that all people are made in the image and likeness of God. It is, first and last, a sin. And finally, the answer cannot be a matter of political machination but only of grace. No one saw this more clearly than St. Paul, who was dealing with the very same issue within the cultural framework of the first century: Jews and non-Jews were at odds, Romans dominated and everyone else obeyed, slavery obtained throughout the ancient Mediterranean world, etc.

Paul came to understand that, strangely enough, a crucified victim of the tyrannical Roman authorities provided a way out: "There is no longer Jew or Greek, there is no longer slave or free, there is no longer male and female; for all of you are one in Christ Jesus" (Gal. 3:28). It would require a lengthy theological tome fully to unpack the meaning of that phrase. Suffice it to say that the Crucifixion of the Son of God disclosed the entire range and universality of human dysfunction: stupidity, violence, injustice, cruelty, victimizing, etc.: "All have sinned and fall short of the glory of God" (Rom. 3:23). And the Resurrection of Jesus revealed the entire range and universality of the divine mercy: "Where sin increased, grace abounded all the more" (Rom. 5:20). In a word, we are all sinners upon whom an amazing grace has been poured out. So let us stop playing games of domination: us against them, racial superiority, masters and slaves. In Christ, all of that has been exposed as fraudulent and swept away.

This is the saving word that the Christian churches can and should bring to this age-old and still-festering wound in the body politic of our nation.

Pentecost
and the Fires in Our Cities

It is in a way providential that the Feast of Pentecost in 2020 arrived just as our country was going through a convulsive social crisis. For the Holy Spirit, whose coming we celebrate on Pentecost, is a power meant to transform the world, or, in the language of Psalm 104, to "renew the face of the earth" (Ps. 104:30 NABRE). Pentecost, accordingly, is never simply for the Church; it is for the world by means of the Church.

One of the principal biblical metaphors for the Spirit is the wind, and indeed, on Pentecost morning, the Apostles heard what sounded like a strong driving wind as the Spirit arrived. But the wind, elusive and unpredictable, is never really known in itself, but only through its effects. On the scriptural reading, the first effect of the Holy Spirit is the formation of an *ekklesia* (a Church), which in turn is designed to transform the wider society into the Spirit's image. In the words of the Nicene Creed—accepted by Orthodox, Catholic, and Protestant Christians—this *ekklesia* is "one, holy, catholic, and apostolic." The wind of the Holy Spirit produces these qualities, and therefore, it is by them that the Spirit's action is discerned. So let us analyze them one by one.

The Acts of the Apostles gives us the great icon for the unity of the Church in the picture of the Apostles gathered in prayer in one place with the Virgin Mary on Pentecost morning. The Holy Spirit is nothing other than the love that connects the Father and the Son, which explains why one of his great titles in the tradition is *vinculum amoris* (chain of love). Thus, the Spirit draws all of the followers of Jesus together in unity. This is not an oppressive or imperialistic oneness, for indeed there is a marvelous variety of personalities, theological schools, and pastoral emphases in the Christian community. But in essentials, the community of Jesus is meant to be united and in that unity to find its power to unify the world. Origen of Alexandria said, "*Ubi divisio ibi peccatum*" (Where there is division, there is sin). Consequently, the Church's missionary task is to overcome division, wherever it might be found. The night before he died, Jesus prayed "that they may be one, as we are one" (John 17:22). In this prayer, he intended not just the Church to become one, but the world by means of the Church.

Secondly, the Church is meant to be holy, and it achieves this quality precisely in the measure that it is filled with the Holy Spirit. And since the Holy Spirit, as we saw, is none other than the love that connects the Father and the Son, holiness consists in love, which is not an emotion but the act of willing the good of the other. Everything in the life of the Church—sacraments, the Eucharist, the liturgy, preaching, the witness of the saints, etc.—is meant to inculcate love. I will confess that I frequently shake my head ruefully when I come across Catholics on the internet who profess passionate commitment to the sacraments, doctrines, and practices of the Church, and yet who are obviously filled with hatred. I want to tell them, "You know, all of your devotions are fine, but in your case, they're not working!" Did not Jesus himself say, "By this everyone will know that you are my disciples, if you have love for one another" (John 13:35)? Willing the good of the other is the great flag of the Holy Spirit.

In the third place, the Church is marked by catholicity, a word derived from the Greek phrase *kata holos* (according to the whole). By its very nature, the *ekklesia* of Jesus is universal in scope and mission, for it is meant to bring the whole world to Christ. Jesus said, "Go therefore and make disciples of all nations, baptizing them in the name of the Father and of the Son and of the Holy Spirit" (Matt. 28:19), and that when the Son of Man is "lifted up," he "will draw all people" to himself (John 3:14, 12:32). To be sure, there is a terrible history regarding attempts to achieve this unity through violence and imposition, but that is simply the story of how nominal Christians refused to cooperate with the Holy Spirit. What is most important to see in this regard is that the Church's task is to be light, salt, and leaven for the whole society (*kata holos*), never suppressing the plurality of cultures, but at the same time, bringing them under the influence of the divine love.

And finally, the Church is apostolic. The word "apostle" is derived from the Greek *apostelein*, which means "to send." The original twelve Apostles were empowered by the Holy Spirit and then sent into the world to evangelize. Though they received the Spirit while they were hunkered down in the upper room, they were never meant to stay hunkered down. From the beginning, there has been an expulsive, centrifugal energy to the *ekklesia*, an instinct for the ends of the earth. The original flame of the Holy Spirit was meant to become a conflagration, for Jesus said, "I came to cast fire upon the earth" (Luke 12:49 RSV-CE). One of the principal themes in the writing and sermonizing of Pope Francis is precisely this missionary nature of the Church. He wants believers in the Lord to leave their sacristies and get out onto the streets, to stir things up, even to overturn what needs overturning.

All of which brings me back to the situation in which we found ourselves on Pentecost. The riots and unrest that were convulsing our country were prompted by the killing of George Floyd, to be sure, but their deeper cause is the racism—systemic and personal—that has bedeviled our society for over four hundred years. Though undoubted progress has been made in the course of these four centuries, there is still irrational hatred in the hearts of far too many in our country. And for all the years that racial tension and violence have endured, from slavery and segregation to the racism both overt and indirect that obtains today, the overwhelming majority of people in our land have been Christians—which is to say, people baptized into the divine life, filled, at least in principle, with the Holy Spirit. In the measure that the scourge of race hatred remains, therefore, we know that the *ekklesia* of Jesus has not been fulfilling its mission, has not been living up to its identity. If Christians have been the dominant presence in our country for all of these centuries, why isn't there more unity? Why isn't there more love? Why is it painfully obvious that so few of us have really gone on mission?

May I offer a challenge to all the members of the *ekklesia* today, Protestant, Catholic, and Orthodox? Celebrate the coming of the Holy Spirit this

Pentecost, but then get out of the upper room! Light the fire of love in the streets, in the halls of government, in the world of communication, in business and industry, in schools, and in the hearts of your friends and neighbors. The stubborn survival of the awful cancer of racism in the body politic proves— and I say it to our shame—that we have not been the *ekklesia* that the Holy Spirit wants us to be.

Martin Luther King Jr.
and the Religious Motivation
for Social Change

A principal reason why the civil rights movement of the 1950s and 1960s was so successful both morally and practically was that it was led largely by people with a strong religious sensibility. The most notable of these leaders was, of course, Martin Luther King Jr. To appreciate the subtle play between King's religious commitment and his practical work, I would draw your attention to two texts—namely, his "Letter from Birmingham City Jail" and his "I Have a Dream" speech, both from 1963.

While imprisoned in Birmingham for leading a nonviolent protest, King responded to certain of his fellow Christian ministers who had criticized him for going too fast, expecting social change to happen overnight. The Baptist minister answered his critics in a perhaps surprising manner, invoking the aid of a medieval Catholic theologian. King drew their attention to the reflections of St. Thomas Aquinas on law, specifically Thomas' theory that positive law finds its justification in relation to the natural law, which finds *its* justification in relation to the eternal law. Aquinas means that what makes a practical, everyday law righteous is that it somehow gives expression to the principles of the moral law, which in turn are reflective of God's own mind. Therefore, King concluded, unjust positive laws, such as the Jim Crow regulations that he was contesting, are not just bad laws; they are immoral and finally offensive to God.

Here is King's own language: "One may well ask: 'How can you advocate breaking some laws and obeying others?' The answer lies in the fact that there are two types of laws: just and unjust. I would be the first to advocate obeying just laws. One has not only a legal but a moral responsibility to obey just laws." But then King contrasts this with obedience to an unjust law: "Conversely, one has a moral responsibility to disobey unjust laws. I would agree with St. Augustine that 'an unjust law is no law at all.'" And in clarifying the difference, he turns to Aquinas: "Now, what is the difference between the two? How does one determine whether a law is just or unjust? A just law is a man-made code that squares with the moral law or the law of God. An unjust law is a code that is out of harmony with the moral law. To put it in the terms of St. Thomas Aquinas: an unjust law is a human law that is not rooted in eternal law and natural law." This is not pious boilerplate; rather, it reveals what gave King's movement its justification and purpose.

The very same dynamic was on display six months later, when King addressed the throng who had gathered at the Lincoln Memorial for the March on Washington. He was not giving a sermon. He was making a political speech, advocating in the public place for social change. But attend to some of the language that he used: "I have a dream that one day every valley shall be exalted, every hill and mountain shall be made low, the rough places will be made plain, and the crooked places will be made straight, and the glory of the Lord shall be revealed, and all flesh shall see it together." He was directly relating the social revolution he was advocating to the mystical vision of the prophet Isaiah (Isa. 40:4–5). And listen to the magnificent conclusion of the address, in which he artfully blends the lyrics of an American patriotic song with the lyrics of a song he and his family sang in church: "And when this happens, and when we allow freedom ring, when we let it ring from every village and every hamlet, from every state and every city, we will be able to speed up that day when *all* of God's children, black men and white men, Jews and Gentiles, Protestants and Catholics, will be able to join hands and sing in the words of the old Negro spiritual: *Free at last! Free at last! Thank God almighty, we are free at last!*" Once again, on King's reading, the political nests within the moral, which nests within the sacred.

Martin Luther King derived from his religious heritage not only the meta-physics that informed his social activism, but also the nonviolent method that he employed. What Jesus reveals in the rhetoric of the Sermon on the Mount—"Love your enemies and pray for those who persecute you" (Matt. 5:44); "If anyone strikes you on the right cheek, turn the other also" (Matt. 5:39); etc.—and even more strikingly in his word of forgiveness from the cross is that God's way is the way of peace, nonviolence, and compassion. As a Christian, King knew in his bones that reacting to oppression with violence would only exacerbate the tensions within society. He sums up this principle in one of his best-known sermons: "Returning hate for hate multiplies hate, adding deeper darkness to a night already devoid of stars. Darkness cannot drive out darkness; only light can do that. Hate cannot drive out hate; only love can do that."

Within the confines of this brief article, I cannot begin adequately to address the social upheaval occurring in our culture today. But I will say simply this: it is indisputably clear that there are severe moral deficits in our society that must be addressed, but the best way to do so is from within a moral and finally religious framework. May Martin Luther King's model of leadership in this regard be a lodestar.

Acknowledging an Abyss,
Finding a Bridge

One of the most remarkable differences between the social protests of the 1960s and those of today is that the former were done in concert with, and often under the explicit leadership of, religious people. One has only to think of the crucially important role played by the Rev. Dr. Martin Luther King Jr. and so many of his colleagues and disciples in the civil rights demonstrations. But we don't find today the same concert between those agitating for social change and the religious leadership. There are many reasons for this phenomenon. Perhaps the most important is simply that the number of people who subscribe to religion, especially in the ranks of the young, has precipitously dropped in our society. But I also think that there is something subtler at play as well, and I have to put on my philosopher's hat to articulate it.

In the 1960s, Dr. King and company were certainly using biblical ideas and terminology to express their critique of injustice and their longing for a righteous society, but they were also more or less confident that, in doing so, they would find a receptive audience among those trained in the political tradition that we might characterize as "classical liberalism." This, broadly speaking, is the public philosophy shaped by such figures as Thomas Jefferson, John Stuart Mill, and especially John Locke. As is evident in some of their principal texts—Jefferson's Declaration of Independence, Mill's *On Liberty*, and Locke's *Two Treatises of Government*, for example—we find a clear sense that human reason can discern certain fundamental moral objectivities, including and especially the truth that all people are endowed with rights and dignity. Furthermore, we find the conviction that objective theoretical truth exists and that it is accessible through the intellectual give-and-take fostered by the political practice of allowing freedom of speech.

Though there were clear points of demarcation between classical liberalism and Christianity (indeed, all of the figures referenced above were, to varying degrees, opposed to biblical religion), nevertheless, on these central points, people trained in the scriptural tradition could find common ground with liberals. Revisit Dr. King's "I Have a Dream" speech to see a master class in how to weave the two traditions together. King used soaring language from the prophet Isaiah, but then effortlessly related it to Jefferson's political philosophy and even to the lyrics of our patriotic songs. Another excellent example of someone who could link together the two schools of thought was John Paul II. In numerous texts and speeches, the great pope happily adopted the human rights language of classical liberalism and lifted it up into the higher context of a biblical anthropology.

The absence of religious leadership in the protest movements of the present moment, and indeed the hostility to religion exhibited by many of the protesters, are a function of a major shift in the culture. The philosophy that undergirds the "woke" perspective is not classical liberalism, but rather postmodernism, indeed a fairly nasty strain of it. The voices behind much of the opposition leadership today are not those of Locke and Jefferson, but rather of Karl Marx, Friedrich Nietzsche, and Michel Foucault—and this makes a crucial difference. Marx, for instance, denies the existence of a stable human nature, insisting that the term simply means "the sum total of one's social relations." Nietzsche asserts the nonexistence of God and hence the relativity of any claim to objective truth or moral value. In the space opened up by this metaphysical collapse, the "will to power," he argued, can and should assert itself. And Foucault—probably the most influential of the three—understands the ideas and forms of discourse of a given society to be nothing more than the cynical means by which a dominant group maintains itself in power. A key practical implication of this theorizing is that the free speech so dear to classical liberalism as a means of coming to truth is appreciated as a means of oppression. And the appeals that religious people used to make to the rights of the individual are typically seen by postmodern theorists as unjustified and ultimately manipulative. As a result of all of this, it is exceptionally difficult for the religiously motivated to get any traction with those formed by postmodernism, and vice versa. The two groups tend to stare at one another across an intellectual abyss.

But all is not lost. If I might suggest one possible bridge between the two worlds, it would be a shared passion for justice. Despite their consistent claim that truth and value are relative and that language is but a subtle means of domination, the schools formed by Marx and Foucault would certainly hold that the oppression of one class of people by another is unjust. To that degree, they inescapably hold to something like an objective moral value, and they would seem to agree that language that articulates that value is something other than merely manipulative. And here, the biblical person can indeed find common ground, for beginning with the Hebrew prophets and coming directly through Jesus himself and then into the great Christian tradition, we find the conviction that seeking justice is congruent with the will of God.

So the conversation between the religious and the revolutionary is tougher today than it was in the 1960s, for a philosophical system more alien to religion than was classical liberalism has come to hold sway in revolutionary circles. But I would urge my co-religionists not to give up. A love for justice might be the bridge.

We're All Becoming Platonists Now—
and That's Not Good

One of the most fundamental divides in the history of philosophy is that between a more Platonic approach and a more Aristotelian approach. Plato, of course, saw the universal or formal level of being as more real, more noble, whereas Aristotle, while acknowledging the existence and importance of the abstract, favored the concrete and particular. This differentiation was famously illustrated by Raphael in his masterpiece *The School of Athens*, the central figures of which are Plato, his finger pointing upward to the realm of the forms, and Aristotle, stretching his palm downward to the particular things of the earth. This archetypal demarcation had (and has) implications for how we think about religion, science, society, ethics, and politics. Just as most Beatles fans separate themselves rather naturally into Lennon or McCartney camps, so most philosophers can be, at least broadly speaking, characterized as either more Platonic or more Aristotelian in orientation. So far, so harmless, for each side complements and balances the other.

However, in the political arena, the option for a Platonic rather than an Aristotelian framework has more dangerous implications, and no one saw this more clearly than the twentieth-century theoretician Karl Popper. In his principal work, *The Open Society and Its Enemies*, Popper identified Plato as the father of modern totalitarianism, for Platonic political thought, he argued, subordinates the individual to a grandly abstract construal of justice. So as to attain the right balance between the three great divisions of society—guardians, auxiliaries, and workers—the guardians, Plato's philosopher-kings, can utterly control the lives of those in their charge, even to the point of censoring music and poetry, regulating pregnancy and childbirth, eliminating private property, and annulling the individual family. Though he reverenced

Plato, Aristotle departed from this conception of the good society and took as his point of departure the aspiration and freedom of the individual—though certainly by our standards he was far from ideal in this area.

Popper contended that the Platonic streak runs perilously through Western history, but manifested itself with particular destructiveness in the totalitarianisms of the twentieth century, which had their roots in Hegel and Marx. These highly influential Germans were, Popper held, basically Platonic in their tendency to subordinate the individual to the abstractions of "history" or "progress" or "the revolution," and their practical political disciples in the twentieth century presided, predictably, over the piling up of corpses.

Why this little tour of the history of Plato's influence on political thinking? I feel obligated to rehearse it because, in many senses, we are all becoming Platonists now—and this should worry us. Under pressure from the "woke," politically correct culture, almost all of us automatically think in terms of generic categories and not in terms of individuals. When considering, for example, an appointment or an election or the constitution of a board of directors, we hardly ever ask the question "Well, who is the best-qualified person?" Rather, we wonder whether a candidate is African American, or Hispanic, or lesbian, or transgendered, or a woman, etc. Or we fret whether the right balance of minority groups will be met by hiring this or that man, or to what degree a given woman represents an intersectional crossing of generic traits. In so doing, we are trying, in the Platonic manner, to satisfy an abstract norm of justice by subordinating the particular qualities of individuals to collective categories.

An upshot of this political and cultural Platonism is that we are tending to reverence equity of outcome over equality of opportunity. The former is a function of compelling conformity to predetermined abstractions, while the latter, congruent with a much more Aristotelian mindset, is a determination to level the playing field as much as possible so as to give each individual a chance to achieve his or her goals. When the Rev. Martin Luther King Jr. expressed his dream that his "little children will one day live in a nation where they will not be judged by the color of their skin but by the content of their character," he was extolling the value of equality of opportunity, not equity of outcome. And he was explicitly distancing himself from the view that we should look first to abstract categories of race and skin color when making determinations of social status.

The "woke" movement today is decidedly Platonist in orientation, and it carries with that Platonism the totalitarian attitude that Karl Popper identified. It thinks in relentlessly abstract terms, seeing individuals only as instances of racial, sexual, ethnic, and economic types, and hence it is altogether willing to reorganize society so as to conform to its conception of justice. Read a book such as Robin DiAngelo's *White Fragility* in order to see the "woke" program laid out with admirable clarity. All white people, she argues, simply by virtue of being white, are bearers of a privilege that they must acknowledge and are, without exception, racist. All black and brown people, again just by virtue of their ethnic heritage, belong to an oppressed class and must consider their white colleagues oppressive. An ethnically African American man who rejects the "woke" ideology is, on DiAngelo's view, not truly "black"! Very much in the Platonist manner, everyone in the society must accept the new ideology or be seen as an opponent of justice. Appeals, such as Martin Luther King's, to a color-blind society and equality of opportunity are pilloried as reactionary and supportive of the racist status quo.

The bottom line is this: any political program that subordinates the individual to collective categories and ideals is dangerous and will conduce, in short order, to oppression and profound injustice. I would suggest that we all take a good, hard look at the Platonic road down which we are heading— and head back the other way.

Canceling Padre Serra

After voting to remove a large statue of St. Junípero Serra that stands in front of their City Hall, the government of Ventura, California (which is in my pastoral region), later considered removing the image of Padre Serra from the county seal. This entire effort to erase the memory of Serra is from a historical standpoint ridiculous and from a moral standpoint more than a little frightening.

Let me address the ridiculous side first. To state it bluntly, Junípero Serra is being used as a convenient scapegoat and whipping boy for certain abuses inherent to eighteenth-century Spanish colonialism. Were such abuses real? Of course. But was Fr. Serra personally responsible for them? Of course not. I won't deny for a moment that Serra probably engaged in certain disciplinary practices that we would rightfully regard as morally questionable, but the overwhelming evidence suggests that he was a great friend to the native peoples; that he sought, time and again, to protect them from mistreatment by civil authorities; and that he presided over missions where the indigenous were taught useful skills and were introduced to the Christian faith. To suggest, as did some of those who were petitioning for the removal of his statue, that Serra was the moral equivalent of Hitler, and his missions the moral equivalent of concentration camps, is nothing short of defamatory.

It is no exaggeration to affirm that from the missions established by Junípero Serra came much of the political and cultural life of the state of California. Many of our greatest cities—San Diego, Los Angeles, San Francisco, Santa Barbara, and yes, Ventura—were built on the foundation of the missions. And I won't hesitate to say it: the spread of the Christian faith in this part of the world took place largely because of the work of Junípero Serra and his colleagues—and this is a good thing! Jesus told his first followers to go into all the world and preach the Good News, not as a message of oppression but of spiritual liberation. It was precisely in response to that apostolic summons that Fray Junípero left Majorca, crossed the ocean, and spent the remainder of his life proclaiming Christ to those who did not know him. Though it is politically incorrect to say it today, this kind of enthusiastic evangelism is to be celebrated, not excoriated. The majority of Catholics in California today have the faith that they cherish because Padre Serra first brought it here.

And this brings me to the morally dangerous side of this issue. When I saw the videos of Serra statues being torn down, burned, spat upon, trampled, and desecrated in San Francisco and Los Angeles, I shuddered—not only because such behavior was boorish and unjustified, but also because it called to mind very similar activities at earlier stages of American history. In the mid to late nineteenth century, anti-Catholicism was rampant in the United States, due in part to prejudices inherited from Protestantism, but also due to the arrival of large groups of immigrants from Catholic countries, who were considered inferior. A powerful political party, the Know-Nothings, was organized precisely around the theme of opposing Catholicism, and in many of the major cities of our country, Catholic convents, parishes, cathedrals, statues, and churches were burned to the ground by unruly mobs. Moreover, in that same period, the Ku Klux Klan, which was active not just in the South but in many northern cities as well, endeavored to terrorize African Americans and Jews, of course, but also, it is easy to forget, Catholics. If you doubt that this sort of knee-jerk opposition to Catholicism endured well into the twentieth century, I would recommend you consult some of the histrionic rhetoric used by the opponents of John F. Kennedy during the presidential campaign of 1960. The dean of American historians, Arthur Schlesinger Sr., summed up this trend in his oft-repeated remark that prejudice against Catholics is "the deepest bias in the history of the American people."

So when I see mobs of people tearing down and desecrating statues of a great Catholic saint, canonized just five years ago by Pope Francis, how can I not see the ugly specter of anti-Catholicism raising its head? We are passing through a Jacobin moment in our cultural history, and such periods are dangerous indeed, for there is no clear indication what can stop their momentum. So in this case, what's next? Shall we tear down the missions themselves, the moral equivalents of death camps? Shall we call into question the Catholic faith and institutions that Junípero Serra brought to these shores? One can only hope that cooler heads will prevail and that responsible people might bring to an end this ridiculous and dangerous attempt to erase Padre Serra.

How the Star Wars Franchise
Lost Its Way

I fell sound asleep for about ten minutes during *Star Wars: The Last Jedi*. This was not only because the narrative had wandered down a very tedious alleyway, but because *Star Wars* in general has lost its way. What began as a thrilling exploration of the *philosophia perennis* has devolved into a vehicle for the latest trendy ideology—and that is really a shame.

Like so many others in my generation (I was seventeen when the first film in the series came out), I was captivated by George Lucas' vision. We all loved the explosions, the spaceships, and the special effects (corny now, but groundbreaking at the time), but we also sensed that there was something else going on in these films, something that excited the soul as much as it dazzled the eyes.

Lucas was a devotee of Joseph Campbell, a scholar of comparative religion and mythology at Sarah Lawrence College, who had spent his career exploring what he called "the monomyth." This is the great story that, despite all sorts of different accents and emphases from culture to culture, remains fundamentally the same and that conveys some pretty basic truths about nature, the psyche, human development, and God. It customarily unfolds as a "hero's quest." A young man (typically) is summoned out of the comfort of his domestic life and compelled to go on a dangerous adventure, either to secure a prize or protect the innocent, or subdue the forces of nature. In the process, he comes to realize and conquer his weakness, to face down enemies, and finally to commune with the deep spiritual powers that are at play in the cosmos. Usually, as a preparation for his mission, he is trained by a spiritual master who will put him quite vigorously through his paces. Campbell was particularly intrigued by the manner in which this story is concretely acted out in the initiation rituals among primal peoples. Lucas' mentor was Campbell, and Campbell's teacher was the great Swiss psychologist C.G. Jung, who had spent his career exploring the archetypes of the collective unconscious that play themselves out in our dreams and our myths.

Now, one would have to be blind not to see these motifs in the original Star Wars films. Luke Skywalker is compelled to leave his mundane home life (remember Uncle Owen and Aunt Beru?), and, under the tutelage of Obi-Wan and Yoda, he overcomes his fears, discovers his inner strength, faces down the darkness, and learns to act in communion with the Force. Attentive Star Wars fans will notice, by the way, that Yoda pronounces a number of the well-known sayings of C.G. Jung. I referenced the *philosophia perennis* (the perennial philosophy) above. This is a standard set of philosophical and psychological insights shared by most of the great spiritual traditions of the world, and it provided the inspiration for Jung, Campbell, and Lucas—and hence the Star Wars films.

Certain elements of all of this remain, of course, in the most recent episodes, but the mythic and archetypal dimensions are all but overwhelmed by an aggressively **feminis**t ideology. The overriding preoccupation of the makers of the most recent Star Wars seems to be, not the hero's spiritual journey, but the elevation of the all-conquering female. Every male character in *The Last Jedi* is either bumbling, incompetent, arrogant, or morally compromised; and every female character is wise, good, prudent, and courageous. Even Luke has become embittered and afraid, bearing the stigma of a profound moral failure. The female figures in *The Last Jedi* typically correct, demote, control, and roll their eyes at the males, who stumble about when not provided with feminine instruction. I laughed out loud when Rey, the young woman who has come to Luke for instruction in the ways of the Jedi, shows herself already in full possession of spiritual power. No Yoda or Obi-Wan required, thank you very much. The movie ends (spoiler alert) with all of the men off the stage and Leia taking the hand of Rey and saying, "We have all we need."

Contrast this overbearing and ham-handed treatment of men and women with the far subtler handling of the same motif in the earlier Star Wars films.

In accord with Jungian instincts, the twins Luke and Leia—both smart, strong, and spiritually alert—represented the play of animus and anima, the masculine and feminine energies, within every person. And the relationship between Leia and Han Solo was such a delight precisely because they were evenly matched. Leia didn't have to dominate Han in order to find her identity. Quite the contrary; she became more fully herself as he pushed back against her. Whereas a sort of zero-sum game obtains in the present ideology—the male has to be put down in order for the female to rise—nothing of the kind existed in the wonderfully Tracy and Hepburn rapport between Leia and Han.

Now, don't get me wrong: I fully understand why, in our cultural context today, women are feeling the need to assert themselves and to put powerful men in their place. I even see why a certain exaggeration is inevitable. It's just disappointing that this concern has hijacked a film series that used to trade in more abiding truths.

"Wokeism" in France:
The Chickens
Coming Home to Roost

will confess that I had a big laugh while reading a recent article in *The New York Times* by Norimitsu Onishi. In this lengthy piece, the author tells us that the current political and cultural leadership in France, very much including President Emmanuel Macron, is alarmed at the rise of "American-style woke ideology," which is effectively undermining French society and fomenting violence. Why, you are wondering, would this produce laughter? Well, what we call "woke" thinking in our American context was almost totally imported from French intellectuals who flourished in the second half of the twentieth century. One thinks of Jean-Paul Sartre, Jacques Lacan, Jacques Derrida, Julia Kristeva, and perhaps especially of Michel Foucault. The thinking that was originally shared in Parisian coffeehouses eventually made its way into the university system of Europe, and then, especially in the seventies and eighties of the last century, into the world of American higher education. Finally, in very recent years, much of this thinking has poured out onto the streets in the form of "wokeism." In the measure that it is threatening French society—as indeed I think it is—the phrase "the chickens have come home to roost" springs rather readily to mind.

In order to make this plain, I should like to concentrate on the one French theorist that has had the greatest impact on the formation of the "woke" mentality—namely, Michel Foucault. When I commenced my doctoral studies in Paris in 1989, just five years after Foucault's death, the philosopher's owlish face looked out from every bookstore window in the city. It was simply impossible to avoid him. Foucault is perhaps best characterized as a twentieth-century disciple of the influential German thinker Friedrich Nietzsche. Famously declaring that God is dead, Nietzsche denied the objectivity of epistemic or moral truth and saw human life as a ruthless power struggle. Decrying Christianity as a "slave morality," the pathetic attempt of the weak to shame the strong, Nietzsche called for the *Übermensch* (Superman or Over-man) to assert his will to power. In a universe void of objective moral values, the *Übermensch* is to embody his own values and to declare his dominance.

Foucault thoroughly embraced Nietzsche's atheism and hence denied any objective grounding to moral values. Instead, he interpreted these, whether espoused by the Church or secular society, as the means by which powerful people maintained themselves in positions of power. Like Karl Marx and Sigmund Freud, Foucault was accordingly a master of suspicion, an unmasker of what he took to be pretentious claims to truth. He unfolded his Nietzschean project in a series of massively influential books from the sixties and seventies: *Madness and Civilization, The Birth of the Clinic, The History of Sexuality*, and *Discipline and Punish*. In all of these texts, he engaged in what he called an intellectual archaeology, digging underneath the present consensus on matters such as the nature of madness, sexual morality, the legitimacy of incarceration, etc. in order to show that in previous ages, people entertained very different ideas in all of these arenas. The upshot of this move was to demonstrate that what appeared to be objective moral principles and high-sounding language were, in fact, the ever-shifting games played by the powerful.

Now, the legion of Foucault's disciples in the Western academy continued this archaeological project after their master's death, looking especially into issues of colonialism, gender, homosexuality, and race. And what they found in all these areas, unsurprisingly, was a Nietzschean power struggle between oppressors and oppressed. Once awakened to this reality (woke), they endeavored to foment confrontation between the powerless and the powerful, and here the influence of Marx cannot be overlooked; indeed, one of Foucault's greatest mentors was the French Marxist Louis Althusser. Appeals to order, social norms, and objective ethical values should be swept aside, for they are but a camouflage for the real social dynamics. *Vive la revolution!*

154

I trust that much of this is sadly familiar to any American who endured the worst of 2020's social upheaval.

Now, are there real injustices that obtain within our society at all levels? Of course. Should the Church and the political establishment be committed to fighting injustice wherever it appears? Of course. But is this Foucaultian "woke" philosophy, which holds to an antagonistic social theory, deconstructs language, denies the objectivity of moral norms, and sees reality simply as an incessant struggle between oppressor and oppressed, the answer? Of course *not*. And perhaps we should be encouraged by the French alarm at the emergence of "wokeism" in their midst, for now the very society that produced the intellectual virus might join the fight against it.

Daniel Berrigan and Nonviolence

On April 30, 2016, Fr. Daniel Berrigan, SJ, passed away at the age of ninety-four. Though many younger Catholics might not remember him, Fr. Berrigan was one of the most provocative and controversial religious figures of his time. Standing in the tradition of principled nonviolence proposed by Mahatma Gandhi, Thomas Merton, Dorothy Day, and others, Berrigan led the charge against America's involvement in the Vietnam conflict and its ongoing participation in the Cold War and the nuclear arms race. He was most famous, of course, for his leadership of the "Catonsville Nine," a group of protestors who, in the spring of 1968, broke into a building and burned draft records with homemade napalm. To say that he was, during that tumultuous time in American history, a polarizing figure would be an understatement.

I had the opportunity to meet and speak with Fr. Berrigan when he came to Mundelein Seminary in the mid-1990s. By that time, he was in his seventies, and much of the firebrand quality that so marked him in his prime had evanesced. I found him very quiet and ruminative. I asked him about the film *The Mission*, in which he played a small role. As you might recall, that great movie ends ambiguously. When the peaceful and religiously vibrant mission was being forcibly closed by corrupt powers, Robert De Niro's character, a Jesuit priest, resisted violently, while Jeremy Irons' character, also a Jesuit priest, resisted nonviolently, holding up the Blessed Sacrament in the midst of his people. Since both men were killed and the mission destroyed, the film doesn't really decide which of them was "correct"; rather, it shows two paths, and invites the viewers to make up their own minds. Well, I asked Daniel Berrigan what he thought of the ending, and he said, with a bit of a weary smile, that it reflected the director's views, not his own. I took him to mean that he didn't fully approve of the unresolved tension between the two paths of resistance to evil, preferring a clear endorsement of nonviolence.

Not many years after I met Fr. Berrigan, I heard Cardinal Francis George speak at the University of Notre Dame. In the course of a question and answer period, he was asked about the theory and practice of nonviolent resistance. The cardinal gave an answer that I had never heard before and frankly have never heard since—namely, that the Church needs pacifists the same way it needs celibates: in order to witness to the eschaton even now in the midst of a fallen world. At the consummation of all things, we will neither marry nor be given in marriage, for marriage will have been transfigured into a mode of love intimate beyond our imagination. The celibacy of clergy and religious here below witnesses to this strange and beguiling state of affairs, which is why it always seems to the citizens of the fallen world a little "off." In a very similar manner, the cardinal was implying, those who live in radical nonviolence even now bear witness to that time beyond time when "the wolf shall live with the lamb" (Isa. 11:6) and when men "shall beat their swords into plowshares, and their spears into pruning hooks" (Isa. 2:4). "Now," Cardinal George went on, "just as I don't want everyone to be celibate, I don't want everyone to be a pacifist!" He meant that it would be irresponsible for police departments, standing armies, and rightly constituted political authorities utterly to eschew violence, since this would be tantamount to a renunciation of their responsibility to protect the innocent. He was, of course, speaking out of the venerable Catholic tradition of just war, which teaches that, under certain stringent conditions, war is permitted so as to secure justice and security.

What I particularly appreciated about Cardinal George's intervention was the deft manner in which he exhibited the Catholic both/and in regard to this famously controverted issue. Even as we hold to the legitimacy of violence under prescribed circumstances, so we hold to the legitimacy of nonviolent forms of resistance, again, under the right circumstances. And to give the advocates of pacifism their due, nonviolence is not tantamount to passivity or dreamy resignation in the face of evil. What becomes eminently clear in the social action of Gandhi, Martin Luther King, Dorothy Day, and John Paul

157

II is that pacifism can constitute a massively efficacious means of battling evil and bringing about real change. Precisely by living now as we will all live in the eschaton, advocates of nonviolence plant the seeds of eternal life in the soil of the fallen world.

In point of fact, Cardinal George's clarification is in rather striking accord with the ending of *The Mission*. The Catholic tradition sides unambiguously with neither Jesuit, and it stands ready to affirm both Jesuits—again, according to circumstances. And therefore is it appropriate to honor the radical and prophetic nonviolence advocated by Fr. Berrigan? Absolutely—as long as we affirm, at the same time, that we don't want everyone to be Fr. Berrigan.

The Surprising Message
of *Downsizing*

When I saw the trailer for Alexander Payne's film *Downsizing*, I thought the movie would be a light-hearted farce, relying principally on visual gags. In point of fact, the jokes based on the contrast between regular-sized people and their five-inch-tall counterparts are surprisingly rare. Most of the film deals with events within the world of the downsized—so everything seems more or less normal. And when I took in the opening scenes, and heard a lot of talk about protecting the environment and the dangers of overpopulation, I thought that *Downsizing* would be a propaganda piece for left-wing causes. Here I was surprised again, for the film amounts, I will argue, to a not-so-subtle critique of that ideology.

Downsizing opens in a Norwegian lab where a group of scientists are testing an experimental technique to reduce animals in size. It soon becomes clear that the purpose of these endeavors is to apply the technology to human beings. The most dramatic scene in the film is the moment when the team presents a five-inch person to a lecture hall of astounded researchers and journalists. We then flash forward several years to discover that downsizing has become a popular trend, though the majority of people undergo the procedure for financial rather than piously environmental reasons. It appears that the dollar goes much further when you have tiny clothes, your nutritional needs are those of a mouse, and you live in a doll house.

At this point, we meet Paul Safranek (played by a rather pudgy-looking Matt Damon) and his wife Audrey (Kristen Wiig in a surprisingly sober turn), who have decided to take the plunge. But on the fateful day, Paul goes through with it while Audrey chickens out, leaving Paul stranded in the land of the tiny. Compelled by his wife's treachery to divorce, Paul finds himself out of his mansion and stuck in a nowhere-job and a small apartment. Just as he hits bottom (literally lying in a stupor on the floor of a friend's apartment after a night of debauchery), he spies Ngoc Lan Tran (wonderfully incarnated by Hong Chau), a noble Vietnamese activist who had been forcibly downsized by her government and who now does menial labor, cleaning the homes of the wealthy. Despite the loss of a leg, Ngoc has devoted herself, in her spare time, to the care of an army of the underclass of the small, who live in a sprawling slum. When she discovers that Paul has some basic medical training, she presses him into service, bringing him to suffering person after suffering person, compelling him to come out of himself. Carrying a Bible and attending enthusiastic religious services, Ngoc is unembarrassedly a Christian, and it is unmistakable that her faith informs her dedication to those in need.

By an odd plot twist (I won't bore you with the details), Paul and Ngoc travel to Norway to commune with Dr. Jorgen Asbjørnsen, the scientist who developed the downsizing technology, and the original commune of the small, who are living like a band of hippies along the shores of a picturesque fjord. They soon discover that this community, convinced that environmental pollution will render the surface of the earth uninhabitable, has actually resolved to retreat to a subterranean world that they have constructed. Beguiled by their romanticism and dedication, Paul decides to go with the community, and he leaves the tearful Ngoc behind. But then, just as the entrance to the tunnel is about to be blown permanently shut, Paul races out and embraces his beloved. The two of them then return to the States and Paul gives himself over to Ngoc's work of service for the suffering poor.

A film of social commentary? You bet, but not the social commentary I was expecting. Is there a better symbol for the downsizing that is currently happening in Europe than the shrinking and disappearance of that original colony of the small? For the past roughly fifty years, the West in general, but Europe in particular, has been experiencing a population implosion, the number of births way below replacement level in England, France, Holland, and Germany. This has been prompted, of course, by a number of factors, but certainly one of them is a conviction that human beings are just bad for the planet, using up too many resources, raping the environment, etc. Wouldn't it be best, many seem to think, if the human race just shrank down and went away? *Downsizing* gives dramatic expression to this conviction and, not so subtly, makes fun of it. I laughed out loud when, at the climactic moment of Paul's escape, the camera pulls back and reveals the "blowing" of the door as a tiny pebble falling about two inches to the ground. Talk about going out not with a bang but with a whimper.

Contrasted to this despairing retreat is the vibrant compassion exemplified by Ngoc. She, too, sees the world as a painful place, but her resolution is not to retreat but to address the pain through love. And it cannot be accidental that the Vietnamese woman's Christian faith is clearly emphasized, while no one on the European side exhibits the slightest interest in religion. In point of fact, it is precisely religious faith that will awaken courage and compassion, and it is precisely the lack of faith that conduces, by a short road, to spiritual and psychological exhaustion—both in the individual and in a culture.

I applaud *Downsizing* for making this contrast clear.

Talking to Some Young Jesuits about Social Justice and Evangelization

I once had a wonderful meeting with around thirty young Jesuits in Chicago, all in their "pre-tertianship" period of formation. This means that these men had already passed through their lengthy education in philosophy and theology and had been involved for some time in a ministry of the Jesuit order. The group I addressed included high school teachers, university professors, journal editors, and doctoral students—and almost all of them were ordained priests. After a simple lunch of soup and sandwiches, we plunged into conversation. We were at it for well over an hour, but I enjoyed the exercise so much, it seemed like about fifteen minutes. They were massively impressive people: smart, articulate, passionate about their work, and dedicated to the Gospel.

They were very interested in my ministry of evangelizing through the social media, and so we spent a good amount of time talking about the "nones," about the cultural challenges to proclaiming the faith today, about the new atheism, and about the pros and cons of the digital world. We also spoke a lot about prayer and the play between one's interior life and one's ministerial commitments. I especially enjoyed telling these young men about the Jesuits who have had an impact on my work: Bernard Lonergan, Henri de Lubac, Michael Buckley, Avery Dulles, the at least erstwhile Jesuit Hans Urs von Balthasar, and Michel Corbin, who was my doctoral director at the Institut Catholique in Paris.

Toward the end of our time together, one of the men posed a question that, he warned, would "put me on the spot." He said, "We Jesuits have been criticized a good deal in recent years. Do you think any of these critiques are justified?" Now, I think it's rather bad form to come into someone's house and offer criticisms, but since I felt so comfortable with them, and since the

162

question had been so directly asked, I responded, "Well, I think perhaps since the council, many Jesuits have embraced the social justice agenda a bit too one-sidedly." No one got up and left, which was a good sign! In fact, the discussion became especially lively and illuminating. I'd like to share some of what I said to these young Jesuits in order to address a general issue that I consider to be of great importance in the life of the Church today.

At its 32nd General Congregation in 1975, under the leadership of the charismatic Pedro Arrupe, the Jesuit order committed itself to propagate the works of justice as an essential part of its mission. And since that time, Jesuits have become renowned for their dedication to this indispensable task. My concern, I told my interlocutors, is that an exaggerated stress on the fostering of justice in the political and economic arena can compromise the properly evangelizing mission of Christ's Church. Mind you, a commitment to doing the corporal and spiritual works of mercy, to righting social wrongs, to serving the poor and needy necessarily *follows from* evangelization. One of the permanent achievements of Vatican II is to show that conversion to Christ entails not a flight from the world, but precisely a deeper love for the world and a desire to alleviate its suffering. There is simply no question about it: an evangelized person works for justice.

But when we squint at the issue from the other end, things get a bit more complicated. On the one hand, striving for justice can indeed be a *door* to evangelization. What attracted so many people in the first and second centuries to take a look at Christianity was none other than the Church's obvious care for the sick, the homeless, and the poor: "How these Christians love one another!" But on the other hand, the commitment to social justice, in itself and by itself alone, cannot be sufficient for evangelization, which is the sharing of the Good News that Jesus Christ, the Son of God, is risen from the dead. The reason for this is obvious: a Jew, a Muslim, a Buddhist, a secular humanist, even an atheist of good will can be an advocate of social justice. One can fully and enthusiastically embrace a program of caring for the poor and the hungry without, in any sense, espousing faith in Jesus Christ. Many statistical studies reveal that young people today understand (and applaud) that the Church advocates for justice, even as they profess little or no belief in God, Jesus, the Resurrection, the Bible as an inspired text, or life after death. I would argue that this disconnect is, at least in part, a result of the hyper-stress that we have placed on social justice in the years following the council.

I told my young Jesuit conversation partners that they ought to follow the prompt of our Jesuit pope and go not just to the economic margins but to the "existential margins"—that is to say, to those who have lost the faith, lost any contact with God, who have not heard the Good News. Go, I told them, into your high schools, colleges, and universities and advocate for the faith, speak of God, tell the young people about Jesus and his Resurrection from the dead. Don't for a minute, I continued, abandon your passion for justice, but let people see that it is grounded in Christ and his Gospel.

Peter Claver vs. Immanuel Kant

One of the greatest heroes of the social justice wing of the Church is, quite rightly, the seventeenth-century "slave of the slaves," St. Peter Claver. Born near Barcelona, Claver joined the Society of Jesus and was known, even as a young man, as a person of deep intelligence and piety. Spurred by what he took to be the direct prompting of the Holy Spirit, the young Spaniard volunteered to work among the poor in what was then known as "New Spain." Arriving in Cartagena, he saw the unspeakable degradation of the captives brought in chains by ship from Africa, and he resolved to dedicate his life to serving them.

We have a wonderful letter that Peter Claver wrote to his Jesuit superior in which he vividly describes apostolic work that he did among the slaves, just after they came ashore in Cartagena. He speaks of hopeless people staggering off the ships, stark naked, starving, and disoriented. Many were so sick that they were barely able to stand. Peter and his colleagues brought them fruits and water, and then, he tells us, they contrived to build a crude shelter using their own coats and cloaks. For the dying, they lit a fire and threw aromatic spices onto the flames so that the sufferers might have a bit of comfort and delight before they died. He adds the touching detail that they employed friendly gestures and signs to communicate concern to those with whom they shared no common language: "This is how we spoke to them, not with words but with our hands and our actions." I cannot imagine any decent person today who wouldn't understand and deeply sympathize with everything that Peter Claver did on behalf of these poorest of the poor. They would be justified in seeing him as a seventeenth-century anticipation of Mother Teresa.

However, as we continue to peruse Claver's letter, we discover something that many today would find puzzling, even off-putting. Immediately after caring for their physical and psychological needs, the saint commenced to instruct the slaves in the rudiments of the Christian faith. Once the new arrivals demonstrated a fundamental understanding, Claver continues, "we went on to a more extensive instruction, namely, about the one God, who rewards and punishes. . . . We asked them to make an act of contrition. . . . Finally . . . we declared to them the mysteries of the Trinity, the Incarnation, and the Passion." In other words, just after ministering to their bodies and their troubled minds, he ministered to their souls.

Now, don't get me wrong: I wouldn't exactly recommend that one move to evangelization quite as quickly as Peter Claver did! And I don't think it's either wise or fair to propose the Christian faith to those who are physically weak and psychologically traumatized. Nevertheless, it is eminently clear that the great saint, the slave of the slaves, did not drive a wedge between the Church's "social justice" ministry and its evangelizing outreach. He most certainly did not think that his care for the marginalized began and ended with attention to their worldly needs. In fact, Peter Claver was proudest of the fact that, in the course of his work with the slaves, he baptized upwards of three hundred thousand.

I bring this up because I'm concerned that afoot in our society and even in our Church today is the unhappy tendency to separate what Peter Claver kept very much together. How often we hear some version of this: "Well, it doesn't really matter what people believe, as long as they are decent and tolerant"; or of this: "Being a Christian finally comes down to helping the poor." Ideas, doctrines, and dogmas seem to be at best private convictions and at worst sources of division and oppression. But all of this reflects, not the Church's authentic self-understanding, but the Kantian prejudice that has formed the modern consensus. The massively influential philosopher Immanuel Kant held, of course, that religion is basically resolvable into ethics, that everything else that preoccupies religious people—liturgy, sacraments, prayer, preaching, pious practice, etc.—is all finally about making us morally upright people.

But as Pope Benedict XVI reminded us, the Church has three funda-mental and mutually implicative tasks: to care for the poor, to worship God, and to evangelize. Each of these calls out to the other two, and all forms of reductionism in their regard ought to be avoided. Keep in mind, too, that Pope Francis, whom no one could ever accuse of indifference to the physical and psychological suffering of the poor, also speaks of those on the "existential margins"—which is to say, those who are alienated from God and unacquainted with the Gospel. The "field hospital" of the Church—and how vividly that imagine calls to mind Peter Claver's work—is meant for those who need care in body, mind, and soul.

Therefore, yes to social justice! And yes to evangelizing! And down with Kantian reductionism!

Dominion, the Values of the West, and the Cross of Christ

The popular historian Tom Holland has written an extraordinary book called *Dominion: How the Christian Revolution Remade the World.* The subtitle sums up his argument. Holland is deeply impatient with the secularist ideology that reigns supreme in the academy and that tends to regard Christianity as a debunked, outmoded religion, a holdover from a primitive, prescientific age, a block to progress both moral and intellectual. In point of fact, he argues, Christianity has been and continues to be the most powerful shaper of the Western mind, though its influence is so pervasive and so deep that it is easily overlooked.

His very effective strategy for bringing this out into the open is first to defamiliarize Christianity through a brutally realistic accounting of what crucifixion meant in the ancient world. To be put to death on a Roman cross was just about the worst fate that anyone at that time could have imagined. The very fact that our word "excruciating," which designates the most agonizing kind of pain, comes from the Latin *ex cruce* (from the cross) fairly gives away the game. But more than the awful physical suffering of the cross was its unsurpassed humiliation. To be stripped naked, nailed to two pieces of wood, left to die in the course of several hours or even days, while exposed to the mockery of passersby, and then, even after death, to have one's body given over to be devoured by the birds of the air and the beasts of the field was just about as degrading an experience as possible. That the first Christians, therefore, proclaimed a crucified criminal as the risen Son of God could not have been a more comical, unnerving, and revolutionary message. It turned upside down all of the ancient world's assumptions about God, humanity, and the right ordering of society. If God could be identified with a crucified man, then even the lowest and most forgotten members of the human family are worthy of love. And that the earliest followers of Jesus not only declared this truth but concretely lived it by caring for the homeless, the sick, the newborn, and the aged made their message even more subversive.

Though he explores many other ways that the Christian philosophy influenced Western civilization, Holland identifies this idea, radiating out from the crucified Jesus, as the most impactful. That we take for granted that every human being is worthy of respect, that all people are bearers of equal rights and dignity, that compassionate love is the most praiseworthy ethical attitude, is quite simply a function, whether we acknowledge it or not, of our Christian cultural formation. Proof of this can be found by looking back to ancient civilization, where none of these notions held sway, and by looking, even now, at societies unshaped by Christianity, where these values are by no means unquestioningly revered.

The bulk of Holland's book is taken up with analyses of key moments in Western history, which reveal the influence of the master idea of the cross. I would put special stress on his reading of the Enlightenment, whose political values are unthinkable apart from the Gospel, and of the contemporary "woke" movements, whose preoccupation with the suffering of victims and the marginalized is the fruit of a culture at whose heart, for two thousand years, has been a crucified and unjustly condemned man. I particularly appreciated his coverage of the Beatles' famous 1967 Abbey Road recording of "All You Need Is Love" in front of a live audience. The sentiment conveyed by that iconic song is one with which neither Caesar Augustus nor Genghis Khan nor Friedrich Nietzsche would be the least bit sympathetic, but which in fact is deeply congruent with the thought of St. Augustine, St. Thomas Aquinas, St. Francis of Assisi, and St. Paul the Apostle. Like it or not, the Christian revolution massively shapes the way that we in the West continue to see the world.

With this part of Holland's argument—and it takes up 90 percent of the book—I am in complete agreement. The point he is making is not only true; it is of crucial importance at a time when Christianity is, so often, put down or set aside. That said, for me, the entire book unraveled at the end, when the author admitted that he believes neither in God nor, obviously, in the divinity of Jesus or his Resurrection. The revolutionary ethic that flowed from those beliefs he finds compelling, but the convictions themselves are, he feels, without warrant. This distilling of an ethical system out of deeply questionable dogmas is a familiar move among the modern philosophers. Both Immanuel Kant and Thomas Jefferson endeavored to do just that. But it is a foolish enterprise, for it is finally impossible to separate Christian ethics from metaphysics and from history. If there is no God and if Jesus did not rise from the dead, how in the world is it the case that every human being is worthy of infinite respect and a subject of inviolable rights? If there is no God and if Jesus did not rise from the dead, how could we not conclude that, through the power of his awful cross, Caesar won? Jesus might be vaguely admired as an ethical teacher with the courage of his convictions, but if he died and remained in his grave, then power politics prevails, and the affirmation of the dignity of every person is just a silly wish fulfillment.

It is instructive that, when the first Christians evangelized, they did not speak of human rights or the dignity of all or of other such abstractions; they spoke of Jesus risen from the dead through the power of the Holy Spirit. They insisted that the one whom Caesar's empire put to death, God had raised up. Tom Holland is absolutely right that many of the best ethical and political instincts of the West have come from Christ. But just as cut flowers will last only a short time in water, so those ideas will not long endure if we deracinate them from the startling facticity of the cross of Jesus.

Stretching Out to Great Things:
A Commencement Address for the
University of St. Thomas

This commencement address was delivered at the University of St. Thomas in Houston on May 8, 2021.

I have the very happy responsibility today of congratulating the University of St. Thomas class of 2021! And also to express my pride in becoming today a member of your class. I'm delighted to be in your company. I would also, of course, like to thank and congratulate your parents, your siblings, your friends, and your professors, who have done so much to bring you to this day and who feel a very justifiable pride in your accomplishments.

My fellow graduates, I would like to reflect with you, very briefly, on the meaning of the formation in the Catholic intellectual tradition that you have received here at UST. A standard view today, on display in practically every nook and cranny of our cultural life, is that the individual person has the prerogative of creating his or her own values. Freedom, especially the freedom of self-determination, is practically unassailable. Frankly, I cannot think of anything more boring!

If we define our own values, our own truth, our own purpose, we effectively lock ourselves into the tiny space of what we can imagine or control. When we follow these prompts of our culture today, we become cramped souls, what the medieval philosophers called *pusillae animae*. The entire point of a Catholic intellectual formation is to produce *magnae animae* (great souls). A great soul doesn't invent her own values; rather, she intuits the marvelous intellectual, moral, and aesthetic values that are found in the objective order—

and then she responds to them with her whole heart. She thereby expands in a manner commensurate with the goods that have captivated her.

The basic purpose of the initiation rituals found among primal peoples around the world was to convince a young person that his life is not about him. Typically, he would be wrested away from his comfortable domestic environment, scarified in some way, instructed in the lore of his tribe, and then, equipped with only a few provisions, cast out into jungle or forest or tundra and told to make it on his own. This was not arbitrary cruelty; it was an invitation to move out of his own space and to discover the objective values in his people's history, in nature, and finally in the spiritual order.

Your time here at the University of St. Thomas has been a kind of ritual of initiation. The point of these last four years has been to break you out of your self-regard and to invite you to an adventurous exploration of new worlds of thought and experience. I am concerned that "safe" and "safety" have become, for the present generation, such conspicuous words. No one would deny, of course, that a modicum of safety is required for any sort of peace of mind or achievement; nevertheless, one would be hard-pressed to say that a religion that places at the very center of our attention a man nailed to a cross is concerned primarily with safety. According to the cliché, ships are safe in harbors, but ships are not meant for harbors; rather, they are meant for the open sea. In a similar way, you are safe within the confines of your own desires and expectations, but you are not meant to live in that small world, but rather in the infinitely wider and more fascinating world of objective value.

Your generation, I would submit, is especially oriented to the realm of value in regard to two areas: the natural sciences and social justice. In the course of my evangelical work, I find that there is, among many young people, a great reverence for the sciences and the technology that they have produced. Even as they demonstrate a certain impatience with other disciplines, they tend to accept physics, chemistry, medicine, and engineering as authoritative. In doing so, they are acknowledging an extraordinarily significant realm of value—namely, objective intelligibility. No scientist—physicist, chemist, astronomer, psychologist, etc.—could get her work off the ground unless she believed that the world she investigated was marked by form, pattern, understandability. The responsible researcher is not inventing intelligibility; she's finding it, following it, rejoicing in it.

And you and your peers are passionate about issues of social justice. You are eager to fight corruption, discrimination, race prejudice, and inequality; you advocate for inclusivity, the acceptance of diversity, and care for those on the margins of society. In so doing, you are acknowledging the existence of certain moral values that you have not invented and that apply in all circumstances. None of you, I wager, would say that racism or sexism or human trafficking are acceptable in some contexts or that opposing these is simply a matter of personal opinion. No, in point of fact, you feel so strongly about these matters precisely because you know that they are moral absolutes that summon your attention and demand your acquiescence. Like the intelligibility of the world, these objective moral truths draw you out of yourself and toward spiritual adventure.

Now let us take one more step. If the patterned structure of nature and moral values are not projections of our subjectivity, or the products of mere social consensus, but rather objective features of reality, we readily ask, "Where did they come from?" The answer of the great Catholic intellectual tradition is that they came from the Creator God, who is intelligibility itself and moral goodness itself, from the God who is supremely wise, supremely good, supremely beautiful—and who therefore ought to engage our attention most completely. The great command found in the sixth chapter of the book of Deuteronomy and reiterated centuries later by Jesus himself gives expression to this conviction: "You shall love the LORD your God with all your heart, and with all your soul, and with all your might" (Deut. 6:5). We can now see the point of a Catholic education: to beguile you with the objective values— epistemic, aesthetic, and moral—that exist in the world and that direct you finally to the divine source of those values. Once you understand this, you're ready for spiritual adventure; you're ready to move the ship out of the safe harbor; you're ready to become a great soul.

How can I address this assembly and not make reference to your patron, St. Thomas Aquinas? In the second part of his magnificent summary of Christian doctrine, the *Summa theologiae*, Thomas discusses the virtue of *magnanimitas* (magnanimity), the quality of having a great soul. He writes, "Magnanimity by its very name denotes the stretching forth of the soul to great things." That pithy definition expresses everything I've been trying to say in this address. What are these "great things" that Thomas references but the objective values that summon the soul? So the key to a spiritually successful life is to go for them, to stretch out toward them. To stay within the musty confines of the self, or to see the values in question but never to reach out toward them, to settle thereby for a kind of spiritual mediocrity— that's the tragedy of being a small soul. Here is St. Thomas again: "For just as the magnanimous person tends to great things out of greatness of soul, so the pusillanimous person shrinks from great things out of littleness of soul."

So my young friends, fellow graduates of the class of 2021, identify a value that you have learned here at UST, some goodness or truth or beauty that has sung to your soul, and then give yourself to it with reckless abandon. Stretch out toward it, and it will give you satisfaction and finally lead you to God. The literature of the world is filled with stories of people who have spent their lives satisfying their egos, building up wealth, pleasure, power, and honor, but neglecting the development of their souls. Perhaps you have met such people: glittering on the outside but atrophied on the inside. And perhaps you have encountered the opposite case: those who have very little in the eyes of the world but who are vibrantly alive, spiritually on fire, for they have cultivated their souls.

There is a story told of Thomas Aquinas that I particularly savor. Toward the end of his life, Thomas was laboring over the section of the *Summa theologiae* dealing with the Eucharist. Though it is commonly taken now for a masterpiece, Thomas himself was uneasy with his treatise, convinced that it did not do justice to the mystery he was attempting to describe. And so he placed the text at the foot of the crucifix and asked for God's help. According to the legend, a voice came from the figure of the crucified Christ: "Thomas, you have written well of me. What would you have as a reward?" The great man could have asked for anything—for fame, for wealth, for a powerful office. But instead he said, *"Non nisi te, Domine"* (Nothing but you, Lord). The patron of this university spent his life discerning and seeking objective values, and he knew that all of those goods find their source in the supreme value of God. His soul stretched out to great things and finally to the Creator of those great things.

The purpose of this university is to make you like Thomas Aquinas. So put the ship out to the perils and possibilities of the open sea. Be great souls!

PART VI

NAVIGATING POLITICAL POLARIZATION

Four Principles for Catholics during Election Season

Every four years, Catholics face an intense dilemma in regard to the vote. There are ardently Catholic Democrats who wonder how their coreligionists could possibly choose a Republican candidate, and there are ardently Catholic Republicans who express precisely the opposite opinion. And both sides, typically, look with eagerness to their bishops and priests to resolve the tension. Each presidential election cycle, the Church endeavors to clarify the issue, usually to the satisfaction of very few. However, under the rubric of "once more unto the breach, dear friends," let me try to provide some direction by articulating four basic principles.

First, Catholic social teaching clearly goes beyond the split between Republican and Democrat, between liberal and conservative, and therefore corresponds perfectly with neither political camp. Anyone who says that either of our political parties perfectly, or even adequately, represents Catholic social thought is simply misinformed. Broadly speaking, the Democratic Party advocates a number of themes and principles reverenced by the Catholic tradition: concern for the underprivileged, for the migrant and refugee, and for the environment, as well as opposition to capital punishment and to all forms of racism. And again, broadly speaking, the Republican Party sides with Catholic teaching in a number of ways: opposition to abortion and euthanasia, defense of the traditional family, advocacy for conscience protection and freedom of religion. Which of the two parties is more "Catholic"? It seems to me impossible to adjudicate the question in the abstract.

Are we left, therefore, simply in a lurch? Not quite, and this leads to the second principle I would like to explicate: among the various values mentioned, a priority must be given to the defense of human life, since life

179

is the most fundamental good of all, the one without which the other goods wouldn't obtain. Therefore, in the political calculus of a Catholic, opposition to abortion, euthanasia, and capital punishment should take pride of place. Now, just to keep things complicated, Republicans are relatively right in regard to the first two and Democrats in regard to the last one, though, to be sure, the number of those threatened by abortion and euthanasia is far greater than the number of those under threat of capital punishment. Sometimes people will say that all lives are equally sacred, but in this context, that observation is something of a red herring. For the relevant question is not which lives are more sacred—those of the unborn, the elderly, the poor, the migrant—but which lives are more direly and directly threatened.

And this leads to a third principle: a Catholic may never vote for a candidate *because* that candidate supports a morally repugnant position, only *despite* that support and only because of balancing considerations. Thus, for example, a Catholic in good conscience could never say that she will vote for a Democrat *because* the Democrat is pro-choice, and by the same token, a Catholic in good conscience could never say that he will vote for a Republican *because* the Republican is for capital punishment. Each would have to say some version of "Despite his unacceptable position, I will vote for him because, in prudence, I have determined that other commitments of his and/or his own character counterbalances his objectionable opinion." Does this lead us into somewhat murky waters? Frankly, yes, but that's necessarily the case when we're dealing not with matters of principle but with matters of prudence.

And this last statement conduces to my fourth and final proposition: Catholics ought never to disagree in regard to moral principles, but they can indeed legitimately disagree about the best means to instantiate those principles. So, for example, I think that every Catholic in America ought to embrace the political ideals that I identified above, some more characteristic of the left and others of the right. *Every* Catholic ought to be for protecting the environment, serving the poor, defending the traditional family, battling social injustice, advocating for religious liberty and freedom of conscience, etc. But not every Catholic is obliged to subscribe to the same means of attaining those ends. Liberal and conservative Catholics can disagree about the Paris Climate Accords, the legitimacy of offshore drilling, the advisability of reforming our health care system, changes to our tax laws, the level of the minimum wage, the best policy in regard to Wall Street regulation, etc., etc. Those latter issues are open to legitimate debate and are matters for prudential judgment.

Perhaps I might, in closing, not so much propose a fifth principle as deliver myself of a *cri de coeur*: vote! Some Catholics are tempted to think—and I will admit to feeling the tug of this temptation—that because things are so complicated politically for those who advocate Catholic social teaching, it is best to say, "A plague on both your houses," and keep to the sidelines. But this is not a tenable position. In the Lord's Prayer, we petition, "Thy kingdom come, thy will be done *on earth* as it is in heaven." The Gospel message does indeed draw us ultimately to eternal life on high with the Lord, but it also has real-world implications here below. If we Catholics don't involve ourselves in the political process, as messy as that often is, we permit Catholic social teaching to remain a set of harmless abstractions.

Governor Cuomo and
God's Noncompetitive Transcendence

In April 2020, Andrew Cuomo, the Governor of New York, made a rather interesting theological observation. Commenting on the progress that his state had made in fighting the coronavirus, and praising the concrete efforts of medical personnel and ordinary citizens, he said, "The number is down because we brought the number down. God did not do that. Faith did not do that." I won't waste a lot of time exploring the hubris of that remark, which should be obvious to anyone. I might recommend, out of pastoral concern, that the governor read the first part of Genesis chapter 11.

What I will do instead is explain the basic intellectual confusion that undergirds Cuomo's assertion, one that, I fear, is shared even by many believers. The condition for the possibility of the governor's declaration is the assumption that God is one competitive cause among many, one actor jostling for position and time upon the stage with a coterie of other actors. On this reading, God does certain things—usually of a rather spectacular nature—and creaturely causes do other things, usually more mundane. Thus, we can clearly parcel out responsibility and credit—some to God and some to finite agents. But this account is deeply unbiblical and alien to the Catholic theological tradition.

To understand the scriptural sense of the play between divine and human causality, it is helpful to consult the cycle of stories dealing with King David in 1 and 2 Samuel. What strikes the attentive reader is that nothing obviously "supernatural" takes place in these accounts. Practically everything that happens to David could be adequately accounted for on psychological, historical, military, or political grounds. However, throughout the narrative, God's activity and involvement are assumed, for the author takes for granted the principle that the true God works not typically in an interruptive way, but precisely through a congeries of secondary causes. Mind you, it is not the case that some explanations of David's story are political or psychological and some properly theological; rather, everything is, at once, natural and supernatural—precisely because God's causality is operating noncompetitively, on a qualitatively different level than creaturely causality. If you want a one-liner summary of this distinctively biblical perspective, you could not do better than this, from the prophet Isaiah: "LORD . . . you have accomplished all we have done" (Isa. 26:12 NABRE).

Now, why should this be true? Here it would be helpful to turn to the Church's greatest theologian, St. Thomas Aquinas. For Thomas, God is not the supreme being (*ens summum* in his Latin), but rather *ipsum esse subsistens*, which means "the sheer act of to be itself." In a word, God is not one more instance of the genus "being," one thing, however exalted, among others; instead, he is the self-explaining source of existence as such, that great font of being in and through which all finite things subsist and act. Therefore, God does not compete for space, so to speak, on the same ontological grid as creatures; a zero-sum game does not obtain in regard to God's activity and creaturely activity—the more we ascribe to one, the less we have to ascribe to the other.

Allow me to ground this rather abstract rhetoric with a very homely example. If one were to ask what is necessary to make a bicycle, the response would be something like this: "Tires, brake pads, a chain, a metal frame, the skill of the builder, perhaps a schematic to guide the building process, etc." No one would ever be tempted to respond as follows: "Tires, brake pads, a chain, God, a metal frame, the skill of the builder, etc." And yet, a smart religious person, upon finishing the project of constructing that bike, would quite legitimately say, "Thank God!" The prayer would be a humble acknowledgement, not that God in a fussily invasive way interfered with the building process, but that God is responsible for the entire nexus of causes and behaviors that made up the process. The upshot is that the two dimensions of causality—one finite and the other transcendent—operate simultaneously and noncompetitively: "You have accomplished all we have done."

All of which brings me back to Governor Cuomo. To claim that "God did not do that" because we did it is simply a category mistake. What brought the coronavirus numbers down? It is perfectly accurate to say, "The skill of doctors and nurses, the availability of hospital beds, the willingness of so many to shelter in place, etc." But it is also perfectly valid to say that God brought those numbers down, precisely by grounding the entire complex of creaturely causality just referenced. This relationship holds at the metaphysical level, but it is perhaps even clearer when it comes to the psychological motivation of those dedicated physicians and nurses. Why, ultimately, were they willing to do what they did? I would be willing to bet a large percentage of them would say that it was a desire to serve others and to be pleasing to God.

So we should thank all of the good people involved in bettering that situation, and we shouldn't hesitate, even for a moment, to thank God as well. There is absolutely no need to play the zero-sum game proposed by the Governor of New York.

A Talk on the Hill

In 2019, I had the distinct privilege of addressing an audience of senators, representatives, and Capitol Hill staffers in a beautiful room at the Library of Congress. This event was made possible by two Congressmen, Rep. Tom Suozzi of New York, a Democrat, and Rep. John Moolenaar of Michigan, a Republican. Both had seen videos of the speeches I had given at Facebook and Google headquarters and wanted something similar for those who work in government.

At the outset of my talk, I specified that I would not be addressing the hot-button issues that so often dominate discussions of religion and politics. I was quick to point out that this is not because I think those questions are unimportant or that they shouldn't eventually be addressed. But I insisted that the rush to those matters around which there is radical polarization effectively precludes the possibility of finding deep points of contact between the spiritual and political worlds. And it was that common ground that I endeavored to explore in my presentation.

I commenced with the idea of vocation. We're accustomed to using this term in an explicitly religious context, but I suggested that, with its full spiritual resonance, it applies just as well to other areas of life. I asked my audience to recall the moment when they first felt the summons to pursue a career in public service. I invited them to bracket the anxieties, disappointments, and opportunities of the present moment and to recover that moment, undoubtedly marked by enthusiasm and idealism, when they decided to enter into politics and to work for justice. The passion to pursue righteousness in particular cases, I told them, is a function of something more basic and more mystical—namely, the call from Justice itself, the summons to be a servant of this great transcendental value. In a similar way, an artist is someone who has heard the call—as James Joyce did, for example—to be a knight for Beauty, and a philosopher or journalist or professor is someone who has heard the summons to serve Truth itself. But in Catholic theology, Truth itself, Beauty itself, Justice itself are simply names for God. Therefore, provided they search out the deepest ground for their commitment, all of these participants in the culture can and should understand themselves as having received a vocation with religious implications.

And once that connection has been made, I told my Washington audience, the great biblical texts dealing with vocation from God open up in a fresh way. I drew their attention to the marvelous story of the call of the prophet Samuel (1 Sam. 3). When just a boy, Samuel heard the voice of God, but did not at first recognize it for what it was. It was only after several repetitions—"Samuel! Samuel!"—and after the helpful intervention of the high priest Eli, that the young man was ready to listen to God. So, I said, God (under his title Justice itself) called you each by name, most likely called you repeatedly until you listened, and probably employed some elder to interpret the meaning of his voice. Next, I referenced the strange and illuminating account in the sixth chapter of Isaiah regarding the call of the prophet. Isaiah says that he saw the Lord in the temple surrounded by angels crying, "Holy, holy, holy" (Isa. 6:3). The Hebrew term here is *kadosh*, which carries the sense of "other." God is not one being among many, not one true thing among true things; rather, he is the source of existence itself, the unconditioned ground of all that is—and this entails that he is greater than all of the particular projects and desires that customarily preoccupy us. His call to us is accordingly greater than career, family, personal pleasure, country, or anything else. Isaiah speaks further of how smoke filled the place where he was and how the foundations shook (Isa. 6:4). Both of these symbols indicate the manner in which the experience of God puts anything finite or conditioned into question. So, I told the senators, representatives, and staffers, the summons to serve Justice itself must trump anything else, any other concern, any merely personal project. It properly shakes the foundation of your life and relativizes everything you once considered supremely important.

To make all of this a bit more pointed, I moved to a consideration of Thomas Aquinas' doctrine of law. For the great medieval Dominican, positive law (the concrete statutes by which a polity is governed) properly nests inside the natural law (that whole range of moral precepts evident to reason), and the natural law nests finally within the eternal law, which is coincident with the divine mind itself. This entails, I argued, that an unjust positive law is not simply a political problem; it is a moral and finally spiritual problem. To legislate unjustly, I concluded, is therefore to stand athwart the God who originally called the legislator to be a servant of Justice. And lest this analysis seem too abstract and distant, I drew their attention to the extraordinary letter that Dr. Martin Luther King Jr. wrote from the Birmingham City Jail in 1963, prompted by a group of white Christian ministers who were questioning King's methods. In response, the great civil rights activist said that just laws ought always to be obeyed but that unjust laws can and should be opposed— always and despite the cost or inconvenience. And for justification, he reached to the very teaching of Aquinas that I just sketched. King was a political agent to be sure, but he had a keen sense that his activism was but an expression of finally moral and religious convictions.

My hope was (and is) that my presentation would both inspire and discomfit my audience. I wanted them to see both the high spiritual dignity of their call and the rather awful responsibility before God that they bear.

One Cheer for George Will's
The Conservative Sensibility

I have been following George Will's thought for a long time. I'm old enough to remember when his column occupied the last page of *Newsweek* magazine every other week and when he sat in the chair of conservative thought on David Brinkley's Sunday morning political talk show. I have long admired his graceful literary style and his clipped, smart manner of speech. Will was always especially good when, with lawyerly precision, he would take apart the sloppy thinking of one of his intellectual or political opponents. When I taught an introductory course in political philosophy at Mundelein Seminary many years ago, I used Will's book *Statecraft as Soulcraft* to get across to my students what the ancients meant by the moral purpose of government.

And so it was with great interest that I turned to Will's latest offering, a massive volume called *The Conservative Sensibility*, a book that both in size and scope certainly qualifies as the author's *opus magnum*. Will's central argument is crucially important. The American experiment in democracy rests, he says, upon the epistemological conviction that there are political rights, grounded in a relatively stable human nature, that precede the actions and decisions of government. These rights to life, liberty, and the pursuit of happiness are not the gifts of the state; rather, the state exists to guarantee them, or to use the word that Will considers the most important in the entire prologue to the Declaration of Independence, to "secure" them. Thus is government properly and severely limited and tyranny kept, at least in principle, at bay. In accord with both Hobbes and Locke, Will holds that the purpose of the government finally is to provide an arena for the fullest possible expression of individual freedom. Much of the first half of *The Conservative Sensibility* consists of a vigorous critique of the "progressivism," with its roots in Hegelian philosophy and the practical politics of Theodore Roosevelt and Woodrow Wilson, that would construe government's purpose as the reshaping of a fundamentally plastic and malleable human nature. What this has led to, on Will's reading, is today's fussily intrusive nanny state, which claims the right to interfere with every nook and cranny of human endeavor.

With much of this I found myself in profound agreement. It is indeed a pivotal feature of Catholic social teaching that an objective human nature exists and that the rights associated with it are inherent and not artificial constructs of the culture or the state. Accordingly, it is certainly good that government's tendency toward imperial expansion be constrained. But as George Will's presentation unfolded, I found myself far less sympathetic with his vision. What becomes clear is that Will shares, with Hobbes and Locke and their disciple Thomas Jefferson, a morally minimalistic understanding of the arena of freedom that government exists to protect. All three of those modern political theorists denied that we can know with certitude the true nature of human happiness or the proper goal of the moral life—and hence they left the determination of those matters up to the individual. Jefferson expressed this famously as the right to *pursue* happiness as one sees fit. The government's role, on this interpretation, is to assure the least conflict among the myriad individuals seeking their particular version of fulfillment. The only moral bedrock in this scenario is the life and freedom of each actor.

Catholic social teaching has long been suspicious of just this sort of morally minimalist individualism. Central to the Church's thinking on politics is the conviction that ethical principles, available to the searching intellect of any person of good will, ought to govern the moves of individuals within the society, and moreover, that the nation as a whole ought to be informed by a clear sense of the common good—that is to say, some shared social value that goes beyond simply what individuals might seek for themselves. *Pace* Will, the government itself plays a role in the application of this moral framework precisely in the measure that law has both a protective and directive function. It both holds off threats to human flourishing and, since it is, to a degree, a teacher of what the society morally approves and disapproves, also actively guides the desires of citizens. But beyond this, mediating institutions—the family, social clubs, fraternal organizations, unions, and above all, religion—help to fill the public space with moral purpose. And in this way, freedom becomes so much more than simply "doing what we want." It commences to function, as John Paul II put it, as "the right to do as we ought." For the mainstream of Catholic political thought, the free market and the free public space are legitimate only in the measure that they are informed and circumscribed by this vibrant moral intuition. George Will quite rightly excoriates the neo-Gnostic program of contemporary "progressivism," but he oughtn't to conflate that dysfunctional philosophy with a commitment to authentic freedom in the public square.

When we come to the end of *The Conservative Sensibility*, we see more clearly the reason for this thin interpretation of the political enterprise. George Will is an atheist, and he insists that, despite the religiously tinged language of some of the Founding Fathers, the American political project can function just fine without reference to God. The problem here is twofold. First, when God is denied, one must affirm some version of Hobbes' metaphysics, for, in the absence of God, that which would draw things together ontologically, and eventually politically, has disappeared. Secondly, the negation of God means that objective ethical values have no real ground, and hence morality becomes, at the end of the day, a matter of clashing subjective convictions and passions. Catholic social teaching would argue that the rhetoric of the Founders regarding the relation between inalienable rights and the will of God is not pious boilerplate, but indeed the very foundation of the democratic political project.

So perhaps one cheer for *The Conservative Sensibility*. Will gets some important things right, but he gets some even more basic things quite wrong.

It's Time for Catholics
(and All Religious People) to Wake Up:
The Real Danger Posed by the
California Confession Bill

This article was released on May 7, 2019. The proposed legislation was dropped the following month.

SB 360, a piece of proposed legislation currently making its way through the California state senate, should alarm not only every Catholic in the country, but indeed the adepts of any religion. In California, as in almost every other state, clergy members (along with a variety of other professionals, including physicians, social workers, teachers, and therapists) are mandated reporters—which is to say, they are legally required to report any case of suspected child abuse or neglect to law enforcement. However, California clergy who come by this knowledge in the context of "penitential communication" are currently exempted from the requirement. SB 360 would remove the exemption. Sen. Jerry Hill, the bill's sponsor, characterized the scope and purpose of his legislation as follows: "The law should apply equally to all professionals who have been designated as mandated reporters of these crimes—with no exceptions, period. The exemption for clergy only protects the abuser and places children at further risk."

I would like to make clear what the passage of this law would mean for Catholic priests in California. Immediately, it would place them on the horns of a terrible dilemma. Since the canon law of the Church stipulates that the conscious violation of the seal of confession results in automatic excommunication, every priest, under this new law, would be threatened with prosecution and possible imprisonment on the one hand or formal exclusion from the Body of Christ on the other. And does anyone doubt that, if this law is enacted, attempts will be made to entrap priests, effectively placing them in this impossible position?

What I hope is clear—not only to Catholics but to any American committed to the First Amendment—is that we are dealing here with an egregious violation of the principle of religious liberty. In its stipulation that Congress shall make no law respecting the establishment of religion, the First Amendment holds off, if you will, the aggression of any religion toward the civil state. But in its further stipulation that Congress shall never legislate in such a way as to obviate the free exercise of religion, it blocks the state's aggression toward religion. The framers of the Bill of Rights were legitimately alarmed at the prospect of the government meddling in the affairs of a religious community, monitoring its beliefs and policing its behavior. But such meddling and monitoring is precisely what SB 360 involves.

I realize that non-Catholics and nonbelievers might not appreciate how precious the sacrament of Confession is to Catholics and why the seal of Confession matters so profoundly. In my last year in the seminary, my classmates and I took a course in the theology and practice of the sacrament of Reconciliation (to give it its proper title). Our professor said something that has stayed with me for all the years of my priesthood, burned into my mind and soul. He told us, "If someone asks, 'Father, would you hear my confession?' the answer is always yes. Even if hearing that confession puts your own life in danger, the answer is always yes." And he went on, "If a person inquires about what was said during a confession, you should act as though the confession never even happened. And if doing so puts your own life in danger, you should still act as though the confession never happened."

Why do we Catholics take this sacrament with such seriousness? We do so because we believe that through this sacramental encounter, a sinner accesses the healing and forgiving grace of Christ. In the context of confession, the priest, we hold, is operating in the very person of Christ, and therefore, the penitent is speaking to and hearing from the Lord himself. Thus, absolutely nothing ought to stand in the way of a sinner who seeks this font of grace. In light of these clarifications, one can understand the indispensable importance of the seal. If a penitent thought that the priest to whom he confessed were likely to share with others what was given in the most sacred confidence, he or she would be reluctant indeed ever to approach the sacrament of Reconciliation. And this is why the Church has striven so strenuously to protect, at all costs, the integrity of confession.

And through the entire course of our country's history, the government has protected the right of the Catholic Church to determine its own sacramental practice and has never sought to compel the violation of the seal. Given this venerable tradition, grounded in the second clause of the First Amendment, an extraordinary burden of proof, it seems to me, lies with those who would seek to dispense with the exemption. But what is impossible to doubt is that religious liberty is indeed under grave threat, especially when we consider the slippery slope onto which SB 360 would invite us. Surely murder, theft, spousal abuse, child neglect, and rape are terrible crimes. Would the state determine that priests are obligated to report these offenses to the authorities, should they hear of them in the confessional?

For some time now, the public institutions of the Church have been under attack from the secular state. The government has been seeking to determine what is taught and practiced in Catholic schools and what is carried out in Catholic hospitals, even when these practices run counter to the Church's formal doctrine. But with SB 360, the secular authorities are reaching into the inner life of the Church, into its sacramental practice and discipline. Catholics should, of course, rise up in strenuous protest against this very aggressive incursion—but so should anyone who cares about the freedom of religion in our society.

Why We Need
a Distribution of Power

A crucially important feature of Catholic social teaching, but one frequently underemphasized or misunderstood, is a clear animus against the concentration of power within a society. This perilous agglomeration can happen economically, politically, or culturally. By a basic and healthy instinct, Catholic social teaching wants power, as much as possible, distributed widely throughout the community, so that one small segment does not tyrannize the majority or prevent large numbers of people from enjoying the benefits that are theirs by right.

We can see this phenomenon perhaps most clearly in the economic order. If one organization manages to monopolize its segment of the economy, it can set prices arbitrarily, hire and fire according to its whim, preclude any competition that might provide better products and/or higher wages for employees, etc. One thinks here of the "trust-busting" work of Theodore Roosevelt in the early twentieth century and the similar concern today for breaking up Google, Facebook, Amazon, and other high-tech conglomerates that exercise an almost unchallenged dominance in their field. A cornerstone of Catholic social teaching is what is traditionally called "distributive justice"—which is to say, the equitable allocation of goods within a society. Now, this can take place through direct government intervention—for example, through anti-trust legislation, minimum wage requirements, programs to aid the poor, taxation, etc.—but it can also happen more indirectly through the natural rhythms of the market. In *Centesimus Annus*, John Paul II observes that profit-making itself can and should signal to prospective entrepreneurs that there is money to be made in that segment of the economy and that they should accordingly get involved. The bottom line is this: spreading out wealth within a society tends to make an economy both more just and more efficient.

We can furthermore see this dynamic in the political realm. If one party comes to dominate a nation, a state, a city, or a community, corruption almost inevitably follows. Unchallenged, the ruling conglomerate can impose its will, compel the acceptance of its vision, and eliminate prospective opponents and critics. It is quite obvious that this sort of arrangement obtains in communist dictatorships and oppressive theocracies, but it is also apparent, to a lesser degree, in local and state governments in our own country. If you doubt me, ask yourself why pro-life candidates in Illinois, Massachusetts, or California could never hope to be elected to office. When a political monopoly couples itself with economic power, the corruption becomes only deeper and more intractable. Once again, according to Catholic social teaching, the desideratum is the breaking up and spreading out of power throughout the society. This could happen in a number of ways: equipping a variety of parties, providing for a greater turnover within legislatures, lifting up various expressions of local government, allowing for mediating institutions, strengthening the system of checks and balances, etc.

Though perhaps less obvious than the first two instances, a third example of this dangerous hyper-concentration of power is in the cultural arena. Under both the Nazi and Soviet dictatorships of the last century, only very definite types of art, music, and literature were acceptable, and any deviation from the norm was quickly squelched by the state. Today, strict censorship of the arts holds sway in many Islamist states, as well as in communist China. But lest we think we in the West are free of this sort of cultural monopoly, take a good look at the kind of strict leftist ideology that exists in practically every film or television program produced in Hollywood. This is not brutal state censorship to be sure, but it is indeed a sort of monopolization of cultural power that effectively excludes rival expressions of the good, the true, and the beautiful. Once again, it is very useful to notice the ways in which this cultural dictatorship allies itself with both political and economic power in order to consolidate its hegemony. Catholic social teaching would like this sort of power to be spread out as widely as possible too, permitting a range of artistic expressions at a variety of levels within the society. How dull it is when only one style of art or only one type of thinking is acceptable.

Someone who was acutely sensitive to the danger of hyper-concentrated power in the society was the great Catholic writer G.K. Chesterton. Accordingly, along with Hilaire Belloc and others, he developed an economic and political program that became known as "distributism," deriving the name from the Catholic preoccupation with the just distribution of wealth. As the great Chesterton commentator Dale Ahlquist has recently pointed out, an alternative name for distributism might be "localism," since the Chestertonian doctrine emphasizes the importance of the many local expressions of political and economic power over any grand project of centralization. If you want to see a vividly narrative presentation of distributism, read Tolkien's *Lord of the Rings*, paying particular attention to the manner of life in the hobbits' Shire in contrast to the political and economic arrangements in Mordor.

What I hope is at least relatively clear is that this uniquely Catholic approach cuts against both the extreme left and the extreme right. Catholic social doctrine advocates neither statist control nor individual freedom run amok. It holds out a wide and just distribution of economic and political power as an at least asymptotically approached ideal.

"Culture Warrior" and
the Fallacy of Misplaced Concreteness

One of the least illuminating descriptors that makes its way around the Catholic commentariat is "culture warrior." The term is invariably used by someone on the left in order to excoriate a right-wing Catholic for his opposition to abortion-on-demand, gay marriage, restrictions on religious liberty, etc. This resistance, we are told, amounts to "negativity," "divisiveness," and of course, "an unwillingness to dialogue." I can only smile when I hear this from representatives of the left, for they seem blithely to overlook their own rather fierce resistance to the culture in regard to a wide range of issues. When people on the port side of the Catholic commentariat hold forth against racism, xenophobia, homophobia, militarism, capital punishment, environmental pollution, the immigration policy of our country, etc., how are *they* not engaging in culture warfare? How are *they* not being, in their own way, negative, divisive, and reluctant to dialogue?

Two champions of the Catholic left—and particular heroes of mine—are Dorothy Day and Martin Luther King. Both of these worthies stood boldly athwart what they took to be dysfunctional features of the culture of their time, and both were willing to endure mockery, marginalization, and imprisonment. One would be hard-pressed to characterize Ms. Day as willing to dialogue with representatives of the military establishment or to describe Dr. King as open to friendly conversation with the keepers of the Jim Crow structure. Both chose forms of confrontation, nonviolent to be sure, but certainly designed to get in the face of their opponents. Both were extremely "divisive," and I would not hesitate for a moment to call them culture warriors. And while we're at it, might I suggest that the current Bishop of Rome is not one to pull any punches when he notices something negative in our society. If you don't think there is a fair amount of culture warfare going on in *Laudato Si'*, *Evangelii Gaudium*, *Amoris Laetitia*, and *Fratelli Tutti*, I would suggest you haven't read them very carefully.

In point of fact, the left isn't any less confrontational than the right; it's just confrontational about different matters. And it's not any more dialogical than the right; it's just willing to dialogue in regard to different subjects. Truth to tell, both left and right are, in their distinctive ways, following the suggestion of St. John Henry Newman that the Church moves through any given culture the same way a foraging animal moves through its environment—which is to say, assimilating what it can and resisting what it must. They just differ in regard to precisely what should be resisted and what can be assimilated. And this brings me to the point of this article—namely, what Alfred North Whitehead called "the fallacy of misplaced concreteness." By this term, the great philosopher meant the tendency to treat pure abstractions as something real, as identical to things, objects, and events. Abstractions can, of course, be useful, but when one mistakes them for the concretely real, one obfuscates rather than clarifies whatever is under discussion.

So consider the abstraction "culture warrior" as used by a left-wing commentator as a negative characterization of his opponent. As we have shown, it can't possibly name anything real, since the accuser is every bit as much a culture warrior as the accused. It therefore functions as a smokescreen for what the accuser really wants to say, and I can think of at least two possibilities: either he doesn't think that the issues his opponent is criticizing should in fact be criticized, or perhaps he feels that the way his opponent is characterizing the issue is unfair. In either case, the *real* matter is obscured, and the use of the term doesn't move anyone even a bit closer to the truth. Infinitely preferable to trading in insulting abstractions that apply as much to oneself as to one's opponent is to engage in the tough work of authentic argument. The Jesuit philosopher Bernard Lonergan urged all thinkers to follow the four epistemic imperatives: be attentive (see what is really there to be seen); be intelligent (form plausible hypotheses to explain a given phenomenon); be reasonable (make judgments so as to determine which of a variety of bright ideas is in fact the right idea); and finally, be responsible (accept the full implications of the judgment made). To do so is to *argue* about concrete matters or, in the language of Aristotle, to stay on the "rough ground" of what is real.

There are many reasons why the Catholic conversation has become dysfunctional, especially in the social media space: tribalism, *ad hominem* attacks, guilt by association, Girardian Twitter mobs, etc. Might I suggest that the fallacy of misplaced concreteness is another key reason? And might I further suggest that whenever you see the term "culture warrior," you might, at least in your imagination, throw a penalty flag, realizing that constructive argument about the real has just been derailed?

PART VII

FACING COVID-19 AND THE PROBLEM OF EVIL

Miracles from Heaven
and the Problem of Theodicy

As any apologist worth his/her salt will tell you, *the* great objection to the proposition that God exists is the fact of innocent suffering. If you want a particularly vivid presentation of this complaint, go on YouTube and look up Stephen Fry's disquisition on why he doesn't believe in God. (Then right afterward, please, do look at my answer to Fry.) But the anguished question of an army of nonbelievers remains: How could an all-loving and all-powerful God possibly allow the horrific suffering endured by those who simply don't deserve it? Say all you want, these critics hold, about God's plan and good coming from evil, but the disproportion between evil and the benefits that might flow from it simply rules out the plausibility of religious faith. The skilled and experienced apologist will also tell you that, in the face of this problem, there is no single, unequivocal "answer," no clinching argument that will leave the doubter stunned into acquiescence. The best approach is to walk slowly around the issue, in the manner of the phenomenologists, illuminating now this aspect, now that.

It is precisely this method that is on display in the surprisingly thoughtful and affecting film *Miracles from Heaven*. The true story revolves around the devout Beam family from Burleson, Texas: Christy, Kevin, and their three daughters. At the age of ten, their middle child, Annabel, develops a devastating disease whereby her intestines are no longer able to process food. After consulting local physicians and surgeons to no avail, Christy and her mother make their way to Boston to see a nationally renowned children's doctor. But after many more months of treatment, her condition remains grave. During this horrific ordeal, Christy's faith in God is seriously shaken, since her ardent prayers have remained, it appears, unanswered. In fact, she explicitly voices to her pastor the confounding puzzle referenced above: How can a loving God permit this innocent and God-fearing child to suffer?

When it seems that things cannot get any worse, Annabel suffers a freak accident, falling headlong down the trunk of a hollowed-out tree. When she comes around after being unconscious for many hours, she is, against all expectations, cured. Unable to account for the sudden improvement, the Boston specialist declares that she is in "complete remission"—just the medical way, he says, of explaining what cannot be explained. Annabel herself, however, tells of an out-of-body experience, a journey to heaven, and God's assurance that she would be fine.

I would like simply to explore a few of the aspects of the problem of suffering—theodicy, to give it its formal title—that are illuminated in the course of this film. First, miracles are rare. As the etymology of the word itself suggests—*mirari* (to be amazed)—miracles don't happen every day, for if they did, we wouldn't "wonder" at or be amazed by them. Indeed, Annabel's hospital roommate, a little girl suffering from cancer and deeply loved by her father, does not receive a miracle. So we shouldn't expect God to intervene any time someone experiences pain or tragedy.

Secondly, God customarily delights in working through secondary causes. To give just one example from the film, the Boston specialist, Dr. Nurko, is portrayed as a man who is not only medically skilled but profoundly compassionate as well. The incomparable good that he does for dozens of children should be construed as an expression of God's loving care, as the vehicle through which God operates. Why would God not act directly? Thomas Aquinas answered that the supreme cause is pleased to involve us in his causality, giving us, as it were, the joy and privilege of sharing his work.

A third lesson is that believers in the God of the Bible should not expect that they will be free of pain; just the contrary. It is actually a bit of a puzzle that so many readers of the Bible seem to think that the love of God is incompatible with suffering, when every major figure in the Scriptures—Abraham, Isaac, Jacob, Joseph, Moses, Joshua, Samuel, David, Solomon, Isaiah, Jeremiah, Ezekiel, Daniel, Peter, James, and John—goes through

204

periods of enormous suffering. And this puzzlement only deepens when we recall that the central person in the Bible is typically displayed to us nailed to a cross and in the throes of death. What becomes clear in the course of *Miracles from Heaven* is that the agony of the Beam family is not meaningless, but rather a participation in the salvific agony of Christ.

A fourth and final insight is that suffering tends to give rise to love. Frequently throughout the film, people perform acts of kindness toward Annabel and her family, precisely because the girl's ordeal has awakened compassion in them. In a word, the girl's pain had a saving effect on those around her; she was, to use the language of the Bible, suffering on their behalf (see Col. 1:24). As Charles Williams pointed out, coinherence—being with and for others—is the master dynamic of the Christian life. Our triumphs and joys are never utterly our own; they are for the sake of others. And the same is true of our tragedies.

Does this film "solve" the problem of innocent suffering? Obviously not. But does it shed light in a creative way on key aspects of it? Yes indeed.

Pain Is Not Metaphysically Basic

In one of my conversations with Jordan Peterson, he commented that pain is somehow metaphysically basic. What he meant was that even the most skeptical philosopher would have to admit the *existence* of pain and would have to deal with it. Try as we might to flee from the world of matter, our bodies and our minds simply will not permit us to set aside the fact and the problem of suffering.

Everyone suffers and at a variety of levels. Babies suffer from hunger and thirst, and their piercing cries remind us of it. We all experience cuts, blisters, bruises, broken bones, infections, rashes, and bleeding. If we live long enough, we develop cancers; our arteries clog up and we suffer heart attacks and strokes. Many of us have spent substantial time in hospitals, where we languished in bed, unable to function. Innumerable people live their lives now in chronic pain, with no real hope of a cure. And as I compose these words, thousands of people around the world are dying, gasping for their last breaths.

But pain is by no means restricted to the physical dimension. In many ways, psychological suffering is more acute, more terrible, than bodily pain. Even little children experience isolation and the fear of abandonment. From the time we are small, we know what it is like to feel rejection and humiliation. A tremendous psychological suffering arises from loneliness, and I have experienced this a number of times in my life, particularly when I started at a new school in a city I did not know. Commencing one's day and having no realistic prospect of human connection is just hellish. And practically everyone has had the dreadful experience of losing a loved one. When the realization sinks in that this person, who is so important to you, has simply disappeared from this world, you enter a realm of darkness unlike any other. And who can forget the dreadful texture of the feeling of being betrayed? When someone that you were convinced was a friend, utterly on your side, turns on you, you feel as though the foundation of your life has given way.

But we haven't looked all the way to the bottom of the well of suffering, for there is also what I might call existential pain. This is the suffering that arises from the loss of meaning and purpose. Someone might be physically fine and even psychologically balanced, but might at the same time be laboring under the weight of despair. Jean-Paul Sartre's adage "*La vie est absurde*" (Life is absurd) or Friedrich Nietzsche's "God is dead" expresses this state of mind. Having surveyed these various levels of pain, we sense the deep truth in the Buddhist conviction that "all life is suffering."

Now I want to take one more important step. There is a very tight connection between pain and sin. Most of the harm that we intentionally do to other people is prompted by suffering. In order to avoid it, avenge it, or preempt it, we will inflict it upon others. And this is the leitmotif of much of the dark and roiled story of humankind. To bring it down to earth, just consider how you behave toward others when you are in great pain.

My gentle reader is probably wondering by now why I have been dwelling so insistently on these dark truths. The reason is simple. The Church places before us an image of a man experiencing practically every kind of pain. The Roman cross was perhaps the most wickedly clever instrument of torture ever devised. The person whose infinitely bad fortune it was to hang from it died very slowly of asphyxiation and exsanguination, even as he writhed in literally excruciating (*ex cruce*, "from the cross") pain. That's how Jesus died: at the limit of physical suffering, covered in bruises and lacerations. But more than this, he died in equally excruciating psychological distress. His closest friends had abandoned, betrayed, or denied him; passersby were laughing at him and spitting on him; the authorities, both religious and political, were mocking and taunting him. And dare I say, he was also in the grip of something like existential suffering. The awful cry "My God, my God, why have you forsaken me?" (Matt. 27:46; Mark 15:34) could only have come from a sense of distance from the source of meaning.

However, the one who hung upon that terrible cross was not just a man; he was God as well. And this truth is the hinge upon which the Paschal Mystery turns. *God* has taken upon himself all of the pain that bedevils the human condition—physical, psychological, and spiritual. *God* goes into the darkest places that we inhabit. *God* experiences the brute metaphysical fact of suffering in all of its dimensions. And this means that pain does not have the final word! This means that pain has been enveloped in the divine mercy. And this implies, finally, that sin has been dealt with. Once we understand that God's love is more powerful than suffering, we have lost, at least in principle, the motivation to sin.

Pain, in point of fact, is not metaphysically basic. The divine mercy is metaphysically basic. And in that is our salvation.

Tragedy, Contingency, and a Deeper Sense of God

have lived in Santa Barbara, California, since 2015. In that brief time, my neighbors and I have experienced a number of real tragedies. In late 2017 to early 2018, the terrible Thomas Fire broke out in my pastoral region, in the vicinity of Thomas Aquinas College (hence the name). For a frightening month it made its devastating way from Santa Paula through Ventura, Carpenteria, Montecito, and eventually commenced to devour the foliage on the hills just north of my home. As I was standing one Saturday morning on my front lawn, staring uneasily at the flames, a retired fire captain stopped his car and yelled out the window, "Bishop, what are you still doing here? Embers are flying everywhere; this whole neighborhood could go up."

We were all relieved when, just days later, rains finally came and doused the flames. But that welcome rain became, in short compass, a deluge, prompting a mudslide in the fire-ravaged hills above Montecito. Twenty-five people were swept to their deaths. In November of that same year, 2018, a disturbed man walked into a crowded restaurant and bar called the Borderline, located in Thousand Oaks, in the far eastern end of my pastoral region. He opened fire at random and killed thirteen people, including a brave police officer who tried to stop him. On Labor Day in 2019, thirty-four people, sleeping belowdecks in a diving boat moored just off the coast of Santa Barbara, died of smoke inhalation as fire roared through their cramped quarters.

I thought of all of these tragedies as we Santa Barbarans, along with the entire country, began dealing with the coronavirus crisis. I think it is fair to say that, at the turn of the year, no one saw this coming. No one would have predicted that millions would be infected by a dangerous pathogen, that hundreds of thousands would die, that we would be shut in our homes, that the economy would go into meltdown. What seemed just a short time ago a fairly stable state of affairs medically, politically, and economically has been turned upside down. Now, I don't rehearse all of this negativity to depress you! I do so to make a theological point.

All of the tragedies that I've recounted are but dramatic examples of a general truth about the nature of things, a truth that we all know in our bones but that we choose, typically, to cover up or overlook. I'm talking about the radical *contingency* of the world, to give it its properly philosophical designation. This means, to state it simply, that everything in our experience is unstable; it comes into being and it passes out of being. Think of every plant, every animal, every insect, every cloud, indeed of every mountain, planet, or solar system, if we allow for a sufficient passage of time: they all come to be and will eventually fade away. And though we habitually divert ourselves from accepting it, this contingency principle applies to each of us. Whenever we get really sick, or a good friend dies, or a weird virus threatens the general population, this truth manages to break through our defenses. Teilhard de Chardin, a theologian-scientist from the last century, said that he acquired a keen sense of his own mortality when, as a boy of three, he saw a lock of his newly cut hair fall into fire and burn up in a split second.

Why shouldn't this perception simply lead to existential despair, a Sartrean sense of the meaninglessness of life? Thomas Aquinas has the answer. The great medieval scholastic said that the contingency of a thing tells us that it doesn't contain within itself the reason for its own existence. This is why we naturally and spontaneously look for the *cause* of a contingent state of affairs: Why did that cloud come to be? What is keeping that insect alive? Why am I writing this article? But if that cause is itself contingent, then we have to look for *its* cause. And if *that* cause is contingent, our search must go on. What we cannot do is endlessly appeal to contingent causes of contingent states of affairs. And thus we must come, finally, to some cause that is not itself caused and that in turn causes contingent things to be. And this, Aquinas says, is what people mean when they use the word "God."

Critics of religion sometimes say that priests and ministers present themselves at moments of sickness and tragedy—in hospitals, nursing homes, and funeral parlors—because they are providing a pathetic crutch to those who can't deal with the sadness of life. But this is hopelessly superficial. Religious leaders do indeed go to those places, precisely because it is there that people experience their *contingency* with particular acuteness, and such experiences open the mind and the heart to God. When we are shaken, we seek by a very healthy instinct for that which is ultimately stable.

At the end of World War II and in the wake of September 11, churches were filled across our country, and I would be willing to bet, when the coronavirus passes, they will be filled again. I would urge you to read this phenomenon not merely psychologically but metaphysically: tragedy sparks an awareness of contingency, and an awareness of contingency gives rise to a deeper sense of God.

Should Suffering Shake Our Faith?

Premier Christian Radio in the UK recently sponsored a survey that investigated how the COVID crisis has affected religious beliefs and attitudes. There were three major findings—namely, that 67 percent of those who characterize themselves as "religious" found their belief in God challenged, that almost a quarter of all those questioned said that the pandemic made them more fearful of death, and that around a third of those surveyed said that their prayer life had been affected by the crisis. Justin Brierley, who hosts the popular program *Unbelievable?*, commented that he was especially impressed by the substantial number of those who, due to COVID, have experienced difficulty believing in a loving God. I should like to focus on this finding as well.

Of course, in one sense, I understand the problem. An altogether standard objection to belief in God is human suffering, especially when it is visited upon the innocent. The apologist for atheism or naturalism quite readily asks the believer, "How could you possibly assert the existence of a loving God given the Holocaust, school shootings, tsunamis that kill hundreds of thousands of people, pandemics, etc.?" But I must confess that, in another sense, I find this argument from evil utterly unconvincing, and I say this precisely as a Catholic bishop—that is, as someone who holds and teaches the doctrine of God that comes from the Bible. For I don't think that anyone who reads the Scriptures carefully could ever conclude that belief in a loving God is somehow incompatible with suffering.

There is no question that God loves Noah, and yet he puts Noah through the unspeakably trying ordeal of a flood that wipes out almost all of life on the earth. It is without doubt that God loves Abraham, and yet he asks that patriarch to sacrifice, with his own hand, his beloved son Isaac. More than almost anyone else in the biblical tradition, God loves Moses, and yet he prevents the great liberator from entering into the Promised Land. David is a man after the Lord's own heart, the sweet singer of the house of Israel, and yet God punishes David for his adultery and his conspiracy to murder. Jeremiah is specially chosen by God to speak the divine word, and yet the prophet ends up rejected and sent into exile. The people Israel is God's uniquely chosen race, his royal priesthood, and yet God permits Israel to be enslaved, exiled, and brutalized by her enemies. And bringing this dynamic to full expression, God delivers his only-begotten Son to be tortured to death on a cross.

Once again, the point, anomalous indeed to both believers and nonbelievers today, is that the biblical authors saw no contradiction whatsoever between affirming the existence of a loving God and the fact of human suffering, even unmerited human suffering. Rather, they appreciated it as, mysteriously enough, ingredient in the plan of God, and they proposed various schemata for understanding this. For instance, sometimes, they speculated, suffering is visited upon us as punishment for sin. Other times, it might be a means by which God effects a spiritual purification in his people. Still other times, it might be the only way that, given the conditions of a finite universe, God could bring about certain goods. But they also acknowledged that, more often than not, we just don't know how suffering fits into God's designs, and this is precisely because our finite and historically conditioned minds could not, even in principle, comprehend the intentions and purposes of an infinite mind, which is concerned with the whole of space and time. Practically the entire burden of the book of Job is to show this. When Job protests against what he takes to be the massive injustice of his sufferings, God responds with a lengthy speech, in fact his longest oration in the Bible, reminding Job of how much of God's purposes his humble human servant does not know: "Where were you when I laid the foundation of the earth?" (Job 38:4).

Once again, whether they half-understood the purpose of human suffering or understood it not at all, no biblical author was tempted to say that said evil is incompatible with the existence of a loving God. To be sure, they lamented and complained, but the recipient of the lamentation and complaint was none other than the God who, they firmly believed, loved them. I don't for a moment doubt that many feel today that suffering poses an insurmountable obstacle to belief in God, but I remain convinced that this feeling is a function of the fact that religious leaders have been rather inept at teaching the biblical doctrine of God. For if human suffering undermines your belief in God, then, quite simply, you were not believing in the God presented by the Bible.

I want to be clear that none of the above is meant to make light of the awful experience of suffering or cavalierly to dismiss the intellectual tensions that it produces. But it is indeed my intention to invite people into a deeper encounter with the mystery of God. Like Jacob, who wrestled all night with the angel, we must not give up on God, but rather struggle with him. Our suffering shouldn't lead us to dismiss the divine love, but rather to appreciate it as stranger than we ever imagined. It is perfectly understandable that, like Job, we might shout our protest against God, but then, like that great spiritual hero, we must be willing to hear the Voice that answers us from the whirlwind.

The Coronavirus and Sitting Quietly in a Room Alone

This article was released in March 2020 in the midst of shutdowns due to the COVID-19 pandemic.

Blaise Pascal said, "All of humanity's problems stem from man's inability to sit quietly in a room alone." The great seventeenth-century philosopher thought that most of us, most of the time, distract ourselves from what truly matters through a series of *divertissements* (diversions). He was speaking from experience. Though one of the brightest men of his age and one of the pioneers of the modern physical sciences and of computer technology, Pascal frittered away a good deal of his time through gambling and other trivial pursuits. In a way, he knew, such diversions are understandable, since the great questions—Does God exist? Why am I here? Is there life after death?—are indeed overwhelming. But if we are to live in a serious and integrated way, they must be confronted—and this is why, if we want our most fundamental problems to be resolved, we must be willing to spend time in a room alone.

This Pascalian *mot* has came to my mind a good deal in recent days as our entire country goes into shutdown mode due to the coronavirus. Shopping malls, movie theaters, restaurants, school campuses, sports stadiums, airports, etc.—the very places where we typically seek out fellowship or *divertissements*— are all emptying out. This is obviously good from the standpoint of physical health, but I wonder whether we might see it as something very good for our psychological and spiritual health as well. Perhaps we could all think of this time of semi-quarantine as an invitation to some monastic introspection, some serious confrontation with the questions that matter—some purposeful sitting alone in a room.

Might I make a few suggestions in regard to our retreat? Get out your Bible and read one of the Gospels in its entirety—perhaps the Gospel of Matthew, which we are using for Sunday Mass this liturgical year. Read it slowly, prayerfully; use a good commentary if that helps. Or practice the ancient art that has been recommended warmly by the last several popes—namely, *lectio divina*. This "divine reading" of the Bible consists in four basic steps: *lectio, meditatio, oratio,* and *contemplatio*. First, read the scriptural text carefully; second, pick out one word or one passage that specially struck you, and then meditate on it, like a ruminating animal chewing on its cud; third, speak to God, telling him how your heart was moved by what you read; fourth and finally, listen to the Lord, discerning what he speaks back to you. Trust me, the Bible will spring to life when you approach it through this method.

Or read one of the spiritual classics during this time of imposed isolation. Keep in mind that, prior to the rise of the physical sciences, the best and brightest people in our Western intellectual tradition entered the fields of philosophy, theology, and spirituality. One of the dark sides of our post-Enlightenment culture is a general forgetfulness of the astonishing richness produced by generations of brilliant spiritual teachers. So take up St. Augustine's *Confessions*, preferably in Maria Boulding's recent translation, which reads like a novel, or Frank Sheed's classic translation. Though he lived and wrote seventeen centuries ago, the spiritual seeker of our time will discern in Augustine's story the contours and trajectories of his own. Or read the *Rule* of St. Benedict, especially the section on the twelve degrees of humility. If you dare, follow St. Ignatius' *Spiritual Exercises*, preferably under the direction of a good guide (who doesn't have the coronavirus!). If these texts and practices seem too dated, spend your quiet time with Thomas Merton's splendid autobiography *The Seven Storey Mountain*, which, in compelling prose, tells the story of the twentieth-century author's journey from self-absorbed worldling to Trappist monk.

And of course, pray. When Merton was once asked what is the most important thing a person could do to improve her prayer life, he replied, "Take the time." Well, now we have more time. Do a Holy Hour every day or every other day. Dust off your rosary, which I think is one of the most sublime prayers in the Catholic tradition. When we pray it well, we meditate on the mysteries of Christ; we call to mind, fifty times, the inevitability of our own passing ("now and at the hour of our death"); and we entrust ourselves to the most powerful intercessor on earth or in heaven. Not a bad way to spend twenty minutes. Take the time at the end of the day to examine your conscience—and not in a cursory manner. Do it carefully, prayerfully, honestly. Ask yourself how many times in the course of the day you missed an opportunity to show love, how many times you did not respond to a grace, how often you fell into a habitual sin.

Now that we're being asked to keep a certain distance from our fellow human beings, embrace the solitude and silence in a spiritually alert way. Go for that long walk on the beach, across the fields, up in the hills—wherever you like to go to be alone. And just talk to God. Ask him what he wants you to do. Pray for your kids or your parents or your friends who might be struggling. Tell him how much you love him and how you want greater intimacy with him. And please put away the iPhones! Open your eyes, lift up your heads, and take in the beauty of God's creation and thank him for it.

If Pascal is right, many of our deepest problems can be solved by sitting, with spiritual attention, alone in a room. Perhaps through God's strange providence, the quarantine we're enduring might be our chance.

The Quarantine's Three Lessons
about the Church

One silver lining for me during the weird coronavirus shutdown of 2020 was the opportunity to return to some writing projects that I had left on the back-burner. One of these is a book on the Nicene Creed, which I had commenced many months ago and on which I was making only very slow progress, given my various pastoral and administrative responsibilities. When I was working in a rather concentrated way on the Creed book, I found myself in the midst of the section on the Church: "I believe in one, holy, catholic, and apostolic Church." I will confess that the peculiar way that we had been forced to express the life of the Church during the quarantine period influenced my ecclesiological reflection.

A first insight is this: we are an intensely, inescapably Eucharistic church. One of the most difficult moments that I've had as a bishop was participating in the decision to close our churches and to shut down the celebration of Mass with a community. Mind you, it was the right decision. I emphatically disagree with those who argue that the bishops caved in to the pressure of the secular state in making this determination. That's nonsense. There are some very real tensions between Church and state and sometimes we have to make a stand—a good example being our vigorous opposition here in California to the legislature's attempt to violate the seal of confession. But this was not one of those cases. Instead, we bishops agreed with the secular authorities that the churches should be closed, precisely for the well-being of our people. Having said that, the suspension of public Mass was painful for everyone—and the principal reason for that pain was the forced fasting from the Eucharist.

Sensing this, innumerable priests and bishops all over the country—indeed, around the world—commenced to livestream or film the liturgy, broadcasting it over Facebook, YouTube, or on television. The reaction to these representations of the Mass was overwhelming. To give just one example, at Word on Fire, we started filming daily Mass on St. Patrick's Day, and we continued to Pentecost Sunday, acquiring in the process well over nine million views from over two hundred countries. Some priests, furthermore, processed through the quiet streets with the Blessed Sacrament, while Catholics looked on from their homes; others placed the monstrance with the consecrated Host in the windows of their residences and rectories so that people could venerate the Sacrament as they walked or drove by. And wasn't the whole Catholic world fascinated by Pope Francis, standing in the rain and facing an empty St. Peter's Square, as he blessed us, via television and social media, with the Eucharist?

To be sure, none of these mitigated encounters with the Eucharistic Lord was a substitute for the real thing—and that's the point. The abstention from the Eucharist—which began, fittingly enough, during Lent—awakened a profound hunger for what Vatican II called "the source and summit of the Christian life." Perhaps too many Catholics had grown indifferent to the Blessed Sacrament, even, as a recent Pew Forum study indicated, ignorant of its deepest significance; and perhaps this forced starvation had a salutary effect.

A second ecclesiological insight is this: priests are in an intensely symbiotic relationship with their people. Everyone knows that priests have been passing through a difficult period, practically without precedent in the history of the Church. The scandals of the past twenty-five years, culminating in the McCarrick outrage, have soured many against priests and have made priests extremely vulnerable to the charge of clericalism. Without denying for a moment that these reactions and impressions are, to a degree, legitimate, I want to insist once again that the vast, vast majority of priests are decent, prayerful men, who want nothing more than to bring Christ to their people. And the coronavirus quarantine powerfully confirmed this for me. During the course of the shutdown, I personally reached out by phone or by Skype or Zoom to all the priests of my region. Like everybody else, they were a little antsy and bored, and their routines were interrupted. But time and again, they told me that their greatest frustration was not being able to have steady contact with their people. Priests indeed bring Christ to their parishioners through preaching, presence, and sacrament, but the people also give life to the priests, sustaining them with prayer and friendship. Keeping the people away from their priests is just bad for both people and priests, for they are, in the Mystical Body, ordered toward one another.

A third and final insight is that the Church is stubbornly incarnational. At the heart of the Catholic sensibility is the conviction that God became *flesh* in Jesus Christ. And Catholicism teaches that the presence of the risen Jesus is made known through words to be sure, but also through physical signs— water, oil, bread, wine, etc.—delivered by human hands and accompanied by bodily gestures. At the liturgy, we are meant to come together in close proximity so that we can pray in unison, sing in unison, process together, embrace one another, gesture in harmony with each other. In all of this, the incarnational quality of the Church becomes concretely expressed. And this is what has made the shutdown so particularly difficult for Catholics. Our faith is not primarily an internal business, something negotiated between the individual and the invisible Lord. Rather, it shows up physically and publicly, through bodies. Once again, I would hope that our fasting from togetherness heightened our appreciation for this incarnational density of our faith.

Perhaps this time of deprivation and abstention awakened a deeper love for the Church in its Eucharistic, symbiotic, and incarnational distinctiveness.

The Book of Exodus
and Why
Coming Back to Mass Matters

In connection with an academic project of mine, I've recently been poring over the book of Exodus and numerous commentaries thereupon. The second most famous book of the Old Testament is concerned primarily with the manner in which God shapes his people so that they might become a radiant beacon, a city set on a hill. On the biblical reading, Israel is indeed chosen, but it is never chosen for its own sake, but rather for all the nations of the world.

I would say that this formation takes place in three principal stages: first, God teaches Israel to trust in his power; secondly, he gives Israel a moral law; and thirdly, he instructs his people in holiness through right praise. The lesson in trust happens, of course, through God's great act of liberation. Utterly powerless slaves find freedom not by relying on their own resources, but rather upon the gracious intervention of God. The moral instruction takes place through the Ten Commandments and their attendant legislation. Finally, the formation in holiness happens through a submission to an elaborate set of liturgical and ceremonial laws. It is this last move that perhaps strikes us today as most peculiar, but that has, I will argue, particular resonance in our strange COVID period.

That education in religion involves moral instruction probably seems self-evident to most of us. And this is because we are, willy-nilly, Kantians. In the eighteenth century, the philosopher Immanuel Kant contended that all of religion is reducible to ethics. What the religious thing is finally all about, Kant argued, is making us more just, loving, kind, and compassionate. In contemporary language, Kantianism in religion sounds like this: "As long as you're a good person, it doesn't really matter what you believe or how you worship."

Now, there is no question that the book of Exodus and the Bible in general agree that morality is essential to the proper formation of the people of God. Those who would seek to follow the Lord, who *is* justice and love, must be conformed to justice and love. And this is precisely why we find, in the great Sinai covenant, injunctions not to steal, not to commit adultery, not to covet, not to kill, etc. So far, so Kantian.

But what probably surprises most contemporary readers of the book of Exodus is that, immediately following the laying out of the moral commandments, the author spends practically the rest of the text, chapters 25 through 40, delineating the liturgical prescriptions that the people are to follow. So, for example, we find a lengthy section on the construction of the ark of the covenant: "They shall make an ark of acacia wood; it shall be two and a half cubits long, a cubit and a half wide, and a cubit and a half high. You shall overlay it with pure gold, inside and outside you shall overlay it" (Exod. 25:10–11). And, as an ornament on the top of the ark, "You shall make two cherubim of gold. . . . Make one cherub at the one end, and one cherub at the other. . . . The cherubim shall spread out their wings above, overshadowing the mercy seat" (Exod. 25:18–20). Next, we find instructions regarding the elaborate furnishings inside of the tabernacle, including a lampstand, a table for the so-called "bread of the presence," pillars, and various hangings. Finally, an enormous amount of space is given over to the description of the vestments to be worn by the priests of Israel. Here is just a sampling: "These are the vestments that they shall make: a breastpiece, an ephod, a robe, a checkered tunic, a turban, and a sash. When they make these sacred vestments . . . they shall use gold, blue, purple, and crimson yarns, and fine linen" (Exod. 28:4–5).

No indication whatsoever is given that the moral prescriptions are somehow more important than the liturgical prescriptions. If anything, the contrary seems to be the case, since Exodus is followed immediately by the book of Leviticus, which consists of twenty-seven chapters of dietary and liturgical law. So what are we post-Kantians to make of this? First, we should observe that the biblical authors do not think for a moment that God somehow requires liturgical rectitude, as though the correctness of our worship adds anything to his perfection or satisfies some psychological need of his. If you harbor any doubt on this score, I would recommend a careful reading of the first chapter of the prophet Isaiah and of the fiftieth Psalm. God doesn't need the ark and the tabernacle and priestly vestments and regular worship, *but we do*. Through the gestures and symbols of its liturgical praise, Israel is brought on line with God, ordered to him. The moral law directs our wills to the divine goodness, but the liturgical law directs our minds, our hearts, our emotions, and yes even our bodies to the divine splendor. Notice how thoroughly the ceremonial instructions of Exodus involve color, sound, and smell (there is an awful lot about incense) and how they conduce toward the production of beauty.

I said above that Exodus' stress on the liturgical and ceremonial has a profound relevance to our time, and here's why. For very good reasons, we abstained completely from public worship, and afterward, our ability to worship together was very limited. In most dioceses in our country, the obligation to attend Sunday Mass was, again for valid reasons, suspended. My fear is that, now that the propitious moment has arrived, and we are again able to return to Mass, many Catholics will stay away, since they grew accustomed to absenting themselves from worship. And my concern takes a more specifically Kantian form: Will many Catholics say to themselves, "You know, as long as I'm basically a good person, what's the point of all of this formal worship of God?"

Could I recommend that you take out your Bible, open to the book of Exodus, especially chapters 25 through 40, and consider just how crucially important to God is the correct worship offered by his holy people? Liturgy has always mattered. The Mass—involving vestments, ritual gesture, smells and bells, song and silence—still matters, big time. Isn't it enough that you're a good person? Not to put too fine a point on it: no.

Come Back to Mass!

The COVID-19 pandemic has been a time of crisis and deep challenge for our country, and it has been a particular trial for Catholics. During this terrible period, many of us were compelled to fast from attendance at Mass and the reception of the Eucharist. To be sure, numerous Masses and Eucharistic para-liturgies were made available online, and thank God for these. But Catholics knew in their bones that such virtual presentations were absolutely no substitute for the real thing. Now that the doors of our churches have opened wide, I would like to urge every Catholic reading these words: come back to Mass!

Why is the Mass of such central importance? The Second Vatican Council eloquently teaches that the Eucharist is the "source and summit of the Christian life"—which is to say, that from which authentic Christianity comes and toward which it tends. It is the alpha and the omega of the spiritual life, both the path and the goal of Christian discipleship. The Church Fathers consistently taught that the Eucharist is sustenance for eternal life. They meant that, in the measure that we internalize the Body and Blood of Jesus, we are readied for life with him in the next world. Thomas Aquinas said that all of the other sacraments contain the *virtus Christi* (the power of Christ) but that the Eucharist contains *ipse Christus* (Christ himself)—and this would help to explain why St. Thomas could never make it through the Mass without shedding copious tears. It is precisely at the Mass that we are privileged to receive this incomparable gift. It is precisely at the Mass that we take in this indispensable sustenance. Without it, we starve to death spiritually.

If I might broaden the scope a bit, I would like to suggest that the Mass is, in its totality, *the* privileged point of encounter with Jesus Christ. During the Liturgy of the Word, we hear not simply human words crafted by poetic geniuses, but rather the words of the Word. In the readings, and especially in the Gospel, it is Christ who speaks to us. In our responses, we speak back to him, entering into conversation with the second person of the Trinity. Then, in the Liturgy of the Eucharist, the same Jesus who has spoken his heart to us offers his Body and Blood for us to consume. There is simply, this side of heaven, no more intimate communion possible with the risen Lord.

I realize that many Catholics during this COVID period became accustomed to the ease of attending Mass virtually from the comfort of their own homes and without the inconvenience of busy parking lots, crying children, and crowded pews. But a key feature of the Mass is precisely our *coming together as a community*. As we speak, pray, sing, and respond together, we realize our identity as the Mystical Body of Jesus. During the liturgy, the priest functions *in persona Christi* (in the very person of Christ), and the baptized in attendance join themselves symbolically to Christ the Head and together offer worship to the Father. There is an exchange between priest and people at Mass that is crucially important, though often overlooked. Just before the prayer over the gifts, the priest says, "Pray, brothers and sisters, that my sacrifice and yours may be acceptable to God, the almighty Father," and the people respond, "May the Lord accept the sacrifice at your hands for the praise and glory of his name, for our good and the good of all his holy Church." At that moment, Head and members consciously join together to make the perfect sacrifice to the Father. The point is that this cannot happen when we are scattered in our homes and sitting in front of computer screens.

If I might signal the importance of the Mass in a more negative manner, the Church has consistently taught that baptized Catholics are morally obligated to attend Mass on Sunday and that the conscious missing of Mass, in the absence of a valid excuse, is mortally sinful. I understand that this language makes many people today uncomfortable, but it shouldn't, for it is perfectly congruent with everything we have said about the Mass to this point. If the Eucharistic liturgy is, in fact, the source and summit of the Christian life, the privileged encounter with Jesus Christ, the moment when the Mystical Body most fully expresses itself, the setting for the reception of the bread of heaven—then we are indeed putting ourselves, spiritually speaking, in mortal danger when we actively stay away from it. Just as a physician might observe that you are endangering your life by eating fatty foods, smoking, and refraining from exercise, so a doctor of the soul will tell you that abstaining from the Mass is compromising your spiritual health. Of course, as I suggested above, it has always been the law of the Church that an individual may decide to miss Mass for legitimate prudential reasons—and this certainly obtains during these waning days of the pandemic.

But come back to Mass! And might I suggest that you bring someone with you, someone who has been away too long or has perhaps been lulled into complacency during COVID? Let your own Eucharistic hunger awaken an evangelical impulse in you. Bring in people from the highways and byways; invite your coworkers and family members; wake up the kids on Sunday morning; turn off your computers. Come back to Mass!

PART VIII

SHINING THE LIGHT
OF THE NATIONS

Pope Francis and the Evangelicals

The whole Christian world watched with fascination as Pope Francis has reached out to evangelicals. Who can forget the mesmerizing iPhone video, filmed by the pope's (late) friend Bishop Tony Palmer, in which the Bishop of Rome communicated, with fatherlike compassion, to a national gathering of American evangelical leaders? His smile, his tone of voice, and the simple, direct words that he chose constituted a bridge between Catholics and evangelicals. What I found particularly moving was the remarkable reaction of the evangelical audience after they had taken in the video: a real prayer in the Spirit.

And who could forget the high-five—reportedly the first of Pope Francis' life—exchanged with Pastor James Robison, after the pope insisted that a living relationship with Jesus stands at the heart of the Christian reality? Many Catholics were surprised when the newly elected Pope Francis asked the crowd gathered in St. Peter's Square to pray for him, but evangelicals from Argentina weren't taken aback, for they had witnessed something very similar. In June of 2006, Cardinal Jorge Mario Bergoglio was attending a meeting of evangelical pastors in Buenos Aires, and after he had spoken to them, he knelt down on the stage and asked them to pray for him and to bless him.

No one doubts that Pope Francis has a genius for the provocative symbolic gesture: washing the feet of women and non-Christians on Holy Thursday, paying his own hotel bill in Rome, opting to reside not in the opulent Apostolic Palace but the far more modest Casa Santa Marta, driving in a tiny car while at World Youth Day in Rio, etc. But does his outreach to evangelicals go beyond the merely symbolic? Is it grounded in more substantial theological commitments? I would argue the affirmative and do so on the basis of Francis' Apostolic Exhortation *Evangelii Gaudium* (*The Joy of the Gospel*).

The third paragraph of that encyclical commences with this ecumenically remarkable sentence: "I invite all Christians, everywhere, at this very moment, to a renewed personal encounter with Jesus Christ." Catholics have tended to be suspicious of the language of personal relationship with Jesus, especially as it has appeared in evangelical Protestant rhetoric over the past half century (accepting Jesus as my "personal Lord and Savior"), and this for two basic reasons. First, it seems to undermine or at least lessen the importance of the properly mediating role that the Church appropriately plays, and secondly, it tends to compromise the communitarian dimension of Christian life. I do not for a moment think that Pope Francis is unaware of those dangers, but I think he is more concerned that a hyper-stress on the ecclesial can render Christian life abstract and institutional. In paragraph 7 of *Evangelii Gaudium*, Francis says, "I never tire of repeating those words of Benedict XVI which take us to the very heart of the Gospel: 'Being a Christian is not the result of an ethical choice or a lofty idea, but the encounter with an event, a person, which gives life a new horizon and a decisive direction.'" Christianity is not a philosophy or a set of ideas, but rather a friendship with Jesus of Nazareth. In paragraph 266, we hear, "It is impossible to persevere in a fervent evangelization unless we are convinced from personal experience that it is not the same thing to have known Jesus as not to have known him."

According to Catholic ecclesiology, the Church is not primarily an institution, but rather the prolongation of the Incarnation across space and time, the Mystical Body of Jesus through which people come to an encounter with the Lord. When this organic relationship between Jesus and his Church is forgotten or occluded, a stifling institutionalism can follow, and this is precisely why Francis insists that we "'cannot passively and calmly wait in our church buildings'; we need to move 'from a pastoral ministry of mere conservation to a decidedly missionary pastoral ministry'" (*EG* 15).

This evangelical urgency, which Pope Francis gets in his bones, is the leitmotif of this entire Apostolic Exhortation. He knows that if Catholicism leads with its doctrines, it will devolve into an intellectual debating society, and that if it leads with its moral teaching, it will appear, especially in our postmodern cultural context, fussy and puritanical. It should lead today as it led two thousand years ago: with the stunning news that Jesus Christ is the Lord, and the joy of that proclamation should be as evident now as it was then. The pope helpfully draws our attention to some of the countless references to joy in the pages of the New Testament: "'Rejoice!' is the angel's greeting to Mary (Luke 1:28).... In her song of praise, Mary proclaims: 'My spirit rejoices in God my Savior' (Luke 1:47).... [Jesus'] message brings us joy: 'I have said these things to you, so that my joy may be in you, and that your joy may be complete' (John 15:11).... In the Acts of the Apostles we read that... wherever the disciples went, 'there was great joy' (8:8)." The pope concludes with a wonderfully understated rhetorical question: "Why should we not also enter into this great stream of joy?" (*EG* 5). Why not indeed? Displaying his penchant for finding the memorable image, Pope Francis excoriates Christians who have turned "into querulous and disillusioned pessimists, 'sourpusses'" (*EG* 85), and whose lives "seem like Lent without Easter" (*EG* 6). Such people might be smart and they might even be morally upright, but they will never be successful evangelists.

Once this basic truth is understood, the rest of the Church's life tends to fall more correctly into place. A Church filled with the joy of the Resurrection becomes a band of "missionary disciples," going out to the world with the Good News. Ecclesial structures, liturgical precision, theological clarity, bureaucratic meetings, etc. are accordingly relativized in the measure that they are placed in service of that more fundamental mission. The pope loves the liturgy, but if evangelical proclamation is the urgent need of the Church, "an ostentatious preoccupation for the liturgy" becomes a problem (*EG* 95); a Jesuit, the pope loves the life of the mind, but if evangelical proclamation is the central concern of the Church, then a "narcissistic" and "authoritarian" doctrinal fussiness must be eliminated (*EG* 94); a man of deep culture, Pope Francis loves the artistic heritage of the Church, but if evangelical proclamation is the fundamental mission, then the Church cannot become "a museum piece" (*EG* 95). This last point calls vividly to mind something that Angelo Giuseppe Roncalli said on the eve of the conclave that would elect him Pope John XXIII: "We are not here to guard a museum, but rather to cultivate a flourishing garden of life."

When he spoke at the General Congregations, the meetings of cardinals in advance of the conclave of 2013, Cardinal Bergoglio reportedly brought to his brothers' attention with great passion the need for the Church to look beyond herself. This preoccupation is echoed in paragraph 27 of *Evangelii Gaudium*: "I dream of a 'missionary option,' that is, a missionary impulse capable of transforming everything, so that the Church's customs, ways of doing things, times and schedules, language and structures can be suitably channeled for the evangelization of today's world rather than for her self-preservation." And this in turn echoes a word that John Paul II spoke to the bishops of Oceania in 2001: "All renewal in the Church must have mission as its goal if it is not to fall prey to a kind of ecclesial introversion." And the mission, once again, is none other than drawing the entire human race into a relationship with the living Christ. There is much here, I would suggest, with which evangelicals can resonate.

Pope Francis realizes that in our postmodern framework, appeals to the true and the good often fall on deaf ears. Indeed, if the dictatorship of relativism obtains, then who are you to tell me what I ought to think or how I ought to behave? This is why the pope calls for an active exploration of the "'way of beauty' (*via pulchritudinis*)" (*EG* 167). It is best for the evangelizer to show the splendor and radiance of the Christian form of life before he or she would get to explicit doctrine and moral commands. This involves the use of classical artistic expressions of the Christian faith as well as contemporary cultural forms. Indeed, says the pope, any beautiful thing can be a route of access to Christ.

If I might end on a note of challenge, or better, of invitation to further and deeper conversation. Along with so many others, I was encouraged by the late Bishop Tony Palmer's outreach to Pope Francis and his ecumenical graciousness. But when he told the gathered ministers that, in the wake of the famous 1999 Joint Declaration on the Doctrine of Justification, Luther's protest is effectively over, I was, to say the least, not convinced. We have made enormous strides in the last fifty years, and as I've suggested here, the papacy of Francis represents another astonishing leap forward. Nevertheless, in the wake of the five hundredth anniversary of the Protestant Reformation, significant differences remain at the doctrinal level, including and especially in regard to the issue of justification and its appropriation. In the early 1940s, the Protestant theologian Karl Barth conducted a seminar in Basel on the texts of the Council of Trent, and to that seminar he invited Catholic thinker Hans Urs von Balthasar. I'm not at all sure that these two giants resolved anything, but I remain entranced by the image of the greatest Protestant theologian of the twentieth century and arguably the greatest Catholic theologian of the twentieth century coming together for serious conversation regarding the central issues of the Reformation. I am exceptionally glad that in many circles we have moved well beyond the stage of hurling invective at one another and that we have indeed found many, many points of contact, especially concerning the centrality of evangelization. But I would still welcome more and more encounters along the lines of the Barth-Balthasar seminar. Toward that end, may we all follow the evangelical drumbeat of Pope Francis.

Laudato Si' Athwart Modernity

When I reread Pope Francis' encyclical letter *Laudato Si'*, I was particularly impressed by the pope's sharply critical assessment of modernity. I think it's fair to say that the Church has had a complex relationship with the modern, coming out strongly against it at the First Vatican Council and in a plethora of statements throughout much of the twentieth century, but affirming many elements of it very enthusiastically at the Second Vatican Council. One has only to consider here Vatican II's document on religious liberty, *Dignitatis Humanae*, or its magisterial document on the Church in the modern world, *Gaudium et Spes*, to see the council's favorable assessment of many key features of modernity. And certainly in the years that I was coming of age in the immediate wake of Vatican II, a positive attitude toward "the world" or the "modern world" was pretty much expected of all right-thinking Catholics.

Modernity is a multifaceted phenomenon, marked by qualities both good and bad, and hence the Church's ambivalence toward it is understandable. To take just two of its principal accomplishments into consideration, I don't know any serious person who wants to reverse the advances that modern thinkers made possible in the physical sciences or in the development of democratic political institutions. On the other hand, as an army of postmodern philosophers and cultural analysts have pointed out, modernity carries with it a shadow—that is to say, emphases and assumptions that are, to say the least, questionable. Though he clearly celebrates the achievements of Vatican II and though he applauds much in the modern project, Pope Francis is also skeptical of modernity, and nowhere is this skepticism on clearer display than in *Laudato Si'*.

Front and center in his analysis of our present situation is a trenchant critique of what the pope calls a "technocratic paradigm" (*LS* 101). By this he means a worldview that privileges technology and what it makes possible over practically any other consideration—over the good of the human family, the needs of the poor, the cause of peace, etc. The effects of this mindset are ubiquitous, but they are especially evident in the rape of the environment and the turning of God's beautiful creation into "an immense pile of filth," in the pope's vivid expression (*LS* 21).

But this paradigm, he reminds us, is made possible by a more fundamental shift in attitude—what Francis terms "modern anthropocentrism" (*LS* 115). This is the tendency, on display in practically all of the great philosophers from the seventeenth to the nineteenth centuries, to place human subjectivity at the center of things, both epistemologically and metaphysically. The consequence of this Copernican revolution is the emergence, the pope argues, of a "Promethean vision of mastery over the world" (*LS* 116). It is instructive in this context to consider the difference between Aristotle's and Descartes' understanding of the purpose of science. For the ancient Greek thinker, philosophy commences in wonder and ends in contemplation of the intelligibilities on display in the world; whereas for the modern French thinker, philosophy begins and ends in a passion to "master nature." No one, including Pope Francis, would want to go back on the real attainments that followed from the Cartesian paradigm shift, but the pope does indeed worry that the turn to subjectivity, at least in its extreme forms, has produced something wicked and dangerous. If nature simply lies before the dominant human subject as a thing to be manipulated, then the integrity of creation is compromised and the objectivity of values that are embedded in nature is disregarded.

Practically every commentator on *Laudato Si'* five years ago remarked that this was the pope's "global warming" encyclical, and indeed that issue is amply discussed in the pages of the text. But what almost every pundit missed was Francis' extraordinarily rich development of the point just made regarding the objectivity of moral values. The same technocratic and anthropocentric prejudice, he says, that gives rise to environmental disaster gives rise as well to population control through artificial contraception and abortion: "Instead of resolving the problems of the poor and thinking of how the world can be different, some can only propose a reduction in the birth rate. At times, developing countries face forms of international pressure which make economic assistance contingent on certain policies of 'reproductive health'" (*LS* 50). Moreover, the setting aside of intrinsic moral values and the concomitant placing of the individual and his needs at the center conduce toward what the pope calls practical relativism: "Hence we should not be surprised to find, in conjunction with the omnipresent technocratic paradigm and the cult of unlimited human power, the rise of a relativism which sees everything as irrelevant unless it serves one's own immediate interests" (*LS* 122). And finally, the domination of the ego over nature also finds expression, says Pope Francis, in a gender ideology that would give to the individual the right to define him or herself even at the physical level. Moreover, there is a clear link between this extravagant claim to freedom and the abuse of the physical environment: "Thinking that we enjoy absolute power over our own bodies turns, often subtly, into thinking that we enjoy absolute power over creation" (*LS* 155).

What this brief survey demonstrates is that the "Fox News vs. CNN" hermeneutic just won't work if we are reading *Laudato Si'* in full. Pope Francis takes positions that annoy both standard-issue liberals and standard-issue conservatives. This is because his overarching opponent is the philosophy of modernity, which in fact has produced both the "conservatism" and the "liberalism" that we know today. His appeal to a worldview that antedates the modern is what makes this encyclical particularly intriguing.

Pope Francis, *Fratelli Tutti,*
and the
Universal Destination of Goods

In the wake of the publication of Pope Francis' encyclical letter *Fratelli Tutti,* there was a great deal of negative commentary regarding the pope's attitude toward capitalism and private property. Many readers interpreted Francis to mean that the capitalist system is, in itself, exploitative, and that the holding of private property is morally problematic. Like most who write in a prophetic mode, Pope Francis is indeed given to strong and challenging language, and therefore, it is easy enough to understand how he excites opposition. But it is most important to read what he says with care and to interpret it within the context of the long tradition of Catholic social teaching.

First, in regard to capitalism, or what the Church prefers to call the "market economy," the pope has this to say: "Business activity is essentially 'a noble vocation, directed to producing wealth and improving our world'" (*FT* 123). He thereby distances himself from any ideology that would simply demonize capitalism, and clearly affirms that a morally praiseworthy economic arrangement is one that not only distributes wealth but creates it through entrepreneurship. Moreover, he argues, a certain self-interest, including the taking of profit, is not repugnant to the moral purpose of economic activity: "In God's plan, each individual is called to promote his or her own development, and this includes finding the best economic and technological means of multiplying goods and increasing wealth" (*FT* 123). In making these observations, Francis stands firmly in the tradition of St. John Paul II, who saw the market economy as an arena for the exercise of human creativity, ingenuity, and courage, and who endeavored to draw ever more people into its dynamism. He also reiterates the teaching of the founder of the modern Catholic social tradition, the great Leo XIII, who, in *Rerum Novarum*, strenuously defended private property and, using a number of arguments, repudiated socialist economic arrangements. So I hope we can put to rest the silly canard that Pope Francis is an enemy of capitalism and a cheerleader for global socialism.

Now, without gainsaying any of this, we must at the same time point out that, like all of his papal predecessors in the social teaching tradition, without exception, Francis also recommends limits, both legal and moral, to the market economy. And in this context he insists upon what classical Catholic theology refers to as the "universal destination of goods." Here is how Francis states the idea in *Fratelli Tutti*: "The right to private property is always accompanied by the primary and prior principle of the subordination of all private property to the universal destination of the earth's goods, and thus the right of all to their use" (*FT* 123). In making the distinction between ownership and use, Pope Francis is hearkening back to St. Thomas Aquinas, who made the relevant distinction in question 66 of the *secunda secundae* of the *Summa theologiae*. For a variety of reasons, St. Thomas argues, people have the right to "procure and dispense" the goods of the world and hence to hold them as "property." But in regard to the *use* of what they legitimately own, they must always keep the general welfare first in mind: "On this respect man ought to possess external things, not as his own, but as common, so that, to wit, he is ready to communicate them to others in their need."

Now, in regard to this distinction, Thomas himself was the inheritor of an older tradition, stretching back to the Church Fathers. Pope Francis quotes St. John Chrysostom as follows: "Not to share our wealth with the poor is to rob them and take away their livelihood. The riches we possess are not our own, but theirs as well." And he cites St. Gregory the Great in the same vein: "When we provide the needy with their basic needs, we are giving them what belongs to them, not to us" (*FT* 119). The simplest way to grasp the distinction between ownership and use is to imagine the scenario of a starving man coming to the door of your house late at night and asking for sustenance. Though you are in your own home, which you legitimately own, and behind a door that you have understandably locked against intruders, you would nevertheless be morally obligated to give away some of your property to the beggar in such desperate need. In short, private property is a right, but not an "inviolable" right—if by that we mean without qualification or conditions—and saying so is not tantamount to advocating socialism.

What we might characterize as something of a novelty in Pope Francis' encyclical is the application of this distinction to the relations between nations and not simply individuals. A nation-state indeed has a right to its own wealth, garnered through the energy and creativity of its people, and it may legitimately maintain and defend its borders; however, these prerogatives are not morally absolute. In Francis' words, "We can then say that each country also belongs to the foreigner, inasmuch as a territory's goods must not be denied to a needy person coming from elsewhere" (*FT* 124). This is not "globalism" or a denial of national integrity; it is simply Thomas Aquinas' distinction between ownership and use, extrapolated to the international level.

Once more, lest we see Pope Francis' teaching here as egregious, I would like to give the last word to Leo XIII, ardent defender of private property and equally ardent opponent of socialism: "When what necessity demands has been supplied, and one's standing fairly taken thought for, it becomes a duty to give to the indigent out of what remains over" (*RN* 22).

Why "What Are the Bishops Doing about It?" Is the Wrong Question

In June 2020, the bishops of California made a statement regarding the attacks on the statues of St. Junípero Serra in San Francisco, Ventura, and Los Angeles. While acknowledging that there are legitimate concerns about racism, both historical and contemporary, we insisted that the characterization of Serra as the moral equivalent of Hitler and the missions he founded as tantamount to death camps is simply unconscionable. I put a link to this statement on my own Word on Fire social media accounts and was gratified to see that many people read it and commented upon it. My purpose in this article is not to examine the specific issues surrounding Padre Serra, but rather to respond to a number of remarks in the comboxes that point to what I think is a real failure to understand a key teaching of Vatican II.

Over and again, perhaps a hundred times, commentators said some version of this: "Well, bishop, making a statement is all fine and good, but what are you and the other bishops going to *do* about it?" Now, almost none of these questioners made a concrete suggestion as to what precisely they had in mind, but I will gladly admit that there are certain practical steps that bishops can and should take in regard to such a situation. We can indeed lobby politicians, encourage legislative changes, and call community leaders together, all of which bishops have been doing. But what struck me again and again as I read these rather taunting remarks is that these folks, primarily lay men and women, are putting way too much onus on the clergy and not nearly enough on themselves.

According to the documents of Vatican II, the clergy are, by ordination, "priests, prophets, and kings." As priests, they sanctify the people of God through the sacraments; as prophets, they speak the divine word and form the minds and hearts of their flocks; and as kings, they order the charisms of the community toward the realization of the kingdom of God. Accordingly, the immediate area of concern for bishops and priests is the Church—that is to say, the community of the baptized. Now, the laity, by virtue of their baptism, are also priests, prophets, and kings (*Lumen Gentium* 31)—but their sanctifying, teaching, and governing work is directed not so much inwardly to the Church but outwardly to the world. For the Vatican II fathers, the proper arena of the laity is the *saeculum* (the secular order), and their task is the Christification of that realm. They are charged to take the teaching, direction, and sanctification that they have received from the priests and bishops and then go forth, equipped to transform the world and thereby find their own path to holiness.

It's worth quoting Vatican II directly here, from *Lumen Gentium*:

> What specifically characterizes the laity is their secular nature. It is true that those in holy orders can at times be engaged in secular activities, and even have a secular profession. But they are by reason of their particular vocation especially and professedly ordained to the sacred ministry. Similarly, by their state in life, religious give splendid and striking testimony that the world cannot be transformed and offered to God without the spirit of the beatitudes. But the laity, by their very vocation, seek the kingdom of God by engaging in temporal affairs and by ordering them according to the plan of God. They live in the world, that is, in each and in all of the secular professions and occupations. They live in the ordinary circumstances of family and social life, from which the very web of their existence is woven. They are called there by God that by exercising their proper function and led by the spirit of the Gospel they may work for the sanctification of the world from within as a leaven. In this way they may make Christ known to others, especially by the testimony of a life resplendent in faith, hope and charity. Therefore, since they are tightly bound up in all types of temporal affairs it is their special task to order and to throw light upon these affairs

in such a way that they may come into being and then continually increase according to Christ to the praise of the Creator and the Redeemer. (*LG* 31)

Great Catholic lawyers, great Catholic politicians, great Catholic university professors, great Catholic physicians and nurses, great Catholic investors and financiers, great Catholic law enforcement officers, great Catholic writers and critics, great Catholic entertainers, each in their special area of competence, are meant to bring Christ to the society and the culture. And when I say "Catholic" here, I don't mean incidentally so or merely privately so, but rather vibrantly and publicly so. This Christification of the culture ought never, of course, to be done aggressively, for as John Paul II said, the Church never imposes but only proposes, but it is indeed to be done confidently, boldly, and through concrete action.

It would be instructive to apply these principles to the present situation in our culture. The crisis precipitated by the brutal killing of George Floyd is one that involves many dimensions of our society: law, the police, education, government, neighborhoods, families, etc. Priests and bishops, to be sure, ought to teach clearly and publicly. The declaration mentioned above and the American bishops' pastoral statement against racism from a year ago, *Open Wide Our Hearts*, are good examples of this. But I would argue that the lion's share of the work regarding this massive societal problem belongs to those whose proper arena is the society and whose expertise lies precisely in the relevant areas of concern—namely, the laity. If I may be blunt, the question ought not be "What are the bishops doing about it?" but rather "What can I and my Christian friends do about it?"

The last thing I would like to do is to stir up any rivalry or resentment between clergy and laity; on the contrary. Following the prompts of the Vatican II documents, I have been stressing the symbiotic relationship that ought to obtain between them. And if I might propose a concrete example of this symbiosis, I would draw your attention to the Catholic Action model that flourished in the years prior to the council but that, sadly and surprisingly, fell into desuetude after Vatican II. In accord with the framework proposed by Cardinal Cardijn, the founder of Catholic Action, a priest would meet with a relatively small group of parishioners who shared a common interest or vocation—say, physicians, or lawyers, or financiers, or business leaders. The spiritual leader would interpret Scripture or lay out some relevant teaching of the Church and then invite his interlocutors to "see, judge, and act." That is to say, he would encourage them to be attentive to the area of their professional interest, then to judge the situations they typically face in light of the Gospel and Church teaching, and finally to resolve to act on the basis of those judgments. When it was functioning at its best, Catholic Action involved priests and laity, each operating in their proper spheres and working together for the transformation of the world.

Not a bad approach to the cultural crisis in which we currently find ourselves.

What Is Synodality?

It was a great privilege for me to participate in the Synod on Young People, the Faith, and Vocational Discernment in the fall of 2018. Along with about three hundred other bishops and ecclesial experts from around the world, I spent four weeks in Rome exploring the complex question of the Church's outreach to the young.

About three weeks into the synod process, a sub-committee of writers presented a preliminary text, meant to reflect our deliberations, questions, and decisions to that point. This draft represented, for the most part, an accurate account of our work, but there were a few pages that troubled a number of us. More or less out of the blue, a vigorous defense of "synodality" appeared in the text, though we had never, either in general session or in the small language groups, so much as discussed the theme. Moreover, the language was so imprecise that it gave the impression that the Church is a kind of freewheeling democracy, making up its principles and teachings as it goes along. Rather alarmed by this section of the draft, a number of bishops and archbishops, myself included, rose to speak against it. We wondered aloud how to square this language with the teaching authority of the bishops, the binding quality of the Church's dogmatic statements, and the practical process of governing the people of God. Mind you, none of us who expressed concern about the language of the text was against synods as such; after all, we were happily participating in one. It was the vagueness and ambiguity of the formulation that bothered us.

Just after our interventions, a well-known and deeply respected cardinal asked to speak. He opined that our objections were baseless and that the texts in question were not threatening to the authority of the bishops or the integrity of the Church's doctrine, though, to be honest, he provided no real argument for his position. When he sat down, applause rang through the synod hall, and we moved on to another topic. At the time, I thought, "Well, you win some and you lose some."

But I will confess that this episode came vividly back to mind in the summer of 2019 when I learned that the German Bishops' Conference was gathering under the rubric of "synodality" and had committed to walk the "synodal path." My attention turned to something closer to alarm when I gathered that they were open to a reconsideration of some of the most fundamental moral teachings and disciplines of the Church, including the nature of the sexual act, the theology of the priesthood, and the possibility of ordination for women. Further, the bishops of Germany were endeavoring to undertake their deliberations in collaboration with the Central Committee for German Catholics, a lay organization, and they were insisting that the decisions of this joint body would be "binding." To state it bluntly, every fear that I and a number of other bishops had when we first read the open-ended language regarding "synodality" in the preliminary document of the Youth Synod now seemed justified. Would it be possible for a local church to establish its own moral rules in such a way that they would then be binding on the Catholics in that region? Could contraception, for example, become ethically permissible in Germany while still remaining morally offensive in other parts of the Catholic world?

It was therefore with a real sense of relief that I learned that the Congregation for Bishops, under the headship of Cardinal Marc Ouellet, had intervened to set limits to the synodality of the German Conference, reminding the bishops that they were not authorized to act in independence of the Holy See. Nevertheless, when the German Bishops' Conference informed the Vatican that they would press ahead on the synodal path, the same fears and hesitations that I experienced at the Youth Synod re-emerged.

All of this was in the back of my mind when, in the company of my brother bishops from Region XI, I met with Pope Francis during the *ad limina* visit. In the course of our conversation, the theme of synods and synodality indeed came up, and Francis was clear and explicit. He told us, in no uncertain terms, that a synod is "not a parliament," and that the synodal process is not simply a matter of canvassing the participants and counting votes. And then he added, with particular emphasis, that the "protagonist" of a synod is not any of the delegates to the gathering, but rather the Holy Spirit. This last observation is of signal importance. The point of a democratic assembly is to discern the will of the people, for in a democratic polity, they are finally sovereign. But in a synod, the point is discerning not the will of the people but the will of the Holy Spirit, for the Spirit in that context is sovereign, or, in the language of Pope Francis, the "protagonist."

Having heard the pope on this score, I couldn't help but hearken back to that moment at the Youth Synod of 2018. Whatever Pope Francis means by "synodality," he quite clearly doesn't mean a process of democratization or putting doctrine up for a vote. He means, it seems to me, a structured conversation among all of the relevant ecclesial players—bishops, priests, and laity—for the sake of hearing the voice of the Spirit.

The Ratzingerian Constants
and the Maintenance
of Harmony in the Church

Some years ago, my friend Msgr. Francis Mannion wrote an article concerning the three essential features of the Eucharistic liturgy—namely, the priest, the rite, and the people. When these elements are in proper balance, rightly ordered liturgy obtains. Further, from these categories, he argued, we can discern the three typical distortions of the liturgy: clericalism (too much of the priest), ritualism (a fussy hyper-focus on the rite), and congregationalism (a disproportionate emphasis on the people). It was one of those observations that just manages to spread light in every direction.

A similarly illuminating remark was made by Pope Benedict XVI concerning the work of the Church, and I would like to spend a little time exploring it. Papa Ratzinger said that the Church performs three basic tasks: it worships God, it evangelizes, and it serves the poor. The religious activities of over a billion Catholics around the globe, he maintained, can be reduced finally to these three fundamental moves. So, for example, the liturgy, the celebration of the sacraments, individual and collective prayer, the singing of monks, the whispered petitions of cloistered religious, praise and worship songs, the recitation of the Rosary—all of these belong under the heading of worshiping God. And the teaching of the *kerygma*, street preaching, catechesis, university-level theology, the evangelization of the culture, proclaiming the faith through the new media—all of that can be categorized as evangelization. Finally, care for the hungry and homeless, outreach to immigrants, Catholic Worker soup kitchens, the work of Catholic charities, hospitals, and orphanages—all of these are expressions of the Church's commitment to serve the poor. The life of the Church consists, Pope Benedict maintains, in the harmonious coming together of these three ministries, no one of which can be reduced to the other two and each one of which implies the other two. Properly evangelized people want to worship God and long to help the needy; helping the needy is a way of proclaiming the Gospel and a vehicle for the teaching of the faith; liturgy by its very nature leads to theology (*lex orandi, lex credendi*) and the instantiation of the kingdom through service.

If I might borrow from Msgr. Mannion, we can also read off of these categories typical distortions in the life of the Church. When the worship of God is exaggerated or exclusively emphasized, the community becomes hyper-spiritualized, disincarnate, and, at the limit, superstitious. What is required is the critical intelligence provided by theology as well as the groundedness provided by the concrete service of the poor. When the evangelical mission is exaggerated, the Church runs the risk of falling into rationalism and of losing affective contact with God. What is particularly needed in that case is the visceral sense of the transcendent provided by the liturgical praise of God. When outreach to the needy is one-sidedly stressed, the Church tends toward a reduction of the supernatural to the natural, becoming, as Pope Francis puts it, just another NGO providing social service. What is required in that case is the robust supernaturalism to which a healthy theology and liturgy give access. The point is that it is in the tensive play among the three elements, each complementing and checking the excesses of the other two, that the Church finds its health and equilibrium.

I don't want to oversimplify the matter, for there are plenty of ideological battles *within* the three "groups": liberal liturgists against conservative liturgists, left-wing approaches to evangelization versus right-wing approaches, etc. But I might suggest that many of our disputes in the life of the Church today have to do with a kind of imperialistic reductionism. I mean that people who are particularly interested in the praise of God sometimes think that the praise of God is *everything*; and that people who are really into evangelization sometimes think that the whole Church should be nothing but evangelism; and that people who are passionate about the service of the poor think that this ministry should take all the oxygen in the room. At its best, the Church resists this kind of imperialism, and you can see it in the lives of the great saints, who seemed to have a feel for the manner in which these three ministries harmonize. Just think of Teresa of Kolkata, pouring herself out in service among the poorest of the poor in the worst slum in the world *and* passing hours and hours in contemplative prayer; or of Edith Stein, one of the premier intellectuals of the twentieth century *and* a woman who spent hours every day in silence before the Blessed Sacrament, and who, at the climax of her life, offered herself as a martyr on behalf of her people; or of Francis of Assisi, who was married to Lady Poverty *and* who, judging from some of the few authentic letters we have of his, was extremely concerned about altar linens and the proper maintenance of tabernacles and churches.

By nature, training, or personal predilection, each of the baptized probably gravitates more readily to one or other of the basic Ratzingerian tasks. I, for example, have long been oriented toward evangelical work: preaching, teaching, writing, communicating, etc. But I cannot tell you how often in the course of my priesthood I have had to battle an anti-intellectualism, usually justified through appeal to the urgency and primacy of social justice work. And I have certainly known advocates of that third path who have endured attacks from liturgy devotees, claiming that service of the poor is "secularist." And indeed I have known passionate liturgists who have been forced to endure taunts for how fussy and out of touch they are with the "real" needs of the people of God, etc.

Could we please cut this out? It is not only stupid; it also crucially undermines the work of the Church, which is a harmonious and mutually correcting interplay of the three Ratzingerian constants. I might close with a word of encouragement to my brother bishops. A major part of our work as "overseers" (*episkopoi*) of the Church is to assure that a symphony among the three basic charisms remains vibrantly in place.

A Case for Priestly Celibacy

There is a very bad argument for celibacy that has reared its head throughout the tradition and that is, even today, defended by some. It runs something like this: married life is morally and spiritually suspect; priests, as religious leaders, should be spiritual athletes above reproach; therefore, priests shouldn't be married. I love Augustine, but it is hard to deny that this kind of argumentation finds support in some of Augustine's more unfortunate reflections on sexuality (original sin as a sexually transmitted disease; sex even within marriage is venially sinful; the birth of a baby associated with excretion; etc.). I once ran across a book in which the author presented a version of this justification, appealing to the purity codes in the book of Leviticus. His implication was that any sort of sexual contact, even within marriage, would render a minister at the altar impure. This approach to the question is, in my judgment, not just silly but dangerous, for it rests on assumptions that are repugnant to good Christian metaphysics.

The doctrine of creation *ex nihilo* necessarily implies the essential integrity of the world and everything in it. Genesis tells us that God found each thing he had made good and that he found the ensemble of creatures very good. Expressing the same idea with typical scholastic understatement, Thomas Aquinas commented that "being" and "good" are convertible terms. Catholic theology, at its best, has always been resolutely anti-Manichaean, anti-Gnostic, anti-dualist—and this means that matter, the body, and sexual activity are never, in themselves, to be despised. In his book *A People Adrift*, Peter Steinfels correctly suggests that the postconciliar reaffirmation of this aspect of the tradition effectively undermined the dualist justification for celibacy that I sketched above.

But there is more to the doctrine of creation than an affirmation of the goodness of the world. To say that the finite realm in its entirety is created is to imply that nothing in the universe *is* God. All aspects of created reality reflect God, point to God, and bear traces of the divine goodness (just as every detail of a building gives evidence of the mind of the architect), but no creature and no collectivity of creatures *is* divine (just as no part of a structure *is* the architect). This essential distinction between God and the world is the ground for the anti-idolatry principle that is reiterated from beginning to end of the Bible: do not turn something that is less than God into God. Isaiah the prophet put it thus: "For as the heavens are higher than the earth, so are my ways higher than your ways and my thoughts than your thoughts" (Isa. 55:9). And it is at the heart of the First Commandment: "I am the LORD your God. . . . You shall have no other gods before me" (Exod. 20:2–3). The Bible thus holds off all forms of pantheism, immanentism, and nature mysticism— all the attempts of human beings to divinize or render ultimate some worldly reality. The doctrine of creation, in a word, involves both a great "yes" and a great "no" to the universe.

Now, there is a behavioral concomitant to the anti-idolatry principle: it is the detachment that is urged throughout the Bible and by practically every figure in the great tradition from Irenaeus and Chrysostom to Bernard, John of the Cross, and Thérèse of Lisieux. Detachment is the refusal to make anything less than God the organizing principle or center of one's life. Anthony de Mello looked at it from the other side and said that "an attachment is anything in this world—including your own life—that you are convinced you cannot live without." Even as we reverence everything that God has made, we must let go of everything that God has made, precisely for the sake of God. Augustine saw to the bottom of this truth, commenting that creatures are loved better, more authentically, precisely when they are loved *in* God. This is why, as G.K. Chesterton noted, there is an odd, tensive, and bipolar quality to Christian life. In accord with its affirmation of the world, the Church loves color, pageantry, music, and rich decoration (as in the liturgy and papal ceremonials), even as, in accord with its detachment from the

251

world, it loves the poverty of St. Francis and the simplicity of Mother Teresa. The same tensiveness governs its attitude toward sex and family. Again in Chesterton's language, the Church is "fiercely for having children" (through marriage) even as it remains "fiercely for not having children" (in religious celibacy). Everything in this world—including sex and intimate friendship—is good, but impermanently so; all finite reality is beautiful, but its beauty, if I can put it in explicitly Catholic terms, is sacramental and not ultimate.

According to the biblical narratives, when God wanted to make a certain truth vividly known to his people, he would occasionally choose a prophet and command him to act out that truth, to embody it concretely. Hence, he told Hosea to marry the unfaithful Gomer in order to sacramentalize God's fidelity to wavering Israel. In *Grammar of Assent*, John Henry Newman reminded us that truth is brought home to the mind, becoming convincing and persuasive, when it is represented not through abstractions but through something particular, colorful, and imaginable. We might be intrigued by the formula of Chalcedon, but we are moved to tears and to action by the narrative of Christ's appearance on the road to Emmaus. Thus, the truth of the non-ultimacy of sex, family, and worldly relationships can and should be proclaimed through words, but it will be believed only when people can *see* it. This is why, the Church is convinced, God chooses certain people to be celibate: in order to witness to a transcendent form of love, the way that we will love in heaven. In God's realm, we will experience a communion (bodily as well as spiritual) compared to which even the intensest forms of communion here below pale into insignificance, and celibates make this truth viscerally real for us now. Just as belief in the Real Presence in the Eucharist fades (as we have seen) when unaccompanied by devotional practice, so the belief in the impermanence of created love becomes attenuated in the absence of living embodiments of it. Though one can present practical reasons for it, I believe that celibacy only finally makes sense in this eschatological context.

I realize that my reader might be following the argument to this point and still feel compelled to ask, "Yes, granted that celibacy is a good thing for the Church, but why must all priests be celibate?" The medievals distinguished between arguments from necessity and arguments from "fittingness." I can offer only the latter kind of argument, for even its most ardent defenders admit that celibacy is not essential to the priesthood. After all, married priests have been, at various times and for various reasons, accepted from the beginning of the Church to the present day. The appropriateness of linking priesthood and celibacy comes, I think, from the priest's identity as a Eucharistic person. All that a priest is radiates outward from his unique capacity, acting in the person of Christ, to transform the Eucharistic elements into the Body and Blood of Jesus. As the center of a rose window anchors and orders all of the other elements in the design, so the Eucharistic act of the priest grounds and animates everything else that he does, rendering qualitatively distinctive his way of leading, sanctifying, and teaching. But the Eucharist is the eschatological act *par excellence*, for as Paul says, "As often as you eat this bread and drink the cup, you proclaim the Lord's death until he comes" (1 Cor. 11:26). To proclaim the Paschal Mystery through the Eucharist is to make present that event by which the new world is opened up to us. It is to make vividly real the transcendent dimension that effectively relativizes (without denying) all of the goods of this passing world. And it is therefore fitting that the one who is so intimately conditioned by and related to the Eucharist should be in his form of life an eschatological person.

For years, Andrew Greeley argued—quite rightly in my view—that the priest is fascinating, and that a large part of the fascination comes from celibacy. The compelling quality of the priest is not a matter of superficial celebrity or charm; that gets us precisely nowhere. It is something much stranger, deeper, and more mystical: the fascination for another world, for that mysterious dimension of existence hinted at sacramentally by the universe here below and revealed to us, however tantalizingly, in the breaking of the bread. I for one am glad that such eschatologically fascinating persons are not simply in monasteries, cloistered convents, and hermits' cells, but in parishes, on the streets, and in the pulpits, moving visibly among the people of God.

There are, I realize, a couple of major problems with offering arguments for celibacy. First, it can make everything seem so pat, rational, and resolved.

I've been a priest now for over thirty years, and I can assure you that the living of celibacy has been anything but that. As I've gone through different seasons of my life as a priest, I've struggled mightily with celibacy, precisely because the tension between the goodness and ephemerality of creation of which I spoke of earlier is no abstraction, but rather runs right through my body. The second problem is that reason only goes so far. As Thomas More said in that wonderful scene from *A Man for All Seasons*, as he was trying to make his daughter understand why he was being so stubborn: "Finally, it isn't a matter of reason; finally, it's a matter of love." People in love do strange things: they pledge eternal fidelity; they write poetry and songs; they defy their families and change their life plans; sometimes they go to their deaths. They tend to be over-the-top, irrational, and confounding to the reasonable people around them. Though we can make a case for it—as I have tried to do—celibacy is finally inexplicable, unnatural, and fascinating, for it is a form of life adopted by people in love with Jesus Christ.

The Question
Behind the Question

On the afternoon of June 14, 2018, a rather spirited, fascinating, and unexpected debate broke out on the floor of the USCCB spring meeting in Fort Lauderdale. At issue was the possibility of reconsidering "Faithful Citizenship," the 2007 statement of the US bishops on the formation of conscience regarding matters political. A group of bishops, including myself, had proposed that instead of producing another lengthy document to succeed "Faithful Citizenship," the bishops ought to write a brief and pointed letter on the political challenges of the present moment and then to create a video or a series of videos bringing forth the salient points of Catholic social teaching. Our thinking was motivated by recent research, which indicates that a very small percentage of Catholics actually read that formal statement from ten years ago. Though it had been taken in and appreciated by the bishops themselves, by lobbyists and political activists, and by members of the Catholic commentariat, it was largely ignored by the very people we were endeavoring to reach.

Once the formal proposal had been made, a number of bishops rose to speak against it and in favor of writing a document to replace "Faithful Citizenship." With considerable eloquence, they reminded us of the shift in emphasis that has taken place with the magisterium of Pope Francis. Concern for the environment, for economic justice, for the poor, for the victims of violence, for refugees and immigrants has been brought to the fore in a new way, and our teaching, they insisted, ought to reflect this change.

About midway through the discussion, I rose to make a clarification. I said that the members of our group were fully aware of what I called "the Franciscan shift" in emphasis and that we very much wanted the bishops' teaching to reflect this change. What was really at issue, I explained, was not so much the content of the teaching but the vehicle for its transmission. I said that practically all of the people in the room are on one side of the page-screen divide, so that we rather naturally privilege written texts and find them more substantive. But the overwhelming majority of those under the age of, say, fifty are, I continued, on the other side of that watershed. They are far more oriented to the screen, far less likely to plow their way through a lengthy written text. I recalled that about fifteen years ago, a member of my staff called to tell me that an article I had written had been accepted by a major Catholic publication. I was delighted, but my excitement was curtailed a bit when he informed me that it would appear on that outlet's online edition and not in the print edition. Sensing my disappointment, my colleague said, "You know, this is much better. You'd rather have it online than in print. It will reach a much wider audience." That little episode was the beginning of a shift in consciousness for me.

With that clarification made, the conversation on the conference floor transposed to a different key, as the meta-question of communication became the focus. One bishop observed that on his flight to Fort Lauderdale, he had noticed that no one around him was reading a book, but practically everyone had his or her eyes glued to a screen. Another bishop, an expert in the use of social media, applauded the shift to digital forms of communication, but also expressed the concern that people will not pay attention to videos longer than a few minutes in length. How can the Church adequately convey its teaching in a sound bite? But still other bishops chimed in to say that nothing prevents us from producing a series of short pieces that together cover a good deal of ground. Finally, some wondered which protocols would govern the approval of videos rather than texts. I will confess that as this part of the lively discussion unfolded, a smile spread across my face, for I have believed for some time that this issue of *how* we communicate is perhaps as important as *what* we communicate—that is, if we are interested in moving the conversation beyond a very narrow circle.

Inevitably, some commentators tried to read the discussion as a fierce disagreement between the "Francis bishops" and their detractors. Nothing could be further from the truth. The overwhelming majority of the bishops wanted the full range of Catholic social teaching to be faithfully defended, and they welcomed Pope Francis' renewed emphasis on the environment and care for the marginal. The far more compelling conversation—and one that clearly engaged the interest of the bishops on the floor of the conference—had to do with how we propagate this teaching as widely and effectively as possible.

The Benedict Option
and the
Identity-Relevance Dilemma

R od Dreher's *The Benedict Option: A Strategy for Christians in a Post-Christian Nation* certainly emerged as the most talked-about religious book of 2017. Within weeks of its publication, dozens of editorials, reviews, op-eds, and panel discussions were dedicated to it. Practically every friend and contact I have sent me something about the book and urged me to comment on it. The very intensity of the interest in the text in one way proves Dreher's central point—namely, that there is a widely felt instinct that something has gone rather deeply wrong with the culture and that classical Christianity, at least in the West, is in a bit of a mess.

Anyone looking for concrete evidence of the crisis doesn't have to look very far or very long. Twenty-five percent of Americans now identify as religionless, and among those thirty and younger, the number rises to 40 percent. The majority of people under fifty now claim that their moral convictions do not come from the Bible, and traditional prohibitions, especially in regard to sex and marriage, are being aggressively swept away. In fact, legally speaking, the momentum has shifted so dramatically that now those who defend classical views on sexuality are subject to harassment, even prosecution. For Dreher, the *Obergefell* Supreme Court decision in regard to gay marriage, which basically unmoored marriage from its biblical and moral foundations, was the straw that broke the camel's back.

It's important to see, moreover, that this was not simply due to a quirk or particularly anti-gay prejudice on Dreher's part. That legal determination had such a powerful impact because it expressed, with crystal clarity, the now

258

widespread conviction that morality is essentially a matter of personal decision and self-invention. A reviewer for *Commonweal* commented that Dreher's reaction to the *Obergefell* decision, though understandable, is disproportionate, given that the twentieth century has witnessed moral outrages far beyond the legalization of same-sex marriage. But this is to miss an essential point. To be sure, atomic bombings and genocide are far graver ethical violations than gay marriage, but in regard to the former, there was, among sane people, a clear consensus that these acts *were indeed* morally wrong. What has changed is that an agreement across the society regarding the objectivity of good and evil has largely disappeared. As G.K. Chesterton put it a hundred years ago, "Man has always lost his way. . . . But now he has lost his address."

And so Dreher recommends the now famous "Benedict Option," named for the sixth-century saint who, at a time of cultural collapse, withdrew to live the Christian life intensely and intentionally. Christians today, Dreher urges, should acknowledge that the cultural war has largely been lost and should stop spending time, energy, and resources fighting it. Instead, they ought, in imitation of St. Benedict, to rediscover, savor, and cultivate the uniquely Christian form of life. This hunkering down is expressed in a variety of ways: homeschooling of children, the creation of "parallel structures"—which is to say, societal forms of resistance to the dominant culture—the opening of "classical Christian schools" where the great moral and intellectual heritage of the West is maintained, the beautiful and reverent celebration of the liturgy, the revival of a sturdy ascetical practice, a profound study of the Bible, the fighting of pornography, challenging the tyranny of the new media, etc. Only through these practices will Christians rediscover who they are; without them, Dreher fears, Christianity will become, at best, a faint echo of the dominant secular culture.

As I was reading the book, I kept thinking of the famously unresolvable "identity-relevance" dilemma. The more we emphasize the uniqueness of Christianity, the less, it seems, the faith speaks to the wider culture; and the more we emphasize the connection between faith and culture, the less distinctive, it seems, Christianity becomes. This problem is on display throughout Church history, as the society becomes, by turns, more or less amenable to the faith. In the era when I was coming of age, the period just after the council, the Church was thoroughly committed to relevance—so committed, in fact, that it came close to losing its identity completely. Part of the spiritual genius of St. John Paul II was that he struck such a dynamic balance between the poles. Who was more of an ardent defender of distinctive, colorful, confident Catholicism than the Polish pope? But at the same time, who was more committed to reaching out to the non-Christian world, to secularism, to atheism than he?

In point of fact, the career of Karol Wojtyła sheds quite a bit of light on the advantages and limitations of the Benedict Option. When Wojtyła was a young man, the Nazis and Communists produced a poisonous, even demonic, cultural context, and he was compelled, consequently, to hunker down. With his friends, he formed a clandestine theater group, which, under cover of darkness and behind locked doors, preserved the great works of Polish drama and poetry, a literature in which the Catholic faith was ingredient. During those dark years, identity was the supreme value. But then, when he became priest, and eventually bishop and pope, he was properly prepared to unleash the energy he had stored. The result was one of the most dramatic transformations of society in modern history. Better than almost anyone in the Church at the time, he knew how to make the ancient faith relevant to the culture.

So do we need the Benedict Option now? Yes, I would say. But we should also be deft enough in reading the signs of the times, and spiritually nimble enough to shift, when necessary, to a more open and engaging attitude.

St. John Henry Newman

As I read the myriad commentaries leading up to the canonization of John Henry Newman in 2019, I was particularly struck by how often he is co-opted by the various political parties active in the Church today—and how this co-opting both distorts Newman and actually makes him less interesting and relevant for our time. I should like to show this by drawing attention to two major themes in Newman's writing—namely, the development of doctrine and the primacy of conscience.

St. John Henry Newman did indeed teach that doctrines, precisely because they exist in the play of lively minds, develop over time. And he did indeed say, in this epistemological context, "To live is to change and to be perfect is to have changed often." But does this give us license to argue, as some on the left suggest, that Newman advocated a freewheeling liberalism, an openness to any and all change? I hope the question answers itself. In his Biglietto speech, delivered upon receiving the notification of his elevation to the cardinalitial office, Newman bluntly announced that his entire professional career could be rightly characterized as a struggle against liberalism in matters of religion. By "liberalism," he meant the view that there is no objective and reliable truth in regard to religious claims. Moreover, Newman was keenly aware that doctrines undergo both legitimate development and corruption. In other words, their "growth" can be an ongoing manifestation of truths implicit in them, or it can be a devolution, an errant or cancerous outcropping. And this is, of course, why he taught that a living voice of authority, some*one* able to determine the difference between the two, is necessary in the Church. None of this has a thing to do with permissiveness or an advocacy of change for the sake of change.

In point of fact, the development of doctrine, on Newman's reading, is not so much a pro-liberal idea as an anti-Protestant one. It was a standard assertion of Protestants in the nineteenth century that many doctrines and practices within Catholicism represent a betrayal of biblical revelation. They called, accordingly, for a return to the scriptural sources and to the purity of the first-century Church. Newman saw this as an antiquarianism. What appears unbiblical within Catholicism are, in fact, developments of belief and practice that have naturally emerged through the efforts of theologians and under the discipline of the Church's Magisterium. His implied interlocutor in the *Essay on the Development of Christian Doctrine* is not the stuffy Catholic traditionalist but the *sola Scriptura* Protestant apologist.

The second issue that particularly draws the attention of commentators today is the role of conscience. Conscience is one of the master ideas in Newman's corpus; he discusses it from beginning to end of his career, and it is the hinge on which many of his major teachings turn. One of the most cited *mots* of Newman's is his clever quip regarding the authority of the pope: "If I am obliged to bring religion into after-dinner toasts, I shall drink—to the Pope, if you please—still, to Conscience first, and to the Pope afterwards." I cannot tell you how many pundits have run with that offhanded remark, concluding that Newman was flouting the pope and advocating a moral subjectivism. Nothing could be further from the truth. In a letter to the Duke of Norfolk, Newman refers to conscience as "the aboriginal vicar of Christ" in the soul—that is to say, the felt presence of "a Supreme Governor, a Judge, holy, just, powerful, all-seeing." Conscience is not the voice of the individual himself, but rather the Voice of Another, who exercises sovereign authority, who makes demands and furnishes both reward and punishment. The pope is indeed the Vicar of Christ in a formal and institutional sense, and the conscience is Christ's representative in an even more intense, more interior, and "aboriginal" mode. This is why toasting the latter before the former by no means implies that they exist in tension with one another; just the contrary.

Now, am I implying through this analysis of two of Newman's central notions that present-day conservatives are right in their claiming of the new saint? Well, sensible conservatives can and should do so, but there are excessive traditionalists in the Catholic Church against whom Newman stands athwart. The idea of real doctrinal development does indeed run counter to a Catholic antiquarianism that would see dogmas as changeless *objets d'art*, and the assertion of the primacy of conscience does indeed run counter to a fussy and hyper-judgmental legalism. As I suggested above, the setting of these discussions within the context of Newman's own time permits us to see how his resolution of these complex matters takes us far beyond the exhausted left-right categories that dominate the present debates.

John Henry Newman in Full

had the great privilege of attending the splendid Mass of canonization—
presided over by Pope Francis and attended by tens of thousands of bishops,
priests, and faithful from all over the world—for John Henry Newman.
Hanging from the central loggia of St. Peter's Basilica during the liturgy was
a marvelous tapestry featuring a portrait of Newman, and I found myself
gazing at it frequently as the Mass progressed. I couldn't help but wonder
what Newman himself would have thought if someone had told him when he
arrived in Rome in 1846 to commence studies for the Catholic priesthood that
one day in the distant future his Mass of canonization would be celebrated
at St. Peter's. He would have been, I'm quite sure, utterly flummoxed. Newly
converted to the faith, seen by many of his former coreligionists as a traitor,
distinctly uneasy in the Catholic intellectual environment, the Newman of
1846 felt more than a little at sea. When he paid a courtesy visit on Pope Pius
IX, Newman bent down to kiss the pope's foot, which was the custom of the
time, and in the process managed to bang his forehead against the papal knee.
This, he said later, rather summed up his relationship with Pius IX, and it also
serves as a fitting symbol of his initial awkwardness and feeling of discomfort
in the Catholic world.

Things didn't get particularly better when Newman returned to England.
Anglicans, who made up the overwhelming majority of the population, were
still, of course, suspicious of him, and Catholics were not quite ready to accept
him fully. Upon becoming rector of the newly established Catholic University
of Ireland, Newman composed the magnificent lectures later gathered as his
book *The Idea of a University*, but he was also met with considerable opposition
from the bishops of Ireland, who wondered why they should entrust their
students to a former Protestant minister. Upon becoming in 1858 the editor

of the *Rambler*, a left-leaning Catholic journal, Newman published an article under the title "On Consulting the Faithful in Matters of Doctrine." It was met with a firestorm of criticism from conservative Catholics convinced that he was democratizing the articulation of the formal teachings of the faith. And those same critics were hardly mollified when they studied Newman's *Essay on the Development of Christian Doctrine*, which struck them as relativizing dogma, or his later *Essay in Aid of a Grammar of Assent*, which clearly departed from the standard scholastic manner of approaching theological questions.

Now, one of the great ironies of Newman's life is that the criticism he received from many Catholics as a "liberal" was rivaled by an equally severe criticism he had received in the first half of his career from his fellow Anglicans as an arch-"conservative." When he was a very young man, still a student at Oxford, he joined the ranks of those calling for a more Catholicizing reading of Anglicanism, an interpretation more in line with the Fathers of the Church than with the Protestant reformers. In his thirties, he became a leader of the so-called Oxford Movement, which sought a deep transformation of Anglicanism, stressing the doctrinal and sacramental elements of the religion. In 1841, Newman published the (in)famous Tract #90, an essay laying out the case that one could interpret the Thirty-nine Articles of Anglicanism—the cornerstone of the English religious and cultural establishment—in a Catholic manner. The reaction to this was so severe that Newman found himself vilified in every corner of the society, condemned from pulpits, criticized in drawing rooms, excoriated in pubs and train cars. In the eyes of his fellow Anglicans, he was a dangerous conservative. And their worst suspicions were confirmed when he converted to Roman Catholicism in 1845.

To be sure, this buffeting from both sides made almost the whole of Newman's life difficult, and it is not hard to see why he saw much of his career as a Sisyphean exercise in futility. But it was precisely this both/and quality that made Newman so attractive to many of the theologians who paved the way for the Second Vatican Council: Balthasar, Ratzinger, Bouyer, de Lubac, Daniélou, to name just a few. They appreciated the great Englishman's obvious devotion to the great Catholic tradition, and they also savored his sense of that tradition as a *living* organism and not a dead letter. Pope John XXIII was entirely in the spirit of Newman when he spoke of the Church not as a museum but as a flourishing garden of life.

The battle over Newman continues to this day. Both liberals and conservatives within the Catholic Church eagerly claim him, and both sides can do so legitimately. I am convinced that it is most helpful to read him in the both/and manner of his preconciliar disciples, to see all sides of him and not to lock him into ideological categories. Best of all, we should read him on his own terms, assess his arguments objectively, take him in full. If we do that, we shall see why he was such an important inspiration to the Second Vatican Council, and why the Church has seen fit to declare him a saint—and one day, I hope, a Doctor of the Church.

Cardinal Etchegaray,
Henri de Lubac, and Vatican II

On September 4, 2019, Cardinal Roger Etchegaray passed away. Perhaps his was not a household name, but this very decent man made a substantive contribution to the life of the Church, serving in a number of different capacities over the years and collaborating closely with Pope St. John Paul II. I had the privilege of meeting him in the mid-1990s when he visited Mundelein Seminary, where I was serving as professor of theology. The cardinal wanted to address the community, but his English was a bit shaky, so I translated for him. But I recall that his smile and evident joy in the Lord needed no translation whatsoever.

The first time I ever laid eyes on Roger Etchegaray was some years before that, on an extraordinary day in Notre Dame Cathedral in Paris: the funeral of the legendary theologian Henri de Lubac. A third-year doctoral student at the time, I had made my way to Notre Dame, hoping against hope that I might be able to participate in the funeral Mass. As I approached the door, I was stopped by a security agent who asked, *"Est-ce que vous êtes membre de la famille?"* (Are you a member of the family?) *"Non,"* I responded. Then he inquired, *"Est-ce que vous êtes theologien?"* (Are you a theologian?) With some trepidation, I said, *"Oui,"* and he promptly directed me to a prime position near the front of the cathedral. To the tolling of the deepest bells in the cathedral, the simple wooden coffin of de Lubac was wheeled down the middle aisle. I noticed, as it passed by my position, that it was topped by de Lubac's red cardinal's biretta.

At the close of the Mass, Cardinal Etchegaray rose to speak on behalf of the pope. He read a beautiful tribute from John Paul II, and then he shared the following anecdote. Soon after his election to the papacy, John Paul came to

Paris for a pastoral visit. He made a special stop at the Institut Catholique de Paris to meet with theologians and other Catholic academics. After his formal remarks, Etchegaray continued, John Paul II looked up and said, "*Où est le père de Lubac?*" (Where is Fr. de Lubac?) The young Karol Wojtyła had worked closely with de Lubac during Vatican II, specifically in the composition of the great conciliar document *Gaudium et Spes*. De Lubac stepped forward, and Pope John Paul, Etchegaray told us, bowed his head to the distinguished theologian. Then, turning to the coffin, Etchegaray said, "*Encore une fois, au nom du pape, j'incline la tête devant le père de Lubac.*" (Once more, in the name of the pope, I bow my head before Fr. de Lubac.)

This is much more than a charming story, for upon John Paul's reverence for Henri de Lubac hangs a very interesting tale of continuing relevance to our time. De Lubac was the most prominent proponent of what came to be called *la nouvelle théologie* (the new theology). Departing from the strict and rather rationalist Thomism that dominated Catholic intellectual life in the first half of the twentieth century, de Lubac and his colleagues turned with enthusiasm to the Scriptures and to the marvelous and multifaceted works of the Church Fathers. This return to the "sources" of the faith produced a theology that was spiritually informed, ecumenically generous, and intellectually rich—and it got de Lubac in considerable hot water with the academic and ecclesial establishment of that time. At the very height of his powers, throughout the 1950s, he was silenced, prohibited from teaching, speaking, or publishing. Rehabilitated by Pope John XXIII, de Lubac played a pivotal role at Vatican II, decisively influencing many of its major documents. It is altogether correct to say that this champion of the reforming Second Vatican Council was no friend of preconciliar Catholic conservatism.

However, in the years immediately following the Council, Henri de Lubac became impatient with the Catholic liberalism, led by such figures as Hans Küng, Karl Rahner, and Edward Schillebeeckx, which was pushing past the texts of Vatican II, accommodating itself far too readily with the environing culture, and losing its mooring in classical Christianity. And so, along with his colleagues Hans Urs von Balthasar and Joseph Ratzinger, he founded the theological journal *Communio*, which was meant as a counterweight to the journal *Concilium*, which published the works of the leading liberals. It was this *Communio* school, this middle path between both a conservative and liberal rejection of Vatican II, that John Paul II enthusiastically embraced. If you seek clear evidence that the Polish pope favored this approach, look no further than the Catechism of 1992, which is filled with the spirit of the *nouvelle théologie*, and to the fact that John Paul specially honored the three founders of *Communio*, making Joseph Ratzinger head of the Congregation for the Doctrine of the Faith, and naming both de Lubac and Balthasar cardinals.

Are both left-wing and right-wing rejections of Vatican II on display today? Just go on the Catholic new media space and you'll find the question readily answered. What is still very much the needful thing is the de Lubac attitude: deep commitment to the texts of Vatican II, openness to ecumenical conversation, a willingness to dialogue with the culture (without caving in to it), reverence for the tradition without a stifling traditionalism. Perhaps I might invite you to muse on that gesture and those words of Cardinal Etchegaray that I took in many years ago: "Once more, in the name of the pope, I bow my head before Fr. de Lubac."

269

The Evangelical Path of
Word on Fire

I commenced my writing career, roughly twenty-five years ago, as a critic of liberal Catholicism, which I referred to, in one of the first articles I ever published, as "beige Catholicism." By this designation, I meant a faith that had become culturally accommodating, hand-wringing, unsure of itself, a Church that had allowed its distinctive colors to be muted and its sharp edges to be dulled. In a series of articles and talks, as well as in such books as *And Now I See*, *The Strangest Way*, and especially *The Priority of Christ*, I laid out my critique of the type of Catholicism that held sway in the years after the Second Vatican Council, as well as my vision of what a renewed and evangelically compelling Church would look like. I emphasized Christocentrism as opposed to anthropocentrism, a Scripture-based theological method rather than one grounded in human experience, the need to resist the reduction of Christianity to psychology and social service, a recovery of the great Catholic intellectual tradition, and a robust embrace of evangelical proclamation. In all of this, I took as my mentor Pope John Paul II, especially the sainted pontiff's interpretation of Vatican II as a missionary council, whose purpose was to bring Christ to the nations.

My media ministry Word on Fire developed as the practical expression of these theoretical convictions. I did not want simply to name a problem and speculate about a solution; I wanted, above all, to contribute concretely to that solution. Hence, I produced videos on a wide variety of theological and cultural themes; created long-form documentaries that conveyed the truth and beauty of Catholicism; preached biblically on radio, television, and the internet; and eventually developed an institute for the formation of lay evangelists in the Word on Fire spirit. All of this constituted a response to the beige Catholicism that I identified as problematic many years before. I have never changed my mind about Catholic liberalism, and I continue to see it as, in the words of my mentor Francis Cardinal George, "an exhausted project."

But the same Cardinal George who strongly criticized the liberal strand within Catholicism also said this: "Conservative Catholicism in some of its reaction takes refuge in earlier cultural forms of faith expression and absolutizes them for all times and all places." Thoroughly imbued with the missionary spirit of Vatican II, the cardinal knew that a hyper-valorization of any particular period of Church history, be it the American Catholicism of the 1950s or the European Catholicism of the thirteenth century, would seriously undermine the Church's present capacity to engage the culture in which it finds itself.

In recent years, a fiercely traditionalist movement has emerged within American Catholicism, finding a home particularly in the social media space. It has come about, partly, as a reaction to the same beige Catholicism that I have criticized, but its ferocity is due to the scandals that have shaken the Church the past thirty years, especially the McCarrick situation. In their anger and frustration, some of it justified, these arch-traditionalist Catholics have become nostalgic for the Church of the preconciliar period and antipathetic toward the Second Vatican Council itself, Pope John XXIII, Pope Paul VI, Pope John Paul II, and particularly our present Holy Father.

The supreme irony, of course, is that these radically traditionalist Catholics, in their resistance to the authority of the pope and their denial of the legitimacy of an ecumenical council, have risked stepping outside the confines of the Church. Theirs is not a beige Catholicism to be sure, but it is indeed a self-devouring Catholicism. Perhaps sensing this contradiction, they remain spitting-mad at anyone who would dare challenge them.

If I might then nail my colors to the mast, Word on Fire represents a "no" to both beige and self-devouring Catholicism. It stands with Vatican II, John Paul II, Pope Benedict XVI, Pope Francis, and the *Catechism* of 1992, and it takes as its mission the New Evangelization. It wants neither to surrender to the culture nor to demonize it, but rather, in the spirit of

St. John Henry Newman, to *engage* it, resisting what it must and assimilating what it can, being, as St. Paul put it, "all things to all people . . . for the sake of the gospel" (1 Cor. 9:22–23). Against self-devouring Catholicism, it is intellectually generous, but against beige Catholicism, it desires to make all thoughts finally captive to Christ. Against the angry denizens of the Catholic right, it seeks not to condemn but to invite; against the representatives of the too-complacent Catholic left, it sees evangelization as the centrally important work of the Church.

Cardinal George said that liberal Catholicism is "parasitical upon a substance that no longer exists," by which he meant that it subsists as a critique of a form of Catholic life that has mostly faded away. I have argued that the extreme traditionalist Catholicism of the present day is self-consuming, for it attacks the very foundations of Catholicism itself. If both of these characterizations are true, then these two critical movements are essentially moribund. I have tried to situate Word on Fire on the path of an evangelical Catholicism, the Catholicism of the saintly popes associated with Vatican II, a living Catholicism.

The Word on Fire Retreat
and
God's Wonderful Providence

Something on clear display in the Bible and in the history of the Church is that a mission that is authentically from God tends to draw people to itself. When Peter and his companions were overwhelmed by the miraculous draught of fishes, other fishermen rushed to the scene to help them. When Mother Teresa made her way into the streets of Calcutta to care for the sick and dying, she was joined, within weeks, by many of her former students.

One of the great privileges of my life has been my involvement with the Word on Fire apostolate. Something I have watched with fascination and deep spiritual joy is that so many people from around the country have been drawn by God's providence into this ministry. In 2019, for the first time ever, we gathered in Santa Barbara all twenty-five members of the Word on Fire team for days of reflection. They came from New York, Chicago, Dallas, Washington, DC, and Los Angeles to the lovely Franciscan Mission in Santa Barbara to pray, to commune with one another, to plan for the future.

Fr. Steve Grunow, the CEO of Word on Fire, was there of course. Fr. Steve was a student of mine at Mundelein Seminary outside of Chicago in the mid-1990s when I had just begun my teaching ministry. He was head and shoulders above the other students: brilliant, insightful, dedicated. In the early years of Word on Fire, he was a close collaborator and advisor, and then, in the late 2000s, Cardinal George formally assigned him as my assistant.

Jared Zimmerer, the Director of the Word on Fire Institute, was on hand for the retreat. I had met Jared through Fr. Steve, who had come upon him online. Father of six, powerlifter extraordinaire, doctoral candidate in the humanities, Jared very competently coordinates the increasingly complex work of our Institute, which is dedicated to forming an army of lay evangelizers.

Robert Mixa was an enthusiastic participant in the retreat. Many years ago, when I was running Word on Fire out of the Chicago office, Bobby emailed me out of the blue. He told me he was a recent philosophy graduate of St. Louis University and a follower of my ministry. He wondered whether he could help in some capacity. Initially, we took him on as a research assistant, and since then he has worn many hats at Word on Fire. Now he is playing a key role in the Institute office in Dallas.

Rozann Carter Lee participated in the retreat. I first met Rozann in 2002 when I was on sabbatical at the University of Notre Dame. During my time at the university, I taught one undergraduate course in theology, and Rozann, a sophomore at the time, was the brightest kid in that class. I was charmed by her smile, her constant cheerfulness, and her very sharp questions. Some years later, we advertised for a position at Word on Fire, and I was delighted to see that Rozann had applied. We hired her right away, and she has supervised almost all of our graphic design work for the past ten years. Some years after Rozann joined us, Sean Lee came aboard. A gifted graduate of Ave Maria University, Sean worked for some years in marketing and now basically runs operations for the entire ministry. More importantly, about six years ago, Sean invited Rozann to accompany him to a Bulls game on a Friday night— and the rest is history. They married five years ago and now have three kids, Kolbe (named for Maximilian Kolbe), Mary Flannery (named for Flannery O'Connor), and Francis George (named for the cardinal who was a sort of grandfather to Word on Fire).

Cassie Pease took part in our days of reflection. When Rozann was looking for some help in the graphic design department, she looked online and found Cassie's extraordinary work, which is simultaneously deeply Catholic and remarkably contemporary in style. Cassie has brought her creative verve and energy to our DVDs, our books, and the Word on Fire Institute Journal.

I could tell you many more stories, but I hope you see what I'm driving at. Like a great artist, the Holy Spirit, in the course of many years, has drawn together a variety of strands, colors, and textures to produce something beautiful. Because God is noncompetitive with his creation, he doesn't supplant our efforts, but rather delights in including us in his work. I do indeed take a father's pride in Word on Fire, and I felt this especially during our retreat, when the whole family was gathered around me. But much more I take an apprentice's delight in seeing what the Master is up to.

Evangelizing through the Good

Anyone even vaguely acquainted with my work knows that I advocate vigorous argument on behalf of religious truth. I have long called for a revival in what is classically known as apologetics, the defense of the claims of faith against skeptical opponents. And I have repeatedly weighed in against a dumbed-down Catholicism. Also, I have for many years emphasized the importance of beauty in service of evangelization. The Sistine Chapel ceiling, the Sainte-Chapelle, Dante's *Divine Comedy*, Bach's *St. Matthew's Passion*, T.S. Eliot's *Four Quartets*, and the Cathedral of Chartres all have an extraordinary convincing power, in many ways surpassing that of formal arguments. So I affirm the path of truth and the path of beauty. But I also recommend, as a means of propagating the faith, the third of the transcendentals—namely, the good. Moral rectitude, the concrete living out of the Christian way, especially when it is done in a heroic manner, can move even the most hardened unbeliever to faith, and the truth of this principle has been proven again and again over the centuries.

In the earliest days of the Christian movement, when both Jews and Greeks looked upon the nascent faith as either scandalous or irrational, it was the moral goodness of the followers of Jesus that brought many to belief. The Church Father Tertullian conveyed the wondering pagan reaction to the early Church in his famous adage: "How these Christians love one another!" At a time when the exposure of malformed infants was commonplace, when the poor and the sick were often left to their own devices, and when murderous revenge was a matter of course, the early Christians cared for unwanted babies, gave succor to the sick and the dying, and endeavored to forgive the persecutors of the faith. And this goodness extended not simply to their own brothers and sisters but, astonishingly, to outsiders and to enemies. This peculiarly excessive form of moral decency convinced many people that something strange was afoot among these disciples of Jesus, something splendid and rare. It compelled them to take a deeper look.

During the cultural and political chaos following the collapse of the Roman Empire, certain spiritual athletes took to the caves, deserts, and hills in order to live a radical form of the Christian life. From these early ascetics, monasticism emerged, a spiritual movement that led, in time, to the re-civilization of Europe. What so many found fascinating was the sheer intensity of the monks' commitment, their embrace of poverty, and their blithe trust in divine providence. Once again, it was the *living out* of the Gospel ideal that proved convincing. Something similar unfolded in the thirteenth century, a time of significant corruption in the Church, especially among the clergy. Francis, Dominic, and their confreres inaugurated the mendicant orders, which is just a fancy way of saying the begging orders. The trust, simplicity, service to the poor, and moral innocence of the Dominicans and Franciscans produced a revolution in the Church and effectively re-evangelized armies of Christians who had grown slack and indifferent in their faith.

And we find the same dynamic in our time. John Paul II was the second most powerful evangelist of the twentieth century, but unquestionably the first was a woman who never wrote a major work of theology or apologetics, who never engaged skeptics in public debate, and who never produced a beautiful work of religious art. I'm speaking, of course, of St. Teresa of Kolkata. No one in the last one hundred years propagated the Christian faith more effectively than a simple nun who lived in utter poverty and who dedicated herself to the service of the most neglected people in our society.

There is a wonderful story told of a young man named Gregory, who came to the great Origen of Alexandria in order to learn the fundamentals of Christian doctrine. Origen said to him, "First come and share the life of our community, and then you will understand our dogma." The youthful Gregory took that advice, came in time to embrace the Christian faith in its fullness, and is now known to history as St. Gregory the Wonderworker. Something of the same impulse lay behind Gerard Manley Hopkins' word to a confrere who was struggling to accept the truths of Christianity. The Jesuit poet did not instruct his colleague by saying "Read this book" or "Consult this argument," but rather, "Give alms." The *living* of the Christian thing has persuasive power.

We have been passing through one of the darkest chapters in recent Church history. The clerical sex abuse scandals have chased countless people away from Catholicism, and a secularist tide continues to rise, especially among the young. Surveying this scene, my mentor, the late, great Cardinal George, used to say, "I'm looking for the orders; I'm looking for the movements." He meant, I think, that in times of crisis, the Holy Spirit tends to raise up men and women outstanding in holiness who endeavor to live out the Gospel in a radical and public way. Once again, I'm convinced that, at this moment, we need good arguments, but I'm even more convinced that we need saints.

Tolkien, Chesterton,
and the
Adventure of Mission

There is a common, and I'll admit somewhat understandable, interpretation of J.R.R. Tolkien's *Lord of the Rings* trilogy that sees the great work as a celebration of the virtues of the Shire, that little town where the hobbits dwell in quiet domesticity. Neat, tidy hobbit holes, filled with comfortable furniture, delicate tea settings, and cozy fireplaces are meant, this reading has it, to evoke the charms of a "merrie olde England" that existed before the rise of modernity and capitalism. As I say, there is undoubtedly something to this, for Tolkien, along with C.S. Lewis and the other members of the Inklings group, did indeed have a strong distaste for the excesses of the modern world.

However, I'm convinced that to see things this way is almost entirely to miss the point. For the ultimate purpose of *Lord of the Rings* is not to celebrate domesticity, but rather to challenge it. Bilbo and Frodo are not meant to settle into their easy chairs, but precisely to rouse themselves to adventure. Only when they leave the comforts of the Shire and face down orcs, dragons, goblins, and finally the power of evil itself do they truly find themselves. They do indeed bring to the struggle many of the virtues that they cultivated in the Shire, but those qualities, they discover, are not to be squirreled away and protected, but rather unleashed for the transformation of a hostile environment.

A very similar dynamic obtains in regard to interpreting G.K. Chesterton. His stories, novels, and essays can indeed be read as a nostalgic appreciation of a romantic England gone with the wind, but a close look at the man himself gives the lie to this simplistic hermeneutic. Though he enjoyed life with his wife and friends in his country home in Beaconsfield, Chesterton was at heart a Londoner, a denizen of the pubs of Fleet Street, where he rubbed shoulders with the leading journalists, politicians, and cultural mavens of the time. He loved to laugh and argue with even the bitterest enemies of the religion he held dear. Most famously, over the course of many years, he traveled the country debating with the best-known atheist of the time, his good friend G.B. Shaw, with whom he typically shared a pint after their joint appearances. The point is that Chesterton didn't hide his Catholicism away; he launched it into the wider society like a great ship onto the bounding main.

Paul Tillich was a quiet and serious student of Lutheran theology, preparing for a life as a preacher, when he was called to serve as a chaplain in the German army during World War I. In the course of five years, the young man saw the very worst of the fighting and dying. He said in one of his letters to his wife that it was like witnessing the collapse of an entire world. In the wake of that horrific experience, he sought a new way of articulating the classical Christian faith for the twentieth century—which is to say, for people whose world had fallen apart. He did indeed spend countless hours with his books, hunkering down to learn the great Christian intellectual tradition, but he insisted that the ultimate purpose of the theologian is to go out to meet the culture *"mit klingendem Spiel,"* which means, roughly, "with fife and drum." Like his one-time colleague Karl Barth, who said that Christians ought never to crouch defensively "behind Chinese walls," Tillich felt that believers in Christ ought to meet the culture head-on.

This general attitude is present from the beginning of Christianity. From the moment the Lord gave the great commission—"Go therefore and make disciples of all nations" (Matt. 28:19)—his disciples knew that the Christian faith is missionary by its very nature. Though it exhibits contemplative and mystical dimensions, it is, at heart, a faith on the move, one that goes out. How fascinating that the Holy Spirit first fell in the heart of a city, and that the greatest figure of the apostolic age, Paul of Tarsus, was an urbane fellow, at home on the rough and tumble streets of Antioch, Corinth, Athens, and Rome.

This, by the way, is why I have a particular affection for YouTube, on whose forums I am regularly excoriated and attacked, and Reddit, where secularists, agnostics, and atheists are happy to tell me how stupid I am. Well, why not? Chesterton faced much worse in Fleet Street bars; Paul met violent opposition wherever he went; Frodo and Bilbo looked into the abyss. Good. We Christians don't stay in hobbit holes; we go on adventure, *mit klingendem Spiel*!

Confirmation and Evangelization

In February 2016, I had the enormous privilege of performing my first Confirmation as a bishop. It took place at Holy Cross Parish in Moor Park, California, a large, bustling, and bilingual parish in my pastoral region. I told the confirmandi—and I meant it—that I would keep them in my heart for the rest of my life, for we were connected by an unbreakable bond. In preparation for this moment, I was, of course, obliged to craft a homily, and that exercise compelled me to do some serious studying and praying around the meaning of this great sacrament.

It is sometimes said that Confirmation is a sacrament in search of a theology. It is indeed true that most Catholics could probably give at least a decent account of the significance of Baptism, Eucharist, Confession, Matrimony, Holy Orders, and the Anointing of the Sick, but they might balk when asked to explain the meaning of Confirmation. Perhaps they would be tempted to say it is the Catholic version of a Bar Mitzvah, but this would not even come close to an accurate theological description.

A survey of the most recent theologizing about Confirmation—the documents of Vatican II, the *Catechism of the Catholic Church*, the 1983 Code of Canon Law, etc.—reveals that this is the sacrament of strengthening, as the term itself (*confirmare* in Latin) suggests. First, it strengthens baptized people in their relationship with the Lord Jesus, and then it further strengthens them in their capacity to defend and spread the faith. The roots of it, of course, are in the great day of Pentecost when, through the descent of the Holy Spirit, eleven timorous and largely uneducated men became fearless evangelists, ready and able to spread the Gospel far and wide. Keep in mind that to proclaim Jesus publicly in that time and place was to take one's life in one's hand—and the disciples knew it. And yet, on the very day of Pentecost, they spoke out in the temple and in the public squares of Jerusalem. With the exception of John, they all went to their deaths boldly announcing the Word. I told those I confirmed that they are, in a certain sense, successors of those first men upon whom the Holy Spirit descended, and that they have the same fundamental task. Their Confirmation, I further explained, is therefore not really for them; it is for the Church and the wider world.

Now, what makes this transformation possible is the third person of the Holy Trinity, who comes bearing a variety of powers, which the Church calls the gifts of the Holy Spirit. These include wisdom, knowledge, understanding, fortitude, counsel, piety, and fear of the Lord. In order to understand these more fully, we must keep in mind their relationship to evangelization and apologetics, to spreading and defending the faith. As I have argued often, a dumbed-down, simplified Catholicism is not evangelically compelling. We have a smart tradition, marked by two thousand years of serious theologizing by some of the masters of Western thought: Origen, Augustine, Jerome, Anselm, Bonaventure, Thomas Aquinas, John Henry Newman, G.K. Chesterton, and Joseph Ratzinger. If one is going to defend the Catholic faith, especially at a time when it is under assault by many in the secular culture, one had better possess (and cooperate with) the gifts of wisdom, knowledge, and understanding.

In order to be an effective evangelist, one also needs the spiritual gift of fortitude or courage. Will the defense of the faith stir up opposition? Watch the news, read the papers, and above all surf the internet, and the question answers itself. It would be tempting indeed to withdraw from the arena and cultivate one's faith privately, but confirmed people, endowed with fortitude, are meant to be soldiers of Christ, engaged in the fight. Some folks suggest that this phrase should not be used as it evokes the terrors of religious violence. However, the struggle of a soldier of Christ is to resist violence, not with the weapons of worldliness but with the weapons of the Spirit—peace, patience, kindness, and forgiveness. Does evangelization put the evangelizer in harm's way? Just ask Peter, Paul, Thomas More, Maximilian Kolbe, and Charles Lwanga. But also consult anyone who has been insulted, joked about, mocked, or excluded because of his faith in Christ. The gift of fortitude empowers the confirmandi to stay in the arena.

Those who would spread and defend the faith also require the gift of counsel, which is the capacity to discern right from wrong, to know what God wants us to do in any given situation. As we move through the day, we perform hundreds of acts. Are we motivated primarily by the worldly desires for wealth, pleasure, power, self-protection, and honor; or are we motivated by a desire to please God? Counsel enables one to make the right moral decisions for the right reason. It is precisely this holiness, this consistent option to follow the will of God, that makes a person radiant and compelling to others—and hence evangelically persuasive.

Finally, the confirmed evangelizer needs the spiritual gifts of piety and fear of the Lord. Though these terms carry a somewhat fussy connotation, they in fact name something strong and bracing. They designate the capacity to place God at the absolute center of one's life, to worship God alone. The person of piety and genuine fear of the Lord (respect for God) does not run after every passing fancy or devote herself to a variety of worldly goods; rather, her heart is set upon God alone, and every other passion or interest in her life is related to that central value. This right ordering of the self conduces toward integrity, and integrity of life makes a person saintly and deeply attractive.

I reminded those I confirmed that their Confirmation was meant to set them on fire with the Holy Spirit, precisely so that they in turn can set the world on fire. Once again, the gifts that they received were not for them.

Paul on the Areopagus:
A Masterclass in Evangelization

The account of St. Paul's address on the Areopagus in Athens, found in the seventeenth chapter of the Acts of the Apostles, is a sort of masterclass in the evangelization of the culture, and anyone engaged today in that essential task should read it with care. The context for Paul's speech is his mission to Greece, which commenced when he crossed over from Asia Minor to the mainland of Europe. As the great Catholic historian Christopher Dawson indicated, this transition of an itinerant Jewish preacher from one side of the Aegean to the other would have excited the interest of no conventional historian or commentator of the time, but constituted, nevertheless, one of the most decisive events in history, for it signaled the introduction of Christianity to Europe and, through Europe, to the rest of the world. A first lesson for us: the evangelist never rests, for the call of the Lord is to announce the Good News to the ends of earth.

After spending time in the northern reaches of the territory—Macedonia, Philippi, Thessalonica—Paul made his way eventually to Athens. It should be noted that though his preaching in the north met with some success, it also stirred up fierce opposition. He was arrested and imprisoned in Philippi and chased aggressively out of Thessalonica by an angry mob. From the very beginning, Christian proclamation has been opposed and Christian preachers have found themselves in danger. Those who venture into the field today should not be surprised that they meet with some pretty rough plowing. But I want to place special emphasis on the fact that Paul went to Athens, arguably the most important cultural center of the ancient Roman world. It is by a sure instinct that Christians—from Paul and Augustine to Thomas Aquinas, John Henry Newman, and John Paul II—have made their way to centers of thought, communication, and the arts. If Jesus' great commission is to be honored, culture must be evangelized.

Upon arriving in the great city, Paul made a beeline—as was his wont—to the synagogue, for his Good News is that God, in Christ Jesus, had fulfilled all of the promises he made to Israel. He knew that Jews were in the best position to understand what he was talking about. We find here another crucial lesson for present-day evangelizers: we must not forget the unbreakable connection between Jesus and the Jews. When we speak of Jesus in abstraction from Torah, temple, prophecy, and covenant, he devolves rather rapidly into a mildly inspiring teacher of timeless truths. But when we announce him as the climax of the story of Israel, our listeners' hearts catch on fire.

Next, we are told that Paul went out "in the marketplace every day" and spoke "with those who happened to be there." Sons and daughters of Israel might be those best disposed to accept Paul's message, but the Gospel is meant for everyone. Thus, his evangelization was extravagant, indiscriminate, offered on the streets and from the rooftops, to anyone willing to listen. Ours should have a like character. I know that even the prospect of it is pretty daunting, but I've always been a fan of street preaching—just getting up on a corner or on a soapbox and announcing Jesus. Will you be roundly mocked? Sure. But so was Paul. And in demonstration of the full extent and range of his outreach, we are told that Paul dialogued with some of the "Epicurean and Stoic philosophers"—which is to say, with the leading philosophical voices of that time and place. The evangelist must be, as Paul himself said, "all things to all people" (1 Cor. 9:22), capable of speaking to the most ordinary and the most sophisticated.

When he arrives at the Areopagus—a rocky outcropping just below the Parthenon—Paul delivered himself of a justly celebrated speech. In accord with the old rhetorical device of *captatio benevolentiae* (capturing the good will of one's audience), Paul compliments the Athenians on their spirituality: "I see how extremely religious you are in every way." There is more here, of course, than mere courtesy, for Paul is in fact appealing to what the Fathers of the Church would later call *logoi spermatikoi* (seeds of the Word)—that is to say, hints, echoes, and indications of the Logos that is fully disclosed in Christ. "For as I went through the city and looked carefully at the objects of your worship, I found among them an altar with the inscription, 'To an unknown god.'" In a word, he elected to build upon a religious foundation already in place in the society he was addressing, assimilating into his distinctively Christian proclamation what he could. My mentor Francis Cardinal George often remarked that one cannot really evangelize a culture that one doesn't love.

At the same time, Paul doesn't simply affirm the society he was addressing. Standing just below the Parthenon—the most impressive temple in the ancient world, which housed a massive sculpture of the goddess Athena—Paul announced, "The God who made the world and everything in it, he who is Lord of heaven and earth, does not live in shrines made by human hands." That must have gotten their attention! There were indeed seeds of the word in the Athenian culture, but there were idolatrous practices and errant theologies as well. The canny evangelist, moving through the culture of his time, assimilates what he can and resists what he must. The dichotomy, so often invoked today, between being "open" to the culture or a "warrior" against it is simplistic and gets us precisely nowhere.

One might think that, in the wake of his magnificent address, Paul brought in boatloads of converts, but in fact the payoff was pretty slim: "When they heard of the resurrection of the dead, some scoffed; but others said, 'We will hear you again about this.'" A handful of people were willing to give Paul the benefit of the doubt—and yet, they were the seeds of European Christianity, and hence of a Christianity that would spread throughout the world. A final lesson for evangelists: in accord with Mother Teresa's principle, don't worry about being successful; worry about being faithful. Announce the Gospel, don't count converts, and leave the increase up to God.